Rachael Roberts, **Heather Buchanan**
and **Emma Pathare**

Series Adviser **Catherine Walter**

Navigate

Coursebook
with video and Oxford Online Skills

B1+ Intermediate

OXFORD
UNIVERSITY PRESS

Contents

Om **Oxford 3000™** *Navigate* has been based on the Oxford 3000 to ensure that learners are only covering the most relevant vocabulary.

1 Trends — page 6

- Talk about things that are changing
- Talk about friendships
- Talk about spending
- Talk about states, thoughts and feelings
- Listen for key words
- Noun suffixes
- Ask for and give opinions
- Write for social media

	GRAMMAR
1.1 **Are you really my friend?** p6	Present simple, continuous and perfect p6
1.2 **Why spending's #trending** p8	State verbs p9
1.3 **Vocabulary and skills development** p10	
1.4 **Speaking and writing** p12	
1.5 ▶ Video *Social media marketing* p14 **Review** p15	

2 What a story! — page 16

- Talk about past experiences
- Use narrative forms
- Sequence events
- Talk about communication
- Understand references in a text
- Use comment adverbs
- Engage a listener and show interest
- Write a narrative

2.1 **I'll never forget that day** p16	Narrative forms p17
2.2 **Unbelievable?** p18	Sequencing events p18
2.3 **Vocabulary and skills development** p20	
2.4 **Speaking and writing** p22	
2.5 ▶ Video *Seven good stories* p24 **Review** p25	

3 Life skills — page 26

- Talk about challenges and success
- Talk about ability
- Talk about work skills
- Talk about obligation, permission and possibility
- Recognize complex noun phrases (1)
- Use compound adjectives
- Give practical instructions
- Write a paragraph supporting an opinion

3.1 **Challenges** p26	Ability p27
3.2 **Faking it?** p28	Obligation, permission and possibility p29
3.3 **Vocabulary and skills development** p30	
3.4 **Speaking and writing** p32	
3.5 ▶ Video *A Woman's life: 1914 vs 2014* p34 **Review** p35	

4 Space — page 36

- Talk about living on water
- Talk about predictions and decisions
- Talk about the natural world
- Talk about probability
- Understand consonant-vowel linking
- Understand idiomatic phrases about places
- Avoid repetition
- Make enquiries

4.1 **Living on water** p36	*will/be going to* for predictions and decisions p37
4.2 **Forest bathing** p38	Probability p38
4.3 **Vocabulary and skills development** p40	
4.4 **Speaking and writing** p42	
4.5 ▶ Video *Songdo* p44 **Review** p45	

5 Entertainment — page 46

- Talk about different genres of films
- *-ing* form and infinitive with *to*
- Describe a video game
- Use present perfect simple and past simple
- Understand linkers
- Use extreme adjectives
- Write a film review
- Compare and recommend

5.1 **Universally popular?** p46	*-ing* form and infinitive with *to* p47
5.2 **Mosquito smasher!** p48	Present perfect simple and past simple p49
5.3 **Vocabulary and skills development** p50	
5.4 **Speaking and writing** p52	
5.5 ▶ Video *Film studies* p54 **Review** p55	

6 In control? — page 56

- Talk about machines in our lives
- Use defining and non-defining relative clauses
- Talk about the climate and extreme weather
- Talk about recent events and changes
- Recognize linkers in conversation
- Understand and use adjective suffixes
- Write a professional email
- Change arrangements

6.1 **Man and machine** p56	Defining and non-defining relative clauses p57
6.2 **Controlling the weather?** p58	Present perfect simple and continuous p59
6.3 **Vocabulary and skills development** p60	
6.4 **Speaking and writing** p62	
6.5 ▶ Video *Mist catchers* p64 **Review** p65	

VOCABULARY	PRONUNCIATION	LISTENING/READING	SPEAKING/WRITING
Friendship p7	Linking p7	▶ Video Vox pops 1 p7	
Spending p8			
Nouns suffixes p11		Listening key words p10	
			Speaking asking for and giving opinions p12 Writing social media p13
Describing past experiences p16	Auxiliary verbs: *had* + *was/were* p17	▶ Video Vox pops 2 p17	
Communication p19			
Comment adverbs p21	Intonation – showing interest p22	Reading references p20	
			Speaking showing interest p22 Writing a narrative p23
Challenges and success p26	Word stress p26		
Work skills p28		▶ Video Vox pops 3 p29	
Compound adjectives p31		Reading complex noun phrases (1) p30	Speaking practical instructions p32 Writing writing an opinion paragraph p33
	Pauses in instructions p32		
Living on water p36			
The natural world p38	Intonation – certainty p39	▶ Video Vox pops 4 p39	
Idiomatic phrases about places p41		Listening consonant-vowel linking p40	
			Writing avoiding repetition p42 Speaking enquiries p43
Going to the movies p46		▶ Video Vox pops 5 p47	
Adjectives to describe a video game p48	Word stress in longer words p48		
Extreme adjectives p51	Extreme adjectives p51	Reading understanding linkers p50	
			Writing a film review p52 Speaking comparing and recommending p53
Machines p56		▶ Video Vox pops 6 p59	
Climate and extreme weather p58	Compound nouns p58		
Adjectives suffixes p61		Listening linkers in conversation p60	
			Writing writing a professional email p62 Speaking changing arrangements p63

			GRAMMAR
7 Ambitions page 66	**7.1 Good prospects** p66		*used to* and *would* p67
■ Talk about working conditions	**7.2 Ask an expert** p68		Question forms p69
■ Talk about finished habits and situations	**7.3 Vocabulary and skills development** p70		
■ Talk about experts and high achievers	**7.4 Speaking and writing** p72		
■ Use question forms			
■ Understand paraphrasing			
■ Use collocations			
■ Write an application letter or email			
■ Ask for and give clarification	**7.5 ▶ Video** *Moving abroad to work* p74 **Review** p75		

8 Choices page 76	**8.1 World happiness report** p76		Real conditionals p77
■ Talk about happiness factors	**8.2 What makes a hero?** p78		Unreal conditionals p79
■ Use real conditionals	**8.3 Vocabulary and skills development** p80		
■ Talk about personality and behaviour	**8.4 Speaking and writing** p82		
■ Talk about unreal situations in the present and future			
■ Recognize changing sounds in linked words			
■ Use prefixes			
■ Take notes while listening			
■ Prepare and give a short talk from notes	**8.5 ▶ Video** *Happiness in Mexico* p84 **Review** p85		

9 Appearances page 86	**9.1 Real beauty?** p86		Comparison p87
■ Describe appearances	**9.2 Paintings** p88		Deduction and speculation p89
■ Make comparisons			
■ Describe paintings	**9.3 Vocabulary and skills development** p90		
■ Speculate and make deductions	**9.4 Speaking and writing** p92		
■ Question a text			
■ Use phrasal verbs			
■ Take part in online discussions			
■ Make effective complaints	**9.5 ▶ Video** *The selfie* p94 **Review** p95		

10 Compete and cooperate page 96	**10.1 Crowd-funding** p96		Passives p97
■ Talk about business	**10.2 Competitive sport** p98		Using articles: *a/an*, *the*, – (no article) p99
■ Talk about how things are done	**10.3 Vocabulary and skills development** p100		
■ Talk about competition			
■ Use articles	**10.4 Speaking and writing** p102		
■ Hear unstressed words			
■ Phrases with *take* and *have*			
■ Write about changes and differences			
■ Make recommendations	**10.5 ▶ Video** *Borussia Dortmund* p104 **Review** p105		

11 Consequences page 106	**11.1 Outlaws** p106		Unreal past conditional p107
■ Talk about crime	**11.2 *I should never have clicked 'send'!*** p108		*should/shouldn't have* p109
■ Talk about unreal situations in the past			
■ Talk about people's behaviour on social media	**11.3 Vocabulary and skills development** p110		
■ Criticize past actions			
■ Hear modal verbs	**11.4 Speaking and writing** p112		
■ Understand words with multiple meanings			
■ Come to a decision			
■ Apologize	**11.5 ▶ Video** *Cyber crime* p114 **Review** p115		

12 Influence page 116	**12.1 Advertising** p116		Reported speech p117
■ Talk about advertising	**12.2 How to persuade and influence people** p118		Reported questions p119
■ Understand and use reported speech			
■ Talk about persuading people	**12.3 Vocabulary and skills development** p120		
■ Understand and use reported questions			
■ Recognize complex noun phrases (2)	**12.4 Speaking and writing** p122		
■ Use dependent prepositions			
■ Agree and disagree			
■ Write an advantages and disadvantages essay	**12.5 ▶ Video** *Starbucks* p124 **Review** p125		

Communication page 126 **Grammar Reference** page 136

VOCABULARY	PRONUNCIATION	LISTENING/READING	SPEAKING/WRITING
Working conditions p66		▶ **Video** Vox pops 7 p67	
High achievers p68			
Collocations p71			
	Sounding polite p73	**Reading** understanding paraphrasing p70	**Writing** an application letter or email p72 **Speaking** clarification p73
Happiness factors p76	Intonation in *if* sentences p77	▶ **Video** Vox pops 8 p77	
Personality and behaviour p78			
Prefixes p81		**Listening** sounds changes p80	
			Writing taking notes p82 **Speaking** giving a talk p83
Describing physical appearance p86	Changing stress p87	▶ **Video** Vox pops 9 p87	
Describing paintings p88	Sentences stress – speculating p89		
Phrasal verbs p91		**Reading** questioning a text p90	
			Writing taking part in online discussions p92 **Speaking** making complaints p93
Business p96	Passives p97		
Competitive sport p98		▶ **Video** Vox pops 10 p99	
Phrases with *take* and *have* p101		**Listening** unstressed words p100	
			Writing changes and differences p102 **Speaking** making recommendations p103
Crime p106		▶ **Video** Vox pops 11 p107	
Behaviour on social media p108	*should/shouldn't have* p109		
Words with multiple meanings p111		**Listening** hearing modal verbs p110	
			Speaking decisions p112 **Writing** apologizing p113
Advertising p116	Linking p117	▶ **Video** Vox pops 12 p117	
Persuading people p118			
Dependent prepositions p121		**Reading** complex noun phrases (2) p120	
			Speaking agreeing and disagreeing p122 **Writing** advantages and disadvantages essay p123

Audioscripts page 160   **Irregular verbs** page 174   **Phonemic symbols** page 175

5

1 Trends

1.1 Are you really my friend?

GOALS ■ Talk about things that are changing ■ Talk about friendships

Grammar & Reading present simple, continuous and perfect

1 Work in small groups. Read the statement and discuss the questions.

> 'Among adult Facebook users, the average number of friends is 338.'

1 Does this statistic surprise you? Why/Why not?
2 Is it possible to really be friends with so many people? Why/Why not?

Photos Like · Comment · Share

Search for people, places and things 🔍

Face-to-face with Facebook friends Like · Comment · Share ∨

How many of your Facebook friends have you seen lately? For Rob Jones, who [1]*is currently meeting* every single friend on his Facebook page, the answer could soon be 700.

His aim to raise money for a children's charity means he has already come face-to-face with 123 internet 'friends' in seven countries, some of whom he has never met before.

[2]*He takes* a photo for his Facebook page with everyone he meets, and persuades them to give to his charity, and he has already raised more than £3,000.

He hopes to have met all 700 within three years, travelling thousands of miles to thirty countries including New Zealand, on the other side of the world, in the process.

People often say that Facebook friends aren't real friends. But Rob met his Polish girlfriend online and [3]*they've now been* together three years. He says [4]*this proves* that the internet is a powerful tool.

'I'm reuniting with friends, and in the process [5]*I'm learning* a lot about myself. I now have good friends in people I have never met before this.'

'Everyone has been great so far; [6]*I generally spend* a day with them and they choose what we do.'

His adventure has taken him across Europe, visiting England, Scotland (top photo), Poland (photo in the centre), Finland, Germany and Switzerland, and [7]*he's also just visited* a distant relative in the USA (bottom photo).

---

2 Read the article. Why is Rob Jones trying to meet all 700 of his Facebook friends? Discuss your ideas with a partner.

3 Read the information in the Grammar focus box and write sentences 1–7 in the article next to the appropriate grammar rule a–f.

> **GRAMMAR FOCUS** present simple, present continuous and present perfect simple
>
> • We use the present simple to talk about
> a things that are always or generally true.
> _____
> _____
> b things that happen regularly/repeatedly.
> _____
>
> • We use the present continuous to talk about
> c things that are happening at/around the time when we speak. _____
> d things that are changing. _____
>
> • We use the present perfect simple to talk about
> e our experience (our lives until now).
> _____
> f things that have already/just happened.
> _____
>
> → Grammar Reference page 136

4a Choose the correct options to complete the questions.

1 What *is Rob trying / does Rob try* to do?

2 How many friends *does he meet / has he met* so far?

3 Why *does he take / is he taking* a photo of everyone he meets?

4 Why does Rob believe that the internet *has been / is* a good way of making friends?

5 What *is Rob learning / does Rob learn* from the process?

6 Who *usually decides / is deciding* what to do when Rob meets a Facebook friend?

7 Which countries *does he visit / has he visited*?

b Discuss the answers to the questions with a partner.

Vocabulary & Speaking friendship

5a **1.1** Listen to two friends, Sarah and Josh, talking about their friendships. Which diagram represents each person's friendship groups?

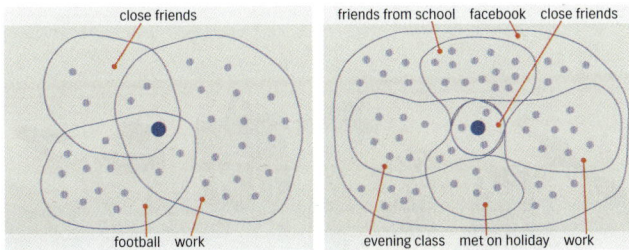

1 _____ 2 _____

b Tell your partner which diagram is more like your friendship groups. Explain why.

6a Work with a partner. Look at the verbs/verb phrases and decide if they are positive (P) or negative (N).

1 get on (well) (with someone) _____
2 meet up (with someone) _____
3 have a lot in common (with someone) _____
4 fall out (with someone) _____
5 help (someone) out _____
6 trust (someone) _____
7 get/keep in touch (with someone) _____
8 make friends (with someone) _____
9 have an argument (with someone) _____

b **1.1** Listen again to Sarah and Josh and check your answers.

PRONUNCIATION linking

> When we speak at normal speed, we link phrases so they often sound like one word.

7a Look at the phrases in exercise **6a**. Mark the way the words link in each phrase.

get_on well with someone

b **1.2** Listen, check and repeat.

8a Complete the statements using the correct form of the verbs/verb phrases in exercise **6a**.

1 I often _____ groups of friends in the evening.

2 You don't need to _____ someone to be friends. It's fine to have different interests.

3 I _____ most people I know. There aren't many people I don't like.

4 A really good friend is someone you can call at midnight and ask them to _____.

5 The friends you _____ at school are often friends for life.

6 I'm always pleased when someone I haven't heard from in ages _____.

7 I'm quite easy-going. I rarely _____ my friends.

8 I'm not speaking to my sister at the moment – we've _____. It seems a bit childish.

9 I can _____ my closest friend with all my secrets.

b **1.3** Listen and check your answers. How many of the statements are true for you? Explain why to a partner.

9 **TASK** Draw a diagram of your friendship groups, like the ones in exercise **5a**. Talk to a partner about some of the people in it. Ask each other questions to get more information.

▶ **VOX POPS VIDEO 1**

1.2 Why spending's #trending

GOALS ■ Talk about spending ■ Talk about states, thoughts and feelings

Vocabulary & Listening spending

1   Work with a partner. Look at the title of the lesson and discuss the questions.

  1   What is happening in the photos?
  2   What does it mean if something is 'trending'?
  3   Why might spending be trending?

2a **1.4**))) Listen to a short radio news item about *Black Friday* and compare what you hear with your ideas from exercise **1**.

 b Does anything you heard surprise you?

3a **1.4**))) Read the statements. Then listen again and decide if the statements are true (T) or false (F). Correct the false statements.

  1   The expression *Black Friday* has been used more than two billion times on Twitter recently.
  2   *Black Friday* only happens in the USA.
  3   Some people have queued overnight.
  4   Shoppers around the world spent more than 11 billion dollars on *Black Friday* last year.
  5   There have been five injuries in the last few years on *Black Friday*.

 b Compare your answers with a partner.

4a Put the words and phrases in the box into the correct groups.

> customer   consumer   deals   discounts   half-price
> items   purchaser   purchases   special offers
> two for the price of one

 b Check your ideas with a partner.

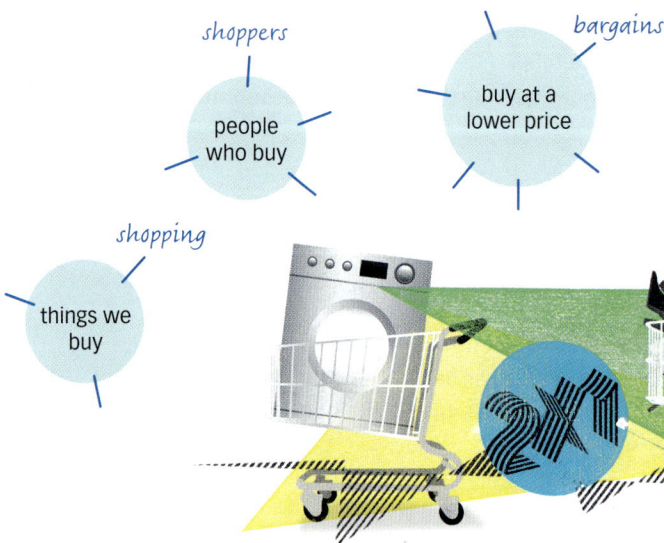

shoppers
bargains
people who buy
buy at a lower price
shopping
things we buy

5   Work with a partner or in small groups. Discuss the questions.

  1   What have you bought recently that was a *bargain*?
  2   Do you look for *special offers* such as *two for the price of one* in the supermarket? How important are they to you in choosing your *purchases*?
  3   Have you ever bought something you didn't need because it was a good *deal*? If so, give an example.
  4   Would you be willing to queue for hours to get a good *discount*? For what kind of *item*?

Grammar & Speaking   state verbs

6 Look at the posters. Do you agree with the message in them? Why/Why not?

7a **1.5**)) Listen to a radio interview with a supporter of *Buy Nothing Day*. Which of the following points does he mention?

> *Buy Nothing Day* is important because it might encourage people not to …
> 1 use shopping as a kind of therapy.
> 2 owe a lot of money.
> 3 support big companies.
> 4 consume more than their fair share of the world's resources.
> 5 buy goods where the workers are badly paid.
> 6 buy goods with unnecessary packaging.

b Which of the points would be most likely to make you think about buying less? Discuss with a partner.

8a Complete extracts 1–7 from the listening with the most appropriate form of the verbs in brackets.

1 Can you explain a little about what *Buy Nothing Day* _____ (mean)?
2 When you really _____ (think) about it, the idea of buying things as a way of spending your leisure time is crazy.
3 We _____ (believe) shopping makes us happy, but it doesn't.
4 Yes, I _____ (agree), that's a good point.
5 We all _____ (own) far too much.
6 Most of the time we _____ (prefer) people to buy locally …
7 Most people _____ (not/understand) how difficult it is …

b **1.6**)) Listen and check your answers.

9a What do all the completed verb forms in exercise **8a** have in common? Read the information in the Grammar focus box and check.

> ### GRAMMAR FOCUS state verbs
> Some verbs are most often used in simple tenses, even if we mean 'just now'. These *state* verbs are often used to talk about:
> - How we think: *know, mean, think,* ¹_____, ²_____, ³_____
> - What we feel: *like, want, hate, love, dislike, feel* ⁴_____
> - What we possess: *have, belong,* ⁵_____
> - What we experience: *be, see, hear, look, smell, taste, seem*
>
> → Grammar Reference page 137

b Put the verbs in exercise **8a** into the correct category.

1

2

10a Look at the posters for *Buy Nothing Day* and complete the text with the best form of the verbs in brackets – present simple or present continuous.

> In Poster 1 there are some people who ¹_____ (stand) inside a shopping basket. I ²_____ (like) this one because I ³_____ (think) it shows the idea of being trapped by shopping very well. It ⁴_____ (seem) to be saying that we ⁵_____ (not/understand) that we are in a cage. It's simple but quite a powerful message. Poster 2 ⁶_____ (look) quite good, but I'm not sure what it ⁷_____ (try) to say. It's obviously based on the *Tetris* video game, and the four blocks at the top that say 'buy' clearly ⁸_____ (fit), but I'm not sure it would make me want to stop shopping. I definitely ⁹_____ (prefer) the first one.

b Compare your answers with a partner.

11a **TASK** Work in small groups. Which of the posters do you think is more effective? Give reasons.

b Decide together on the design of your own poster to promote *Buy Nothing Day*. Which of the points in exercise **7a** could you focus on? How will you make it effective? Present your ideas to the class.

Vocabulary and skills development

GOALS ■ Listen for key words ■ Noun suffixes

Listening & Speaking key words

1a How has the internet changed people's lives? Work with a partner and make a list of 5–10 things which have really changed since the internet was invented.

b Compare your list with another pair. Has life changed for the better? Are any aspects of life worse since the internet was invented?

2 Look at the cover of a recent book about the internet. Do you think the author is positive about the effect of the internet or negative? Read the book description and check your ideas.

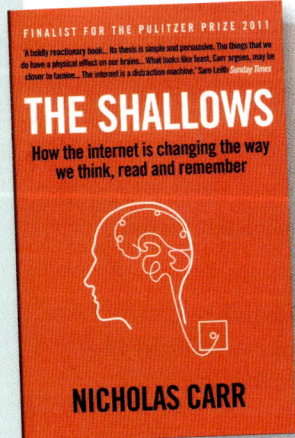

FINALIST FOR THE PULITZER PRIZE 2011

'A boldly reactionary book… Its thesis is simple and persuasive. The things that we do have a physical effect on our brains… What looks like Carr argues, may be closer to famine… The internet is a distraction machine.' *Sam Leith, Sunday Times*

THE SHALLOWS
How the internet is changing the way we think, read and remember

NICHOLAS CARR

This is a fascinating book. We all know that the internet is changing the way we do things, but Carr believes that it is also changing the very way our brains work. With the printed book, he argues, our brains learnt to think deeply. In contrast, the internet encourages us to read small bits of information from lots of different places. We are becoming better and better at multitasking, but much worse at concentrating on one thing.

3 **1.7** Read and listen to the information in the Unlock the code box about listening for key words.

> 🔓 **UNLOCK THE CODE**
> listening for key words
>
> Key words carry the most important information. They are generally nouns and verbs and are usually spoken more loudly and clearly than other words. For example:
>
> **three** times a **week**
> I **send** a **lot** of **emails**
> I **like** looking at **shopping websites**.

4a Look at these phrases from the review in exercise **2**. Which do you think are the most important words in each phrase? Discuss with a partner, and underline them.
1 This is a fascinating book.
2 We all know that the internet is changing the way we do things, …
3 … but Carr believes that it is also changing the very way our brains work.
4 With the printed book, he argues, our brains learnt to think deeply.
5 In contrast, the internet encourages us to read small bits of information from lots of different places.
6 We are becoming better and better at multitasking, …
7 … but much worse at concentrating on one thing.

b **1.8** Listen and check your ideas.

5 **1.9** Listen and complete these opinions about the internet with the missing key words.
1 Shopping and _____ _____ is _____.
2 Looking at _____ all day is _____ for our _____.
3 People will _____ how to _____ to each other.
4 People don't _____ enough _____ _____.
5 Online _____ is not always _____.
6 Hyperlinks in _____ _____ are very distracting.
7 We are now using _____ more _____ to _____ all our _____.
8 Multitasking online makes us _____ less _____.

6a **1.10**))) Listen to part of a radio programme about the book. Which of the opinions in exercise **5** do you hear mentioned?

b **1.10**))) Listen again. According to the speakers, which of the opinions in exercise **5** would Nicholas Carr agree with?

7a Which of the opinions in exercise **5** do *you* agree with? Discuss in small groups.

b What arguments *in favour* of the internet can you think of? Make a list in your group. Compare your list with another groups'.

noun suffixes

8 Read the extract from a review of *The Shallows*. Name one thing the writer likes about the book, and one thing he dislikes.

Book Review: The Shallows
by Nicholas Carr | ★★★✫★

As someone who started working long before the internet arrived, I was shocked by the main ideas in *The Shallows*. The book says that even though the digital age has resulted in amazing improvements in the ways we can get information, it is also causing us to lose our ability to do one thing at a time. It made me think hard about the way I use the internet and manage my relationships with people online.

However, although Carr raises many interesting questions, I am not convinced that the solutions to the problems he raises are as difficult as he suggests. Since I read the book, I have, for example, been keeping Facebook and my email inbox closed while I work, to prevent myself from being distracted. Surely, all we need is a little careful judgement and good sense?

9a Read the information in the Vocabulary focus box and find nouns in the review that end in *-ship, -ment, -ion* and *-ity*.

VOCABULARY FOCUS noun suffixes

- Suffixes often change the class of the word (verb, noun, adjective, etc.).
  secure (adjective) → *security* (noun)
  achieve (verb) → *achievement* (noun)
  connect (verb) → *connection* (noun)
  Notice how the spelling can change:
  communicate → communication;
  able → ability
- Sometimes the word class stays the same, but the meaning is different.
  She is my best friend. (noun)
  We have a close friendship. (noun)

b Add the nouns from the review to the mind map.

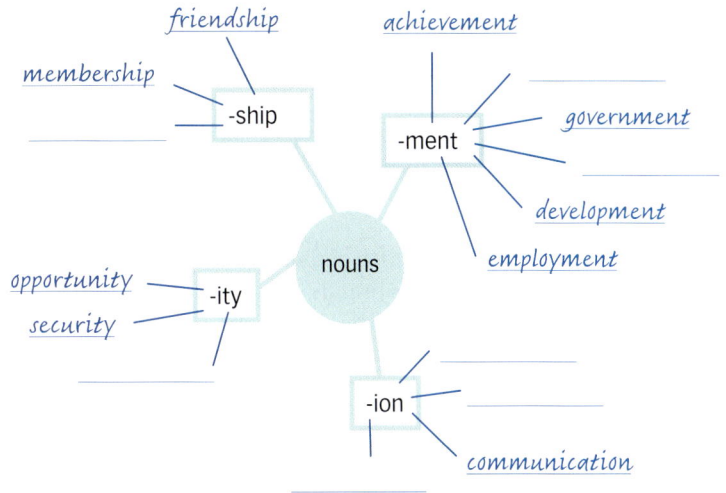

10 Match nouns in the mind map to the definitions.
1 the state of having a job
2 connections with friends, family, etc.
3 change which makes something better
4 ways to deal with a problem
5 forming an opinion/making sensible decisions
6 _____ a thing you have done successfully
7 _____ having the chance to do something you want to do

11 Add noun suffixes to the words in brackets to complete the sentences.
1 The internet, and especially Skype, has improved _____ (communicate) with friends who live abroad.
2 The _____ (develop) of smartphones has made a huge difference to the way we all access information.
3 I am always extremely careful about my personal _____ (secure) online.
4 I think I'm lucky because I've always had a very close _____ (relation) with my sister.
5 I don't have gym _____ (member) because I can't afford the time.
6 Many people think the _____ (govern) should have some control over the _____ (inform) we can get on the internet.
7 The internet offers great opportunities for finding _____ (employ).

12 **TASK** Which of the sentences in exercise **11** are true for you? Compare your answers with a partner and give reasons.

1.4 Speaking and writing

GOALS ■ Ask for and give opinions ■ Write for social media

Speaking & Listening   asking for and giving opinions

1   Look at the photos. Which of these do you think could be described as 'guilt-free brands'? Discuss your ideas with a partner.

Home Tips About us Contact us   🔍 SEARCH

THE LATEST CONSUMER TREND: GUILT-FREE BRANDS

Diamond ring

Tesla electric car

Fairphone

2a   **1.11**))) Listen to a radio programme about guilt-free brands and check your ideas.

b   **1.11**))) Listen again and make notes in the table.

Reasons people might feel guilty about what they buy	Arguments in favour of guilt-free brands	Arguments against guilt-free brands.

c   Which speaker do you agree with more, Gosia or Jem? Why? Discuss with a partner.

3a   Complete the phrases from the conversation.
1   So, Jem, what do you _____ the idea?
2   Well, as _____, anything which makes people think …
3   There's a lot more awareness, but _____ it would be better if …?
4   I'm _____ that if people really understood …
5   Well, _____ the people who make Fairphone …
6   If you _____, we have to give people the option …

b   **1.12**))) Listen and check your answers.

4a   Divide the phrases in exercise **3** into three categories:
• giving your opinion
• talking about other people's opinions
• asking for someone's opinion

b   Check your answers in the Language for speaking box.

LANGUAGE FOR SPEAKING asking for and giving opinions

Giving your opinion
As far as I'm concerned, …   *I'm convinced/certain …*
If you ask me …   *Personally …*

Talking about other people's opinions
Some people say that …   *According to (someone), …*

Asking for someone's opinion
1   Negative questions (we expect someone to agree)
Don't you think …?   Shouldn't …?
2   Other ways:
What do you think (about) …?   How do you feel about …?
What are your views on …?

5 Complete the conversations with appropriate phrases from the Language for speaking box. Compare your ideas with a partner.

1 **A** _____ the fact that guilt-free brands are often more expensive?

B _____ it's fine to pay a bit more to know that the environment isn't being harmed.

2 **A** Most of us can't afford electric cars. _____ people who buy electric cars are showing off how rich they are, rather than actually caring about the planet?

B You may be right, but _____ everyone will drive electric cars in the future.

3 **A** _____ we should just buy less stuff. What do you think about that?

B _____ that's a good idea. We all have far more than we really need.

4 **A** _____ the government make electric cars less expensive so everyone can afford one?

B Yes, definitely.

6 Ask your partner for their opinions on the questions in exercise **5**.

Reading & Writing   social media

7 Read the post from social media page *#haveyoursay*. Which of the following statements do you agree with? Discuss with a partner.

1 Not everyone can afford to buy more expensive clothes.

2 Fashion changes quickly, so it's important to be able to buy cheap clothes you can throw away when they go out of fashion.

3 If you don't buy clothes made in poorer countries, you are putting people out of work.

4 It should be easier to find out which companies look after their workers properly.

5 People buy far too many things these days.

8 Now read the comments underneath the post and match them to the statements in exercise **7**.

9 Read the information in the Language for writing box, then rewrite the comments as full sentences.

LANGUAGE FOR WRITING
informal language for social media

When we write for social media, we often:
- miss words out, especially grammar words such as *a/the/I/ my/is/am/it*, e.g. *Sitting on bed* (**I'm** *sitting on* **my** *bed*)
- use abbreviations or short forms, e.g. people = *ppl*, with = *w/*, especially = *esp*, should = *shld*
- use letters or numbers for words which sound the same, e.g. you = *u*, are = *r*, see = *c*, for = *4*

Search for people, places and things 🔍

Are cheap clothes ethical?
#haveyoursay

Like · Comment · Share ⌄

Cheap clothes can be made using children working in poor conditions. So should we stop buying cheap clothes, or simply be more careful about finding out how and where they were made?

Comments

IM **Ian Martin:**
Every1 shld just buy less.

CO **Cristina Oliveira:**
2 keep up w/ fashion u need 2 buy cheap clothes. Can't afford expensive ones.

PJ **Pippa Jones:**
Ppl need jobs, esp in poorer places. If u don't buy, they don't work.

JB **James Brook:**
Some ppl can't afford 2 pay higher prices 4 clothes.

YW **Yumi Watanabe:**
Difficult 2 know which companies r OK 2 buy from.

10a **TASK** Write your own comment on the post, using informal language.

b Look at the comments written by two other students in your class and reply to each one, using informal language.

Social media marketing

1 Match the two halves of the sentences.

  a My company doesn't broadcast advertisements on
  b Nowadays companies prefer posting advertisements on
  c Online discussions show how advertisers engage
  d Advertisers need to find a successful way of reaching
  e I saw billboards advertising the product as I was walking

  1 with consumers.
  2 their target audience.
  3 social media sites to advertising on TV.
  4 through the city centre.
  5 TV any more.

2 Work with a partner and discuss the different advertising methods you can see in the photos. Can you think of other ways companies could choose to advertise their products?

3 ▶ Watch the video. Which three things does the video talk about?

  a The history of social media marketing
  b how to get a job in advertising
  c changes in the advertising industry
  d more interaction with customers
  e the process for creating a social media advertisement
  f How to upload an advertisement on social media

4 ▶ Watch again. Correct the sentences.

  a Most American advertising companies had an office in Madison Avenue in the 1950s.
  b 'Mad Men' is a common name for people who work in advertising these days.
  c *Madwell* designs and develops social media sites.
  d It can take a whole month to write a short social media post.
  e Advertisers will always engage in a conversation with clients these days.
  f Nowadays, the principal effects of social media are well known.

5a TASK Work with a partner. Think about something you'd like to advertise on social media. It could be an event, product, company or charity. Note down five key points you want the public to know about it.

  b Write an advertisement to go on Twitter. It must be no longer than 140 characters.

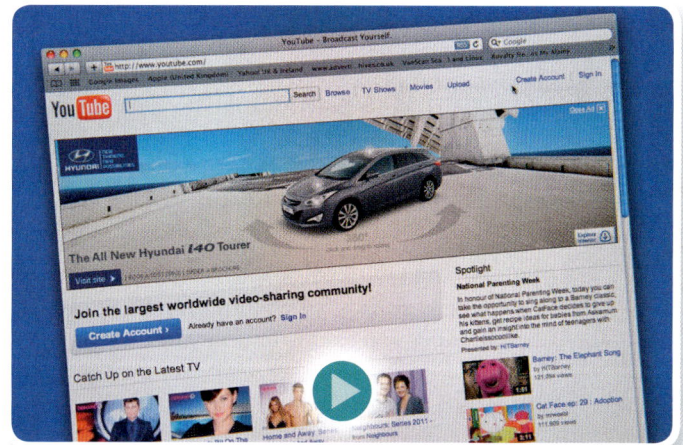

Review

1a Complete the advice about friendship with the correct form of the verbs in brackets. Use the present simple, present continuous or present perfect.

1 If your life _____ (change) recently, your friends might need to change too.
2 If you _____ (just/move) to a new area, it's a good idea to join some clubs.
3 People usually _____ (make) friends at work, so try inviting some work colleagues out socially.
4 Don't automatically say no to an invitation, even if you _____ (get) ready for bed when the phone rings. If you keep saying no, people will stop inviting you.
5 Try to meet your friend's friends. They _____ (like) them, so you probably will, too.
6 When someone _____ (refuse) your invitation, try again another time.

b Work with a partner. Which pieces of advice do you agree with? Why/Why not? Can you add one more piece of advice?

2a Choose the most appropriate form to complete each sentence. Sometimes both forms are possible.

Social networking sites **1** *do not seem / are not seeming* to help people make close friends, according to researchers who studied how the websites **2** *change / are changing* friendships.

Although social networking **3** *means / is meaning* that many people now **4** *have / are having* hundreds or even thousands of 'friends', the researchers **5** *believe / are believing* that to become a real friend, it is still important to actually meet up. Social networking **6** *has become / is becoming* very popular recently, but although people **7** *now keep in touch / are now keeping in touch* with more friends online, the researchers found that we still usually have only around five close friends. We only develop real friendships when we **8** *know / are knowing* we can trust someone.

b Work with a partner and explain why you chose each form.

3a **1.13**)) Listen to six questions and write them down.

b Work with a partner. Ask and answer the questions.

4a Choose the word which is different from the others.

1 purchaser   seller   consumer   customer
2 special offers   bargains   items   deals
3 full price   half-price   discount   two for the price of one

b Work with a partner and explain your answers.

5a Complete the sentences using the noun form with a suffix of one of the words from the box.

develop   happy   inform   member   relation   secure

1 _____ is more important than having lots of money.
2 My _____ with my boss has never been very good.
3 How can you afford the _____ at the tennis club?
4 He gave me some very useful _____ about the new apps that are available for my phone.
5 Have you seen the new _____ of houses by the river?
6 I don't really like my job, but I need the _____ of a regular salary.

b Work with a partner. Try to think of at least one more noun that ends with each of the five suffixes used in exercise **5a**.

6a Choose the correct word to complete each phrase.

1 *Personally / Definitely*, I think …
2 *Shouldn't / Mustn't* people …?
3 I really *ask / feel* that …
4 … if you *tell / ask* me.
5 *According / Along* to …
6 As *far / long* as I'm concerned, …

b Look at these quotations about friendship.

'A friend is someone who knows all about you and still loves you.' Elbert Hubbard

'It's the friends you can call up at 4 a.m. that matter.' Marlene Dietrich

Work with a partner. Discuss how you would define friendship, using the phrases in exercise **6a**.

What a story!

2.1   I'll never forget that day

GOALS ■ Talk about past experiences ■ Use narrative forms

Vocabulary & Reading describing past experiences

1   Look at the photo and the headline of the article and discuss the questions.

   1   What do you consider to be a bad day at work?
   2   How could a hippo be related to a bad day at work?

2   Read the magazine article. Were your ideas close to what actually happened?

3   Read the article again and choose the correct verbs.

A bad day at work

I'll never ¹*forget / remind* that day. It started out as just an ordinary day at work. I never ²*expected / wondered* that within a few hours I would be in great danger!

I was 27 and had been a river guide for several years, taking people down the Zambezi River. The sun was setting and we were reaching the end of the tour one evening, when something knocked into the boat.

Thinking it was the other boat, I turned round to push it away, when suddenly everything went dark. I was stuck inside something. I managed to free one hand and felt around – my hand touched a hippo's nose. It was only then that I ³*believed / realized* I was underwater, my upper body actually in the hippo's mouth! I tried to move as much as I could, and when he opened his mouth, I managed to swim away. But seconds later, he struck again, pulling me under the water. I ⁴*remember / remind* looking up at the surface of the water, and ⁵*recognizing / wondering* which of us could hold his breath the longest.

Suddenly the hippo released me. By chance, a medical team was nearby, and they helped me to reach a hospital. Meanwhile, the hippo had quietly ⁶*appeared / disappeared*.

I ⁷*believe / expect*, though, that I met him one more time. Two years later I was travelling down the Zambezi again. Being there obviously ⁸*recognized / reminded* me of what had happened. Then, just as we were going past the same place in the river, a huge hippo suddenly ⁹*appeared / realized*.

I ¹⁰*screamed / whispered* so loudly that those with me said they'd never heard anything like it. He went back under the water and was never seen again. I'm sure I ¹¹*recognized / realized* the same hippo, still just as angry.

4a Complete the questions with the verbs in the box.

> believe   expect   realize   recognize   remember
> remind   wonder

1 When did the writer _____ that his head was inside a hippo? How do you think he felt?
2 Why do you think the writer _____ so clearly what he was seeing and _____ about while he was underwater?
3 Do you _____ the writer really _____ the same hippo two years later, or did it just _____ him of the hippo that attacked him?
4 Did you _____ the writer to return to being a river guide after what happened? Would you?

b Discuss your answers with a partner.

Grammar & Speaking   narrative forms

5 Work with a partner. Match verbs 1–5 to descriptions a–c.
1 I was 27 and **¹ had been** a river guide for several years.
2 The sun **² was setting** and we **³ were reaching** the end of the tour one evening, when something knocked into the boat.
3 ... something **⁴ knocked** into the boat. Thinking it was the other boat, I **⁵ turned round** to push it away ...

a Setting the background to the story: _____ _____
b The main events in a story: _____ _____
c An event that happened before the main events in the story: _____

6a Read the Grammar focus box to check your ideas.

b Add **one** more example of each form from the article to the box.

GRAMMAR FOCUS   narrative forms

- In narratives, we use the past simple for the main events in a story.
  *Something **knocked** into the boat.*
  1 _____
- We use the past continuous for background events, or longer actions interrupted by a shorter event.
  *The sun **was setting** ...*
  *We **were reaching** the end of the tour one evening, when something knocked into the boat.*
  2 _____
- We use the past perfect for events that happened before the main past time we are talking about.
  *I was 27 and **had been** a river guide for several years.*
  3 _____

→ Grammar Reference page 138

7a Complete the story with the correct form of the verbs in brackets.

A lucky escape

That reminds me of another story I heard about a man who had a lucky escape. He ¹_____ (be) at a barbecue restaurant on top of a mountain, and after the meal he ²_____ (decide) not to take the cable car down with his friends, but to walk down instead. While he ³_____ (look) for the path, he ⁴_____ (fall) into a stream and ⁵_____ (break) his leg. Unable to move, he ⁶_____ (try) to phone for help, but his mobile ⁷_____ (work) because he ⁸_____ (drop) it in the stream. Knowing he was missing, teams of people ⁹_____ (look) for him, but it was twenty-four days before they ¹⁰_____ (find) him. Luckily he ¹¹_____ (bring) a bottle of barbecue sauce with him to the barbecue, and he ¹²_____ (survive) by drinking water mixed with the barbecue sauce.

b 2.1))) Listen and check your answers.

c Work with a partner. What could the man have said about his lucky escape a few years later?

PRONUNCIATION   auxiliary verbs: *had + was/were*

8a Look at these two sentences from the story. What is the difference between the two underlined verbs? How will their pronunciation be different?
1 That reminds me of another story I heard about a man who <u>had</u> a lucky escape.
2 He<u>'d</u> been at a barbecue restaurant.

b How are *was* and *were* pronounced in these sentences? Why?
3 While he <u>was</u> looking for the path ...
4 Knowing he <u>was</u> missing, teams of people <u>were</u> looking for him ...

c 2.2))) Listen, check and repeat.

9 TASK Work with a partner. Student A, turn to page 126. Student B, turn to page 132.

▶ VOX POPS VIDEO 2

Unbelievable?

Grammar & Reading   sequencing events

1a Work with a partner. Look at the photos and match them to the three short articles 1–3.

HOME / STORIES

Hoaxes   🔍 SEARCH

1 Recently a picture has been circulating on the internet of a bright blue watermelon, described as a Japanese moon melon. It seems the fruit grows in Japan and eating it will change the taste of anything you eat afterwards, making sweet things taste sour, and so on. Each watermelon is supposed to cost about $200, but no one is actually offering it for sale, because it doesn't exist.

2 On October 15, 2009, the media reported that a six-year-old boy was inside a large silver balloon floating high in the sky. When the balloon landed, the boy was nowhere to be found, leading to fears that he had fallen out. However, it was later discovered that the whole story had been made up by the boy's parents, in an attempt to get a reality TV deal.

3 In the early twentieth century, scientists were keen to find some evidence that would prove the link between early man and apes. In 1912, it seemed the evidence had been found in Piltdown, England, when Charles Dawson dug up a human skull with an ape-like jaw. For more than thirty years, everyone believed that this skull, known as 'Piltdown Man', was genuine; but in 1953 a team of researchers discovered that it was, in fact, a fake, made from an ancient human skull and a modern ape jaw.

■ **skull** the bones in the head of a human or animal
■ **jaw** the two large bones in your skull that contain your teeth

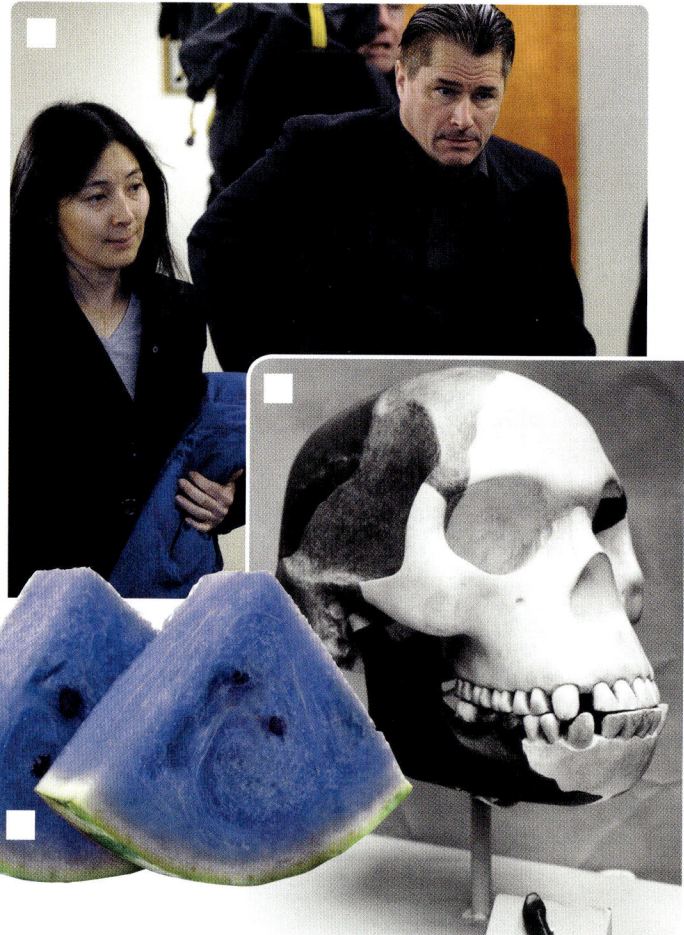

b What do all three stories have in common?

2 Read the stories again. Which story …?
 1 is the oldest
 2 is going round online
 3 did people believe for the longest time
 4 was a result of someone wanting to be famous

3 Work with a partner and discuss these questions.
 1 Have you heard any of these stories before, or any similar ones?
 2 Why do you think people carry out hoaxes like these?

4a 2.3))) Listen to a radio programme about hoaxes. Did they mention any of your reasons?

b Work with a partner. List three of the reasons for carrying out the hoaxes that are mentioned in the programme.

c 2.3))) Listen again and check your answers.

5a Complete the extracts about the first hoax mentioned in the radio programme, using the correct linking word or phrase from the box. Use each word or phrase only once.

> as soon as   by the time (that)   during   meanwhile   until   while

1 A couple, Richard and Mayumi Heene, let a large gas balloon float off into the air and then, _____ it was high in the sky, they claimed that their six-year-old son was inside the balloon.

2 The police were informed and helicopters were sent up to track the balloon _____ they could find a safe way of getting him down.

3 _____ the balloon landed an hour or so later, about 80 km away, the story was live on television.

4 When the boy was not found inside, the media reported that he had fallen out _____ the flight, and a huge search started. _____, the boy was actually safe at home, hiding. The parents suddenly announced that they had found him at home, asleep.

5 We can't say for sure because the couple never admitted it, but _____ reporters were interviewing the family on TV, the boy accidentally mentioned that they'd done it to be on TV. He was supposed to keep quiet about that.

b 2.4))) Compare your answers with a partner. Listen and check your answers.

6 Read the sentences in exercise **5a** again. Choose the correct option to complete the information in the Grammar focus box.

GRAMMAR FOCUS time linkers

We use time linkers to describe how the timing of events in a story relates to one another.

1 *until / while* describes **when** something happened but not for how long

2 *as soon as / by the time (that)* describes an event that happens **immediately after** an event

3 *until / meanwhile* describes a contrasting event that happens **while** something else is happening

4 *by the time (that) / during* describes an action that happened **before** the main events

5 *during / as soon as* describes an action that happens at a point **within** this period of time

6 *during / until* describes an action that continued **up to** a point and then stops

→ Grammar Reference page 139

7a Read the story of the Piltdown Man and choose the best time linker options.

> [1] **During / While** the early twentieth century, scientists were keen to find some evidence that would prove the link between early man and apes. In 1912 that evidence seemed to have been found [2] **meanwhile / while** Dawson and Woodward were digging on a site in Piltdown, in the south of England. [3] **As soon as / Until** they saw the jawbone and the skull, they decided that this must be the evidence science needed. Woodward claimed that both bones belonged to a human being who had lived about half a million years ago, [4] **by the time / during** what is known as the Lower Pleistocene period. Most scientists accepted this opinion [5] **until / while** nearly forty years later, when it was discovered that the Piltdown Man was a fake. [6] **By the time / Meanwhile**, Dawson, who most people consider responsible for making the fake, had died.
>
> The Piltdown Man hoax truly damaged science because [7] **while / by the time** the hoax was discovered, scientists had wasted nearly forty years believing a lie.

b 2.5))) Listen and check your answers.

Vocabulary & Speaking communication

8a Work with a partner. Look back at the extracts from the radio programme in exercise **5a** and find the verbs which describe different ways of communicating or not.

b Now complete the news items with the most appropriate verbs from the box in the correct form.

> announce   claim   interview   mention   tell

> Police [1] _____ yesterday that calls to the emergency 999 number had risen sharply in recent months. They [2] _____ the public to ignore a hoax story which [3] _____ that dialling 999 will charge your phone battery.

> admit   inform   invent   keep quiet   report

> The newspaper which recently [4] _____ that Beijing was showing digital sunrises on huge screens because air pollution was too bad for people to see the real thing has now [5] _____ that a journalist actually [6] _____ the story.

9 **TASK** Work with a partner or in small groups. Go to page 126. Choose one of the stories about a hoax.

Reading & Speaking   references

1   Work with a partner. Discuss your reactions to the quotation below.

> '**EXPERT: A MAN WHO MAKES THREE CORRECT GUESSES CONSECUTIVELY.**'
> DR L. J. PETERS (AMERICAN EDUCATIONALIST AND WRITER)

2a Read the sentences. What does the underlined word in each sentence refer to?

1   We all read the article, but none of us liked <u>it</u>.

2   We all had to study science up to the age of sixteen at school, and <u>so</u> do students at secondary school nowadays.

3   <u>He</u> may be the most famous scientist of all time, but Albert Einstein only got his first scientific job when he was twenty-nine.

b   What is different about the way the reference word is used in sentence 3?

3a Read the information in the Unlock the code box.

🔒 **UNLOCK THE CODE**
understanding references

* We use reference words (e.g. *she, us, those, one, so*) to refer to a word or group of words in a text. Sometimes these words refer to a noun or phrase that came before them.

  We all ate the pizza, but none of us liked it.

  The boss left early and so did we.

* Sometimes they refer to something after them.

  When they arrested the men, the police were very satisfied.

---

b   Now read paragraph 1 of the article.

1   Underline the reference words.

2   What do they refer to?

4   Read the article. What is the main point it is making?

1   Women are better musicians than men.

2   Even experts are influenced by what they see.

3   Orchestras have improved the way they choose their musicians.

Home	News	World	Sport	Culture	Finance

Film	Music	Art	Books	TV and Radio	Theatre

Not as expert as they think

1   In his book *Blink*, the Canadian author Malcom Gladwell tells a wonderful story. It shows, he says, that even if they are very experienced and intelligent, experts can be wrong. It's about music, but it's true for all kinds of other situations.

2   Before the 1980s, when <u>they</u> wanted to find and employ a new musician, orchestras used a very simple system. A group of three 'judges' from the orchestra would sit in a room. One musician after another would come in and play their instrument in front of <u>them</u>, and then the judges would choose <u>the best</u>. Under this system, most of the musicians who were chosen were men. Naturally, since the judges were all experts, nobody thought much of <u>this</u>: they must be able to tell a good musician from a bad <u>one</u>. Men were probably simply better musicians.

3   But then, for a number of reasons, in the 1980s, orchestras started putting up screens in the rooms where these auditions took place, so the judges couldn't see if the musicians were men or women. Amazingly, orchestras started hiring many more women. In fact, [1]_____ hired *more* women than men, which suggested that women were better musicians!

4   The conclusion was that the judges were deciding not on what they could hear, but what they could see. Their judgement probably changed according to whether [2]_____ were seeing a man or a woman. Personally, I find [3]_____ very worrying – the idea that even experts are strongly influenced in this way. Gladwell even jokes that when [4]_____ looks around his classes at the best colleges in the USA, he thinks that every student has been chosen because [5]_____ is the *prettiest*, not the best.

5a Read paragraph 2 of the article and decide what the underlined words refer to. Check your answers with a partner.

they (line 1)	_____	*them* (line 5)	_____
the best (line 6)	_____	*this* (line 8)	_____
one (line 9)	_____		

b Read paragraphs 3 and 4. Add the words below in the correct place and draw an arrow to the noun they refer to. Check your answers with a partner.

> he   he/she   it   they   they

6 Work in small groups and discuss the questions.
1 Why did orchestras start hiring more women?
2 What do you think people judge other people on?
3 What do you notice when you first meet people?

Vocabulary & Speaking   comment adverbs

7a Look at the sentence from the article on page 20. Underline the word which gives the writer's opinion.

> 'Amazingly, orchestras started hiring many more women.'

b What does the writer feel about orchestras hiring women like this?

8 Read the information in the Vocabulary focus box. Underline two more examples of comment adverbs in the magazine article.

VOCABULARY FOCUS   comment adverbs

- Some adverbs tell us the view or opinion of the speaker, e.g. *curiously, luckily, remarkably, sadly, surprisingly, unfortunately*
- Comment adverbs usually go at the beginning of sentences.
  Surprisingly, *orchestras started hiring many more women.*
- Sometimes comment adverbs can go in the middle of a sentence.
  Orchestras, **curiously**, *started hiring women left, right and centre.*

9 How does the choice of comment adverb affect the meaning of these sentences?
1 *Interestingly / Fortunately*, I know lots of people who want to work on television.
2 I got to the bus stop about five minutes after the bus was due, but *luckily / remarkably* all the buses were running late.
3 *Remarkably / Sadly*, none of the students passed the final exam.
4 *Personally / Curiously*, I find learning new things easy.

10a TASK Work with a partner. Choose a situation or think of one of your own when things went wrong or something unexpected happened.
- a meal in a restaurant
- missing a train/plane
- thinking you recognize someone you know but actually don't know

b Tell your partner about them, using some of the comment adverbs.

2.4 Speaking and writing

GOALS ■ Engage a listener and show interest ■ Write a narrative

Speaking & Listening showing interest

1a Work with a partner. Look at the pictures and words. What do you think happened in this true story?

b Ask your teacher *yes/no* questions to find out more about the story.

c When you think you have enough facts, work together with your partner to tell the whole story.

2 2.6))) Listen to the story and compare with your ideas.

3 Which of these statements do you agree with? Why? Discuss with a partner.
- Coincidences are often meaningful and 'meant to happen'.
- Coincidences are just maths. If enough people are involved, many odd-seeming coincidences will happen. For example, at a typical football match with 50,000 people, statistically 135 people will share your birthday.

4a 2.6))) Listen again and write down the phrases the speakers use to engage the listener and show interest.

b Check your answers in the Language for speaking box.

LANGUAGE FOR SPEAKING engaging the listener and showing interest

Engaging the listener
I heard this incredible story about …
Someone told me about …
You're not going to believe this, but …

Showing interest
Really?
How amazing/surprising …!
That's awful/incredible …!
What, you mean …?
No way!
You're joking!

PRONUNCIATION intonation – showing interest

5a 2.7))) Listen to the ways of showing interest. For each one, mark if you think the speaker sounds interested or not interested. What makes their voice sound interested?
1 What happened?
2 Oh no, that's awful.
3 You're joking.
4 What, you mean the ring was on the carrot?!
5 Really?
6 No way! That's incredible!

b 2.7))) Listen and repeat.

6 Work with a partner. Student A, turn to page 127. Student B, turn to page 133.

Reading & Writing a narrative

7a Put the sections in the right order to make a logical story.

A As soon as he told his son, they hugged each other and went for a coffee to talk. Barry had lost contact with his family while he was working abroad.

B After a while, the woman happened to notice Barry's identity card, hanging up in the cab. 'Isn't that funny,' she said to her boyfriend, 'you've got the same name as the taxi driver.'

C The man then said, jokingly, 'Is your first name Barry?' In an instant, the taxi driver's mouth went dry. He waited until there was somewhere safe to park, pulled the car over and said, 'Yes.' The taxi driver had realized that the man in the back of his cab was his son, who he had not seen for thirty-four years.

D Colin said, 'I didn't recognize him at all, but it is great to have my dad back.'

1 E A few years ago, a taxi driver called Barry Bagshaw had a life-changing experience when he went to work one day.

F It seemed like any other day. Barry picked up a man and his girlfriend from a hotel in the seaside town where he lived.

G By an amazing coincidence, it turned out that his son, Colin, who had been living in South Africa, had recently arrived to take up a new job in the same small town where his father lived.

b Which sections relate to the narrative structure from the Communication exercise in Lesson 2.1?

1 Announcing a story is about to start
2 Giving background information
3 Main events
4 Conclusion
5 Final comment

8a Read the story again and underline any words and phrases used to say *when* something happened.

b How many of the time expressions in the Language for writing box did you find?

LANGUAGE FOR WRITING time expressions

In a narrative it is important to say *when* events happened, as well as how quickly they happened. Try to use a variety of time expressions.

After a while/In the end/In an instant/Just then
A few years/months/weeks/days/hours ago
Recently
Straightaway

9 Complete the second sentence so that it has a similar meaning to the first, using a time expression from the Language for writing box. There is one expression you do not need.

1 As soon as he heard the news, he rang her.
   When he heard the news, he _____.
2 Not long ago he had changed his job.
   He had changed his job _____.
3 At that moment, the car suddenly stopped.
   _____, the car suddenly stopped.
4 Finally, he went back to Australia.
   _____, he went back to Australia.
5 Within seconds, everything had changed.
   _____, everything had changed.
6 A short time later, he picked up his bag and left.
   _____, he picked up his bag and left.

10 Use the following story skeleton, or your own ideas, to write a story about a coincidence. Think about the order of events, and how to use time expressions to link the events together.
- Man paints picture and sends it to a gallery.
- Man finds picture thrown into his garden.
- Did gallery owner really hate it?
- Man rings gallery owner/asks why she did this.
- Gallery owner says she really likes picture.
- Picture and other things stolen from her car.
- Thieves kept valuables/threw picture away into a garden.
- Thieves threw picture away into artist's garden!

11 Read your partner's version of the story and answer the questions.
1 What time expressions have they used?
2 How is their story the same as or different from yours?

2.5 Video

Seven good stories

1 Match the questions to the answers.

1 Does the story have an exciting plot?
2 Does the story make you laugh?
3 Does the story make you cry?
4 Is it a frightening story?
5 Are there any surprising moments in the story?
6 Do you like the ending?

a Yes, it's a really funny comedy.
b Yes, because the characters all live happily ever after!
c Yes, it's a tragedy. The couple die in each other's arms.
d Yes, one man goes on an adventure. He meets many people, and some amazing things happen to them.
e Yes, it's a shock when we discover that the hero of the story is actually the little boy who lives next door.
f Yes, it is. You believe the villain is going to kill everyone.

2 Work with a partner. Match a photo with one of the stories from the list below. What do you know about these stories?
• *Macbeth*   • *Jaws*   • *Dracula*
• *Aladdin*   • *The Wizard of Oz*   • *Harry Potter*
• *Cinderella*

3 ▶ Watch the video. Note down the seven types of stories. Match these to the stories in exercise 2.

4 ▶ Watch again and choose the correct options to complete the text.

> [1] *Everyone / Certain* people believe that stories are all based on seven types of plot. In *Cinderella*, *Aladdin* and *Harry Potter*, the main characters all [2] *win and lose / lose* something before learning a lesson about life. Villains [3] *always / normally* die at the end of tragedies. In sagas, the main characters go on a great journey. At the end of these stories, they usually [4] *reach / fail to reach* their destination. In a 'voyage and return' story, the main character will usually return home with [5] *nothing at all / a greater understanding of the world*. You will always find [6] *a romantic tale / some funny characters* in a comedy.

5a **TASK** Work with a partner. Choose a story you know well. The story can be from a film or a book. Ask each other questions about your story. Use the questions from exercise 1 to help you.

b Decide which of the seven plot types your partner's story belongs to.

Review

1a Complete the sentences with the correct form of the verbs in brackets: past simple, past continuous or past perfect simple.

A bad day

1 Last Tuesday my computer broke while I _____ (try) to finish an important piece of work.
2 So I _____ (call) a friend who knows about computers, and he came over straightaway.
3 He _____ (have) a look at it, but he couldn't fix it.
4 He _____ (take) my keys so he could come back to fix it the next day while I was at work.
5 The next morning when I _____ (try) to leave for work, I discovered that he _____ (lock) my front door from the outside, and I couldn't get out of the flat.
6 My parents _____ (travel) abroad, and no one else I know _____ (have) a spare key.
7 I tried to call my friend, but he _____ (leave) his phone in my flat. It _____ (ring) right next to me.
8 I _____ (have) to wait for him to arrive, and so I was very late for work.

b Work with a partner. Circle *had*, *was* and *were* in the completed sentences. Decide together which should be pronounced as a 'weak' form.

c 2.8⟩⟩ Listen and check your answers. Practise reading the sentences aloud together.

2a Each of the sentences comes from a different story. Choose the correct option to complete each sentence.

1 *By the time / As soon as* he arrived, she had already left.
2 *While / During* the summer, he worked in an ice cream van.
3 He stayed there alone *by the time / until* it got dark, then, feeling sad, he went home.
4 He walked off happily. *Meanwhile / While*, she was already planning her revenge.
5 *As soon as / During* he got home, he turned on the news.
6 *By the time / While* I was walking to work, I saw something very strange.

b Work with a partner. Choose one of the sentences and decide together what happened before and after this sentence. Write it as a short story, using some different time linkers.

3a 2.9⟩⟩ You will hear definitions for each of the verbs below. Number each word as it is defined.

appear	___	recognize	___
expect	___	remind	___
forget	___	scream	___
realize	___	wonder	___

b Work with a partner. Choose five of the verbs and write sentences using them. Vary the topics and tenses you use.

c Work with a different pair. Read out your sentences, leaving out the verbs. The other pair has to put in the correct verbs in the correct form.

4 Complete the sentences with an appropriate verb from the box in the correct form.

admit announce claim inform keep quiet mention

1 Lucy _____ you had a new job, but she didn't say much about it.
2 At first he denied having taken the money, but in the end he _____ it was him.
3 'Ladies and gentlemen, I am very happy to _____ that the winner of the award is ...'
4 He _____ he had once worked for the Queen, but I didn't believe him.
5 If you can't say anything nice, you'd better _____.
6 'I'm sorry to _____ you that the company is closing down.'

5a Add a comment adverb to show your attitude to each statement.

1 _____, women in most countries earn between 70% and 90% of what men earn.
2 _____, 55% of university graduates in the UK are women.
3 _____, women talk almost three times as much as men.
4 _____, women live longer than men.

b Discuss the statements with a partner.

6a 2.10⟩⟩ Listen and write down four statements.

b Read the statements to your partner and respond to each one by showing interest.

3 Life skills

3.1 Challenges

GOALS ■ Talk about challenges and success ■ Talk about ability

Vocabulary & Listening challenges and success

1 Work with a partner. What do you find difficult to resist? For example: buying clothes, spending too much time online, eating junk food.

2 Work with a partner. Look at the photo. The children are trying to resist the temptation to eat the marshmallow. Which child do you think is more likely to succeed? Why?

3 3.1))) Listen to the first part of a talk on the Marshmallow Test results. What was Mischel's experiment?

4 3.2))) Listen to the rest of the talk and answer the questions. Check your answers with a partner.

1 How long did the children have to wait without eating the marshmallow?
2 How many of them failed the test?
3 In what ways were the children who didn't eat the marshmallows more successful in later life?
4 How did the successful children manage not to eat the marshmallow?
5 Why is it important to be able to wait for something you want?

5 3.3))) Complete the phrases in the text with the verbs in the box in the correct form. Then listen and check your answers.

> avoid be deal give make (x2) prefer ~~resist~~ rise succeed in wait

PRONUNCIATION word stress

6a Work with a partner. Say the verbs in the box aloud and mark the stress on each verb.

> achieve avoid manage observe prefer resist succeed

b What is the most common stress pattern in verbs with two syllables?

c 3.4))) Listen, check and repeat.

The Marshmallow Test

In the Marshmallow Test, researchers left four-year-old children alone in a room with a marshmallow. If the children managed to ¹ _resist_ **temptation** and not eat the marshmallow, the researcher promised them a reward of two marshmallows. However, most of the children found it difficult to ² _____ **patient** and ³ _____ **in** before the time was up. They ⁴ _____ **to have something immediately** rather than ⁵ _____ **for** what they really wanted. The researchers found that, as adults, those children who could ⁶ _____ **to the challenge** were generally much more successful than the others.

The best technique was to ⁷ _____ **thinking about** the marshmallow at all. The successful children ⁸ _____ **with the problem** by looking away or covering their eyes. If they didn't think about the marshmallow, they didn't have to ⁹ _____ **an effort** not to eat it.

When Mischel taught a different set of children this technique, nearly all the children ¹⁰ _____ **waiting** the full time. Learning these techniques can help in adult life because being able to wait helps us to ¹¹ _____ **the right choices**.

Oxford 3000™

7 Work with a partner and discuss the questions.

1 What kind of things do children find hard to wait for?

2 What happens if children get everything they want immediately?

3 How can children learn to be patient?

4 What techniques do you use when you need to resist temptation? For example, avoid thinking about it, promise yourself a reward later, …

Grammar & Speaking ability

8 Read the information in the Grammar focus box. Match sentences a–e to 1–5 in the box.

a Some ate it straightaway, some **managed to** wait a while before giving in.

b Only 30% of the kids **were able to** wait the full fifteen minutes.

c The kids who **couldn't** resist temptation were generally less successful.

d When he taught the children some simple techniques … nearly all the children **succeeded in** waiting the full fifteen minutes.

e … you **will be able to** make better decisions about your future.

GRAMMAR FOCUS ability

Present and past

- To talk about general ability, we use *can/can't* + infinitive or *am/are/is able to*.
- To talk about doing or not doing something with some difficulty, we use *(don't/doesn't) manage to* + infinitive/ *succeed in* + *-ing*.
- In the past we use:
  a *could/couldn't* or *was(n't)/were(n't) able to* + infinitive (general ability) [1]____
  b *was(n't)/were(n't) able to* (on a specific past occasion) [2]____
  c *(didn't) manage(d) to/succeed(ed) in* (with some difficulty on a specific past occasion) [3]____ [4]____

Future

- To talk about future ability we use:
  a *will/won't be able to* + infinitive (general ability and on a specific future occasion) [5]____
  b *will/won't manage to* + infinitive/*will/won't succeed in* + *-ing* (with some difficulty on a specific future occasion) *If you work hard, I'm sure you'll manage to get the grades you need.*

→ Grammar Reference page 140

9a Work with a partner. Complete the tips in the blog using *can/can't, could/couldn't, (not) manage to, (not) succeed in,* and *(not) be able to* in the correct form.

Home > Success > How to succeed

How to succeed

▶ **Remember that you** [1]____ **choose to resist temptation if you want to.** Just because you [2]____ stop yourself yesterday, doesn't mean you [3]____ never do it.

▶ **Think about something else.** If you [4]____ turning your attention away from the chocolate for a while, you may forget about it altogether.

▶ **Stop for a minute.** Perhaps you felt you [5]____ spare the time to go for a run yesterday? But if you stopped and really thought about it, you'd see it was much more important than many of the things you did [6]____ do.

▶ **Think ahead.** Plan for the future and you will [7]____ achieving your goals.

▶ **Never buy things on impulse.** Go home and think about it. If you really like it, you [8]____ (still) buy it tomorrow, or next week.

▶ **Spend time with people who are** [9]____ **resist temptation themselves.** Pick up some valuable lessons by observing someone whose patience you admire.

b Work with a partner or in small groups. Which are the most useful tips? Put them in order of usefulness.

10 **TASK** Work with a partner. Tell your partner about …

- something you can do now that you couldn't do a few years ago.
- a time when you succeeded in resisting temptation.
- a time when you managed to deal with a problem successfully or make the right choice.
- something you hope you will be able to do in the future and how you plan to do it.

3.2 Faking it?

Vocabulary & Reading · work skills

1 Work with a partner. Look at the two jobs in the photos and decide what skills, apart from cooking skills, are needed for each job.

2 Work with a partner. Read the newspaper review of a recent television programme and discuss these questions.

1 Did the participant succeed in his challenge?
2 What difficulties did he face?

3 Would you enjoy learning to do something completely new in four weeks? Why/Why not? Discuss with a partner.

4 Look at the list of skills below (1–13).

1 being a good leader	8 solving problems
2 being confident in yourself	9 being reliable
3 making decisions	10 managing a team
4 managing (tight) schedules	11 multitasking
5 persuading people to do things	12 setting goals
6 taking responsibility	13 working hard
7 working well under pressure	

Which skill(s) is/are about …?

- working with other people
- managing limited time
- using your intelligence
- being a good boss
- being a good worker

Some skills can be in more than one category.

5 Work in small groups. Decide together which skills Ed needed for both jobs. Give reasons for your choices.

Sunday, 20 April

Review

Last night's TV

The best thing on TV last night was *Faking It*. It takes someone with no experience in a particular job and sends them to live and train with an expert for four weeks. They then have to take part in a contest against professionals, and a panel of expert judges decides which participant is the 'faker'. At the beginning of the programme, we met Ed working in a fast food van in all weathers, selling chips and burgers. In this job he didn't need to do much apart from arrive at work on time and be reasonably pleasant to people. All this changed as he had to learn how *not* to be pleasant to people as a head chef in a top London restaurant.

According to Ed's teacher, one of London's top chefs, to succeed as a chef you must have a passion for food, the ability to run a team, confidence, work to very precise times, and be able to cook.

So, could Ed cook? He explained his technique was to 'wait until the burger went brown on both sides'; [1] *he didn't have to do much more.* To test his skills, his teacher asked him to cook the food in his fridge, [2] *telling Ed he could prepare it any way he wanted.* The results were not good. Even the vegetables were overcooked, as Ed didn't realize that [3] *he didn't need to boil carrots for an hour or more.*

But Ed's biggest problem was that he hated telling people what to do. As the top chef explained to Ed, [4] *'he couldn't be a head chef and be nice'.* Ed was shocked to realize that [5] *he couldn't say please and thank you all the time* if he wanted the team to respect him. [6] *He also had to learn how to walk* and stand more confidently.

Amazingly, after four weeks of hard work and quite a few problems, none of the judges realized that Ed was a complete beginner. In fact, one offered him a job as a chef.

Grammar & Speaking obligation, permission and possibility

6 Read the information in the Grammar focus box. Look at phrases 1–6 in the review on page 28 and match them to rules a–f in the box.

GRAMMAR FOCUS obligation, permission and possibility

Present
- If something is necessary or obligatory, we use **must** when talking about the feelings and wishes of the speaker, and **have to** to talk about obligations that come from someone or somewhere else.
- If it is necessary or obligatory NOT to do something, we use **mustn't**, and **don't have to/don't need to** if it isn't necessary or obligatory.

Past
- If something was necessary/obligatory, we use **had to**.

a _____

We can't use 'must' with this meaning in the past.

- If something wasn't necessary, we use **didn't have to/didn't need to**.

b _____

c _____

permission and possibility – could/couldn't

Present
We use **can/can't** if something is/isn't allowed or possible.

Past
If something was/wasn't allowed or possible, we use **could/couldn't**.

d _____

e _____

f _____

→ **Grammar Reference** page 141

7a Complete the text which compares Ed's old job with his new one, using the verbs from the Grammar focus box. Sometimes more than one answer is possible.

When he was working in the burger van, Ed **1**_____ be reliable and turn up for work on time. He also **2**_____ be polite to the customers. However, he **3**_____ take much responsibility as his boss dealt with the money. He **4**_____ get up early because the van opened at 11 a.m. When he wanted to, he **5**_____ even take a day off work.

Now that he's training to be a chef, it's very different. He **6**_____ manage a team, even though he finds it difficult to tell people what to do. It's also a very high-pressure job, so he **7**_____ work to tight deadlines. However, he **8**_____ work outside any more, and he **9**_____ take home really nice food when the restaurant has closed.

b 3.5)) Listen and check your answers.

8 Work with a partner. Student A, turn to page 127. Student B, turn to page 133.

9a Make a list of six work skills you feel you possess.

b How did you acquire these skills? For example:

I'm good at working in a team. I used to be captain of the football team. I had to take responsibility for choosing the right players. I could …

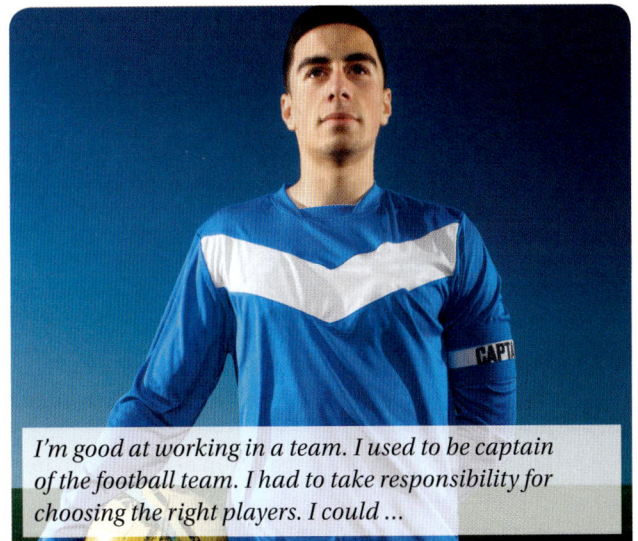

Make similar notes about each of the skills you chose.

c TASK Work with a partner. Ask each other these questions.
- What are your three most important skills?
- What three positive things would your last boss/team colleagues/friends say about you?

Give full and convincing answers, with reasons and examples.

▶ **VOX POPS VIDEO 3**

3.3 Vocabulary and skills development

Reading & Speaking complex noun phrases (1)

1 Work with a partner. Have you ever done any of these things? How did you feel?
   a taken a very important exam
   b made a speech or presentation to a large number of people
   c sung in public
   d had an interview for a job you really wanted

2a Read the information in the Unlock the code box about recognizing complex noun phrases.

> 🔒 **UNLOCK THE CODE**
> recognizing complex noun phrases (1)
>
> Sometimes the subject of a sentence can be very long or contain another verb.
>
> | Subject | Main verb | |
> | --- | --- | --- |
> | Making a speech | is | sometimes hard to do. |
> | Learning these new techniques | helps | in later life. |
> | One of the test groups | experienced | symptoms of stress. |
> | One group who took part in the experiment | were told | nothing. |
>
> When you read, it is important to be able to identify the subject and the main verb quickly.

b Look at the statements. Underline the subjects and circle the verbs.
   1 Stress can actually be good for you.
   2 Taking an important exam often causes people to lose sleep.
   3 Speaking in front of a large group of people can be very stressful.
   4 People who are most under stress show physical signs such as shaking or sweating.

3a Look at the photos and the title of the article. What do you think the article will say? Discuss with a partner.

b Read the article. Were your ideas in the article?

4a Look at the numbered sentences in the article. Underline the subject and circle the verb.

b Decide if the statements are true (T) or false (F). Correct the false statements.
   1 It's difficult to find information on the internet about how to reduce your stress.
   2 The Social Stress Test is a way of measuring stress.
   3 The signs of stress show that you are ready for a difficult experience.
   4 Only one group had some damage to their body.
   5 Some people think these results are difficult to prove.

5 Work with a partner and discuss the questions.
   1 How would you feel in the situations in the Social Stress Test?
   2 Do you agree that stress can sometimes be good for you?
   3 How do you feel after a challenging experience?

Health and Fitness > Stress

Stress could be good for you – if you believe it is

Have you ever given a talk or speech to a large group of people? If so, you'll probably remember it as a very stressful experience … you sweat, your mouth goes dry, your heart starts beating fast.

Vocabulary & Speaking compound adjectives

6a Look at these compound adjectives from the article. Which nouns do they describe?

  a stress-producing
  b five-minute

b Can you think of compound adjectives which match definitions 1–6?

1	describes somebody who uses their left hand to write	_____-handed
2	another word for beautiful or handsome	good-_____
3	the opposite of part-time	_____-time
4	an adjective which means that something lasts two minutes	two-_____
5	describes a shirt which has short sleeves	short-_____
6	describes a person who works hard	hard-_____

Like · Comment · Share

And most people believe that stress is bad for you. **1** *Putting 'reduce your stress levels' into Google gets you 34 million hits.* Articles in the newspapers or on health websites are always telling us how to reduce our stress levels. **2** *Titles like '23 scientifically proven ways to reduce stress right now!' are common.* But what if it isn't actually true?

3 *Experiments with a technique called the Social Stress Test suggest that stress is only harmful if you believe that it is.* In the experiment, two groups of people were asked to perform a series of stress-producing actions, such as doing a maths test while the 'instructor' shouted, 'Faster! faster! That's not very good!' Or giving a five-minute talk to a group of 'experts' who were pretending to be bored.

But the two groups had been treated differently before they took the test. The first group had not been told anything, whereas the second group were told that stress is *good* for you, and that **4** *the dry mouth and beating heart are the body's way of preparing you for a challenge.*

Amazingly, the results were quite different. **5** *The people who had been told nothing showed signs of damage to the blood vessels around the heart*, while those of the other group were normal – as if they were not under stress at all.

6 *These results have been confirmed by other tests.* It seems that the effects of stress depend on what you believe about stress!

---

c Read the information in the Vocabulary focus box about compound adjectives and check your answers.

VOCABULARY FOCUS compound adjectives

Compound adjectives are generally made up of two words, usually either becoming a single word or joined by a hyphen. Here are some of the most common forms they can take.

1 ending in a past participle: *left-handed, short-sleeved*
2 ending in -*ing*: *good-looking, hard-working*
3 ending in a noun: *two-hour, full-time*

7a Add a word from the box to make a compound adjective.

| going   hand   known   made   page   priced |
| speaking   star |

1 easy- _____   5 500- _____
2 home- _____   6 second- _____
3 five- _____   7 English- _____
4 over- _____   8 well- _____

b Work with a partner. What do you think the compound adjectives mean?

c **3.6**))) Listen and mark the main stress in each one.

d **3.6**))) Listen again and practise saying the words.

8 Complete the questions with the compound adjectives in exercise **7a**. Sometimes more than one answer is possible.

1 Have you ever bought a _____-_____ car?
2 When you were young, did you ever wear _____ clothes?
3 Would you rather read a _____ novel or watch a six-hour film?
4 When was the last time you thought something was _____ in a shop?
5 Who is the most _____ musician in your country? Do you like him/her? Why/Why not?
6 Do you prefer a very strict or a very _____ teacher? Why?
7 Have you ever stayed in a _____ hotel? Where? When?
8 Can you name five _____ countries?

9 **TASK** Work with a partner. Ask and answer the questions in exercise **8**. Report the most interesting answers to the class.

3.4 Speaking and writing

GOALS ■ Give practical instructions ■ Write a paragraph supporting an opinion

Listening & Speaking practical instructions

1 Look at the photos. What do you think a 'Litre of Light' is?

Alfredo Moser, a Brazilian mechanic, invented the 'Litre of Light' in 2002. Many thousands of homes around the world now have light for free, using no electricity.

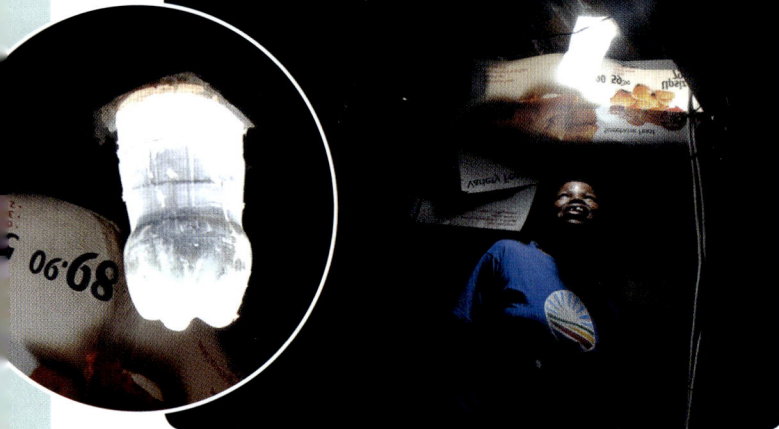

2a Look at the illustrations. Describe what you see in each.

b 3.7))) Listen to the instructions and complete 1–6 with one word in each gap.

1 _____ a hole in the metal sheet.
2 _____ the plastic bottle with sandpaper.
3 _____ the bottle in the hole in the metal and _____ it in place.
4 _____ the bottle with water and _____ ten millilitres of bleach.
5 _____ the _____ on the bottle.
6 _____ a hole in the roof the same size as the bottle.

3a 3.8))) Listen and complete the instructions.

1 _____ you do is cut a hole in the metal.
2 _____ done that, put the bottle in the hole in the metal ...
3 _____ the glue's _____, fill the bottle with water ...
4 _____ that, it's time to go to the roof.

b 3.8))) Compare your answers with a partner. Listen again and check.

PRONUNCIATION pauses in instructions

We often put pauses in instructions to help people understand.

4a 3.9))) Listen and finish marking the pauses in the instructions below.

Next, // rub the bottle with sandpaper. // When you've done that, put the bottle in the hole in the metal and glue the bottle in place.

b Practise giving the instructions clearly.

5 **TASK** Work in small groups and give instructions on how to do something.

1 Choose a skill you are good at and make brief notes on how to do it. Include five steps.
2 Use the information in the Language for speaking box. Add pauses to make the instructions clearer.
3 Work in small groups. Give each other the instructions. When you listen, ask questions to make sure you understand.

LANGUAGE FOR SPEAKING giving instructions

Putting instructions in order

The first thing you do is ...	While you're doing this, ...
When you've done this, ...	After doing this, ...

Explaining or showing

You do it like this.	Let me show you.
Let me give you an example.	Make sure ...

Asking questions

How do you ...?	OK, what next?
Can you say that part again?	Can you show me?

Reading & Writing   writing an opinion paragraph

6   Work in small groups and discuss the questions.

1   What was the last thing you learned to do?

2   Do you think it's important to learn new things as we get older? Why/Why not?

7   Read the paragraph from an article in an educational magazine.

1   What is the writer's general opinion?

2   Which phrase shows the writer is giving their opinion?

TECHNOLOGY – OPINION

Nowadays the idea that learning is only for children is obviously not true. It seems to me that as an adult you can't rely on what you learnt in school to get by any longer. Technology at work and at home, such as computerized household appliances, tablets and mobile phones, are an essential part of everyday life. On top of that, all these devices are constantly developing. So, if you want to be able to function in the 21st century, you have to keep learning and developing, too!

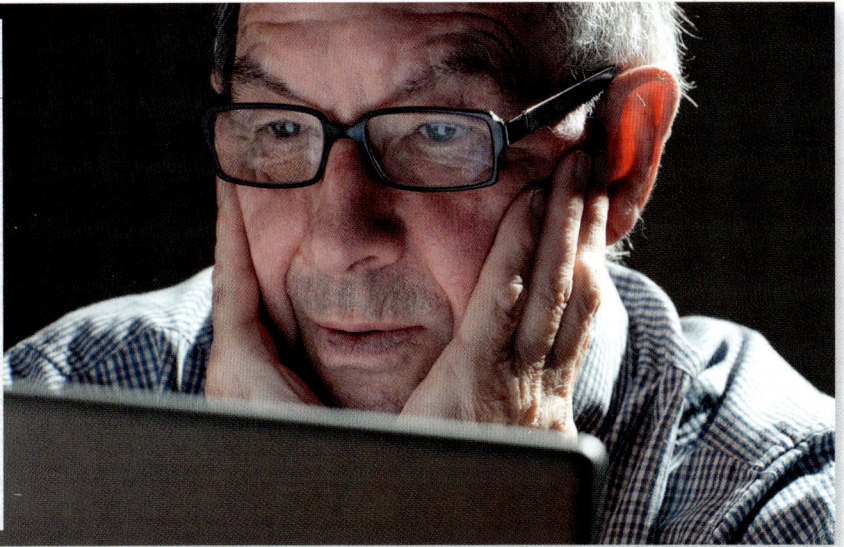

8a   Read the paragraph again and underline one phrase for *adding information to support the idea* and one for *giving an example*.

b   Compare with your partner. Then read the information in the Language for writing box to check.

LANGUAGE FOR WRITING   supporting an opinion

Support an opinion by adding more information and giving examples.

Adding more information

• On top of that, …/In addition, …

  It's important to learn new things. **In addition**, it seems that learning new things is actually good for your brain.

• … also …   … as well.

  It's important to learn new things and it seems it's actually good for your brain **as well**.

Giving an example

• … such as …   for instance, …   for example, …

  People used to have to learn English or French, but nowadays other languages. For example, Chinese and Arabic are becoming more and more essential in business.

9   Work with a partner. Choose the correct options to complete these sentences on the same topic as in the article.

1   Some people say that older people who continue to learn new things, *such as / as well* language and computer skills, stay healthier.

2   Research seems to show that learning new skills is good for our brains; *for instance / on top of that*, the activity of learning improves our memory.

3   A new hobby gives us something to talk about with our friends and family. *Too / In addition*, research has shown that our happiness levels increase as we learn.

4   Learning helps us to stay interesting, *too / such as*, because it gives us new experiences and makes us solve new problems.

10a   **TASK**   Work with a partner. Choose a topic and discuss your opinions.

• Everyone should learn how to do something new after the age of fifty.

• Companies should pay for their employees to receive training and education.

• Adults can be better at learning new things than children.

b   Make a note of three main points to support your opinion. Think of examples for each point.

c   Now write the paragraph. Use the phrases in the Language for writing box to support your opinion with extra information and examples.

3.5 Video

A woman's life: 1914 vs 2014

1   Look at the photos. Work with a partner and discuss the possible connection between the three photos.

2   How do you think life was different for women in Britain one hundred years ago? Discuss your ideas with a partner. Write one idea for each heading.

- Family Life
- Marriage
- Work
- Women's Rights

3   ▶ Watch the video. Did the presenter mention any of your ideas from exercise 2?

4   ▶ Watch again and choose the correct options to answer the questions.

1   How many people visit the museum every year?
   a   About half a million.
   b   Nearly a million.

2   Why didn't many women receive a full education about one hundred years ago?
   a   Only a few schools allowed girls to complete their education.
   b   It was unusual for girls to stay at school until eighteen years old.

3   What had the suffragettes achieved by 1914?
   a   They had changed the lives of many women.
   b   They had persuaded society to pay more attention to women's rights.

4   Which women got the vote in 1918?
   a   The women who had carried out certain jobs during the First World War.
   b   Property-owning women who were also over a certain age.

5   What does the presenter say about women in Britain today?
   a   There are more working women than at any other time in history.
   b   The number of women at work is increasing faster than the number of men.

5a   **TASK**   Work in small groups. Make a list of five skills needed in society one hundred years ago. Then make a list of five skills needed today. Are the lists very different?

b   Compare your lists with another group. Which skills do both groups agree are important in society today?

Review

1a Cross out the options which are not possible.

1. I *couldn't / can't / wasn't able to* swim until I was nearly ten.
2. It was difficult, but I finally *succeeded in / managed to / was able to* learning.
3. However, I still *couldn't / can't / can* swim very far.
4. I *managed to / could / succeeded in* pass my driving test the third time I took it.
5. I was quite good at driving, but I *couldn't / wasn't able to / managed to* park correctly.
6. After I passed, I *can / was able to / managed to* drive to see my parents.

b Work with a partner. Explain why the forms you crossed out are incorrect.

2a **3.10**)) Listen and write the sentences you hear.

b Work with a partner. Decide if the sentences are about obligation (O), lack of obligation (LO), permission (P) or lack of permission (LP).

3a Match 1–5 to a–e to make expressions.

1. be   a temptation
2. deal   b the right choice
3. make   c with a problem
4. resist   d to a challenge
5. rise   e patient

b Choose one of the completed phrases and tell your partner about a time in your life when you did this.

4a Which verb can be used with each group of phrases?

1. *be / have* _____ a good leader, confident in yourself, reliable
2. *deal / manage* _____ a team, tight schedules
3. *make / work* _____ hard, well under pressure

b Which three skills are most important for a manager? Discuss with a partner.

5a **3.11**)) Listen to the first part of six compound adjectives and complete them with a word from the box.

-going -hand -known -looking -speaking -working

b Write a sentence using each completed compound adjective. Compare your answers with a partner.

6a Complete the conversation with the phrases in the box.

Make sure   let me show you   What next
The first thing you do is   While you're doing that
How do you   you do it like this

A ¹_____ to put some flour in a bowl, with a little salt. Then you crack an egg into the bowl.
B I'm not very good at that. ²_____ crack the egg without getting bits of shell in the bowl?
A No problem, ³_____. Look, you crack it on the edge of the bowl, like this. Then you mix it in and add the milk. ⁴_____ you mix it very thoroughly, so there aren't any lumps.
B ⁵_____?
A Then you have to wait for about thirty minutes. ⁶_____ you can get ready whatever you want to put on the pancakes. Then you heat some oil or butter and put some mixture in the pan. When the first side is cooked, you flip it over. Look, ⁷_____.
B Wow! That's clever.

b **3.12**)) Listen and check your answers.

c Work with a partner. Write a similar conversation explaining how to do something, using the phrases in exercise **6a**.

35

4.1 Living on water

Lake Titicaca

Bangkok

Bangkok

Maldives

Vocabulary & Speaking
living on water

1 Work with a partner. Look at the photos and use the words in the box to describe them.

at sea beach canal coast ferry float inland
island lake mainland ocean reeds sand waves

2a Read the article from a business magazine and look at the photos. What does the article say about each of them? Discuss your answers with a partner.

b How many of the words in exercise 1 can you find in the text? Underline them.

3 Work with a partner or in small groups and discuss the questions.
1 What do you think are the advantages and disadvantages of living on water?
2 Do you agree that large numbers of people will start living on water, rather than on land? Why/Why not?
3 Would you like to live on water? Why/Why not?

NEWS **BUSINESS** MONEY ARTS+LIFE PEOPLE

Living on water

As cities become bigger, those who can't move inland are starting to consider moving out, onto the sea itself. There are already cultures where a life on water is nothing new. Islands made from reeds float in the middle of Peru's Lake Titicaca, home to an ancient community. Venice is made up of 118 islands; and the Thai capital, Bangkok, with its canals, is famous for its floating markets. Fishermen live at sea for long periods, but could large numbers of people really move onto the water?

Koen Olthuis, the Dutch founder of *Waterstudio.nl* and a floating architecture expert, thinks so. His company is involved in a project in the Maldives, a group of islands just 1.5 metres above sea level. By 2100, their beautiful beaches and white sand could be completely underwater. However, before the architects can solve this problem, some cash has to

Grammar & Speaking *will/be going to* for predictions and decisions

4a Work with a partner. Complete the sentences with the correct form of *will/be going to* to make predictions.

1 The rise in sea levels _____ cause huge problems.
2 Look at those black clouds. It _____ rain.

b Complete the sentences with the correct form of *will/be going to* for decisions.

3 You look a bit confused. Don't worry, I _____ help you.
4 Tony _____ go to California next spring.

c Check your answers with a partner.

d Read the Grammar focus box and choose the correct options to complete the rules.

GRAMMAR FOCUS
will/be going to for predictions and decisions

Predictions
- When we want to talk about what we **believe or think about the future**, we use ¹ *will / be going to*.
- When there is some **evidence in the present** to support the prediction, or an action is starting or clearly on the way, we use ² *will / be going to*.

Decisions
- When we make a **decision at the moment of speaking**, we use ³ *will / be going to*.
- When we have **already made a decision**, we use ⁴ *will / be going to*.

→ **Grammar Reference** page 142

be raised. To do this, Waterstudio will create a luxury floating development (with a conference centre, golf course, 185-villa resort), and use the money from this to develop artificial islands to provide houses for the Maldives' poorer citizens.

As well as building on the water, architects are now starting to think about building *under* the water. AT Design have produced plans for a 10 km² floating city off the coast of Hong Kong, with islands above the water connected by underwater tunnels and walkways. If and when it is completed, the city will have gardens, a huge entertainment arena for sports matches and concerts and even its own farms, making it self-sufficient. People will be able to travel back and forth from the mainland by ferry, and the designers predict that it will be a huge tourist attraction.

So, it seems that a life at sea will have a lot to offer!

5a Complete the blog entry about a trip to Peru using *will* or *be going to* and the verbs in brackets.

Travel Blog
Destinations Themes Shop Bookings Insurance

So, yesterday we took the train from La Paz, Bolivia, into Peru, stopping at Puno, and today we ¹_____ (visit) the floating islands on Lake Titicaca. I can't wait. Ever since I first heard about these islands in a geography class many years ago, I've wanted to see them. Actually, I don't really enjoy boat trips, but I'm sure the water on the lake ²_____ (be) quite calm, as it's a clear sunny day. It's quite cold, though, so I ³_____ (take) an extra sweater to keep warm.

I'm really interested in finding out more about how people live there. I believe that we ⁴_____ (be able to) ask them questions through a guide. I'd love to know what people eat – a lot of fish, I suppose! I'd also like to know what they think the future holds for them and their families. Do they think their children ⁵_____ (stay) on the islands? What effect ⁶_____ technology _____ (have) on their lives? I know they already have solar power and even black and white TVs.

Just thought! It would be great to have some photos for the blog, so I ⁷_____ (take) my camera, too. Just hope I don't drop it in the water …

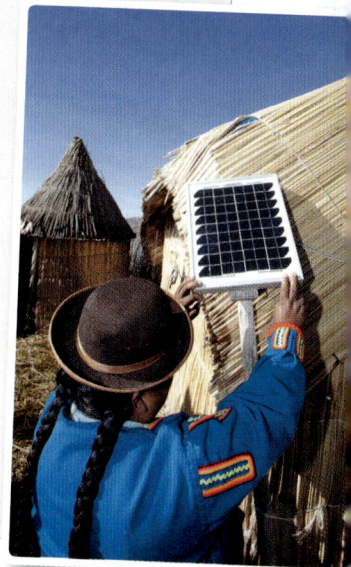

b Compare your answers with a partner and give reasons for your choices.

c **4.1** Listen and check your answers.

6 TASK Work with a partner. Look at the interview questions. Imagine you are someone who lives in one of the four places pictured in exercise 1, and write a conversation, answering the questions (don't mention the name of the place).

- What is the best thing about living here?
- Are there any disadvantages?
- Tell me about a typical day. What are you going to do today, for example?
- Do you think you'll ever move away? Why/Why not?
- What do you think life will be like here in fifty years?

7 Read your conversation to another pair. Can they guess where the person being interviewed lives?

4.2 Forest bathing

GOALS ■ Talk about the natural world ■ Talk about probability

Vocabulary & Speaking the natural world

1a **4.2**))) Listen to two people who have each been to one of the places in photos 1–4. Which ones has he/she been to?

b Which words helped you decide?

2 Choose one of the other photos and make some notes describing it using the words in the box.

> cliffs greenery forest fresh air pools landscape
> peaks season scenery soil steep sunset sunshine
> rocks valley(s) waterfalls

3 Take turns to listen to your partner's description and decide which photo he/she is describing.

Grammar & Listening probability

4 Read the quotation. What do you think might be the benefits of forest bathing? Discuss with a partner.

'Shinrin-yoku, or forest bathing, is simply visiting the forest (or other natural area) and walking slowly, taking in everything that you can see, hear, smell and even taste.'

5a **4.3**))) Listen to a radio interview and note down three benefits of spending time in green spaces.

1 _____
2 _____
3 _____

b Compare your list with a partner.

6a Work with a partner. Look at the predictions and complete them with the numbers in the box.

> 3 8.5 30 50 52 61 92

1 In the US people now spend _____ hours a day looking at a screen, and this trend **will definitely** spread around the world as smartphones become more common.

2 The percentage of British people living in cities **is likely to** rise to _____% by 2030.

3 Countries such as Botswana, where in 1950 only _____% of people lived in a city, **may** end up in a similar situation.

4 Nowadays _____% of Botswana's population lives in cities and this percentage **will probably** rise further.

5 Walking in a forest for _____ minutes improves mood and **might** even stop you getting ill.

6 After a two-hour walk some people showed a _____% increase in the white blood cells needed to help fight disease.

7 The Japanese government **will** build _____ more forest bathing trails within the next ten years, and other countries **may** follow.

b **4.4**))) Listen and check your predictions.

7a Look at the sentences in exercise **6a**. Read the information in the Grammar focus box and choose the correct options to complete the rules.

> **GRAMMAR FOCUS** *will/may/might* to talk about probability
>
> - **Modal verbs**
>   We can use the modal verbs *will*, *may* and *might* to talk about how sure we are about something. *Might/may* suggests a [1] **smaller** / **greater** possibility than *will*.
> - **Adverbs and adjectives**
>   We can also use the adverbs *probably*, *possibly* and *definitely* and the adjectives *likely* and *unlikely* to give more information about how sure we are.
>
>   *Definitely*, *probably* and *possibly* come [2] **after** / **before** the modal verb in positive sentences and [3] **after** / **before** the modal verb in negative sentences.
>
>   *Likely* and *unlikely* are followed by [4] **infinitive + *to*** / **infinitive without *to***.
>
> → Grammar Reference   page 143

b Compare your answers with a partner and give reasons for your choices.

> **PRONUNCIATION** intonation – certainty
>
> Our intonation can often signal how certain we feel about what we are saying.

8a 4.5))) Listen to four statements and write them down.

b Answer questions 1–3.

1 In positive statements, does the stress fall or rise on the modal verb (*will/may/might*) or on the adverb (*probably/possibly/definitely*)?

2 Is it the same in negative statements?

3 Where does the stress fall in sentences using *(un)likely*?

c 4.5))) Listen again and repeat.

9a Write the predictions so they agree with your own opinions about the future, using a probability phrase from the Grammar focus box.

1 By 2030 / eighteen cities / have more than twenty million inhabitants.

2 Pollution / increase.

3 Food prices / rise as we need more space for people to live.

4 Food / on the top of tall buildings.

5 Cities / more green spaces.

6 People / get much fresh air.

7 Every block of flats / a communal garden.

8 People / spend as much time in nature.

b Compare your ideas with a partner. Give reasons for your opinions.

10 **TASK** Work in small groups and discuss your ideas.

- How often do you get out into green spaces? Can you describe a time you did? What made it memorable?
- How important do you think access to nature and green spaces is? Why?
- Do you think this access to nature will become more or less important in the future? Why?

▶ **VOX POPS VIDEO 4**

4.3 Vocabulary and skills development

Listening & Speaking
consonant-vowel linking

1a Look carefully at the photo for one minute. Then close the book and tell your partner as many things as possible that you remember seeing in the photo.

b Work with a partner and discuss the questions.
1 What adjectives would you use to describe the room?
2 Why do you think people hoard things in this way?
3 What would it be like to live with someone who did this?

2a **4.6**))) Listen to two phrases. How many words do you hear?

1 _____   2 _____

b What happens to the words when you say them at normal speed?

c **4.7**))) Read and listen to the information in the Unlock the code box about consonant-vowel linking.

> 🔓 **UNLOCK THE CODE**
> understanding consonant-vowel linking
>
> When one word finishes on a consonant, and the next word begins with a vowel (or the other way round), the consonant often becomes 'attached' to the vowel. This means that it is difficult to hear the correct words:
>
> The person you are listening to actually said: *I'll ask her* /ælæskə/, but you hear: *Alaska*.
>
> While you are listening, you have to check that what you hear makes sense in the situation.

3a **4.8**))) Listen to six phrases and write down what you hear. Compare what you have written with a partner.

b **4.9**))) Listen again to the same phrases in sentences. Practise saying the phrases linking the words naturally.

4 **4.10**))) Listen to an interview with Maurice, a person who hoards things, and answer the questions.
1 What kinds of things does Maurice hoard?
2 What does he keep in the garden?
3 How does his wife feel about it?

5 **4.10**))) Listen again and complete the sentences from the interview.
1 I just can't _____.
2 I'm starting to _____ space.
3 They might _____ one day.
4 I've _____ newspapers, too, going back to 1995.
5 So your house must _____, then?
6 To be honest, she's not very happy. But _____?

6 Work with a partner and discuss the questions.
1 What kinds of objects do you keep for a long time?
2 Why do you keep them?
3 Is your room/office/house tidy or untidy?
4 Do you get stressed when your living space is very untidy?

Vocabulary & Speaking idiomatic phrases about places

7 Read the conversations. Choose a or b as the better meaning for the idiomatic phrases in **bold**.

1 **A** How's the new job? Do you **feel at home** yet?
B I'm starting to. But I'm not used to working nine to five!
a feel healthy
b feel relaxed and comfortable

2 **A** I think we need to move to a bigger office.
B I agree. We've **run out of** space here!
a We don't need more.
b We've used it all.

3 **A** What's your journey to work like?
B It's awful, we're **packed in like sardines** on the Tube.
a uncomfortably crowded
b smelling a lot

4 **A** Do you live in the city centre?
B Well, actually, we live **miles from anywhere**.
a in the suburbs
b far from other people

5 **A** Are you sure you know how to get there?
B Relax, **I know** this part of town **like the back of my hand**.
a be very familiar with a place
b be new to a place

6 **A** Have you lost something?
B I can't find my glasses, I've looked **all over the place**.
a everywhere in this room
b in every room

7 **A** Have you heard? Carlo's buying a house.
B Yes, he told me a while ago that he and Liza were thinking of **settling down**.
a choosing a permanent home
b buying a bigger house

8 Read the Vocabulary focus box.

> **VOCABULARY FOCUS** idiomatic phrases
>
> It is often easier to learn idioms in a topic group; for example, places.
>
> I **feel at home** here.
> They're thinking of **settling down**.
> They are generally fixed phrases.
> I've looked **all over the place** NOT I've looked ~~over all the place~~.

9a Look at the photo. Can you use any of the idioms in exercise **7** to describe what you see?

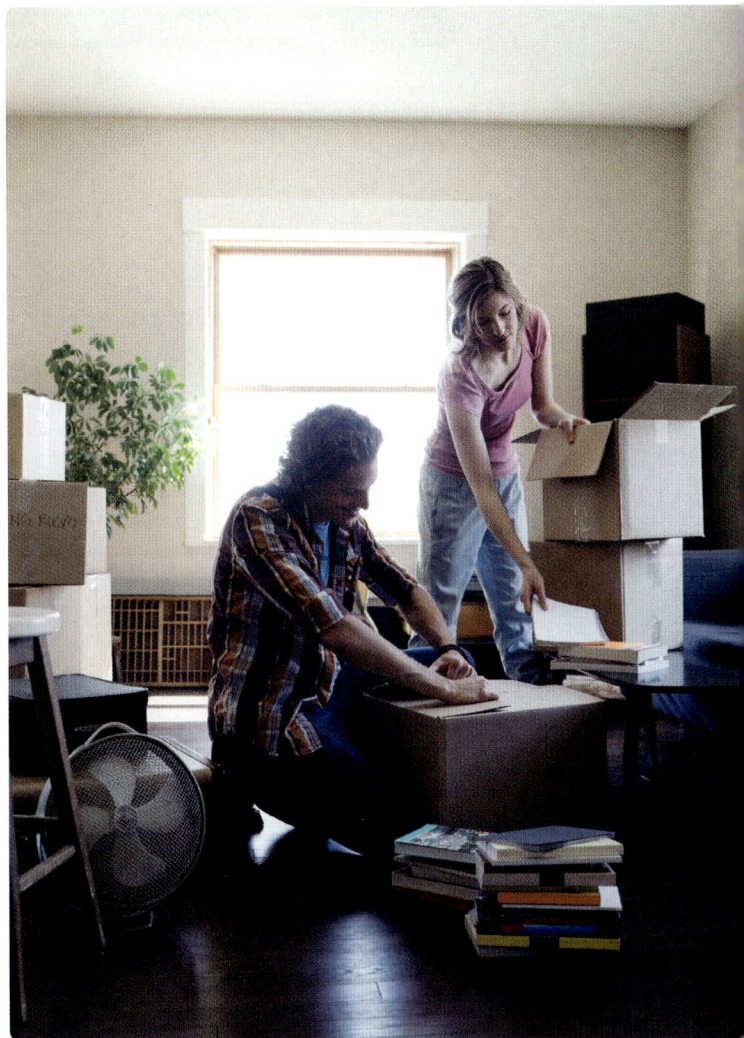

b 4.11)) Richard's friend Abby is visiting him on his first day in his new flat. Listen to the conversation. What problem did Richard have?

c 4.11)) Listen again. What do you think these phrases mean?
- make yourself at home
- make room
- have (got) a lot of room
- take up space
- get rid of (something)

10a TASK Complete these sentences so they are true for you.
1 If your work space is in a mess, it's a sign …
2 It's important to make room in your life for …
3 The thing in my home I would most like to get rid of …
4 I don't/didn't want to settle down until …
5 The place I feel most at home is …

b Work in small groups. Discuss your sentences and see what you have in common.

4.4 Speaking and writing

Tobermory, Scotland

Reading & Writing   avoiding repetition

1a Read the description taken from a travel website. Which place in the photos do you think it is describing?

The Traveller   **BLOG**   **ABOUT**   **CONTACT US**   ➕ @ ☸

Wandering through _____ is like stepping back in time. Narrow streets and houses with orange-red roofs are surrounded by mountains and green fields. In spring the meadows are full of brightly coloured wild flowers.

Perhaps the best view of the ancient city, and the nearby countryside, is found by walking around the top of the medieval city walls. Still in excellent condition, they are a lovely place to walk, shaded by trees. Or enjoy the sunshine by strolling through the beautiful seventeenth-century gardens of the Parco Villa Reale. If you're lucky enough to visit on the third weekend of the month, don't

miss the fascinating antique market, selling silver and brass, furniture and rare books.

Fancy a picnic? Stop off at Forno A Vapore Amedeo Giusti for home-made sandwiches, made with tasty local produce. Or sit outside at Vineria I Santi and watch the world go by while you eat a variety of delicious snacks.

Lucca, Italy

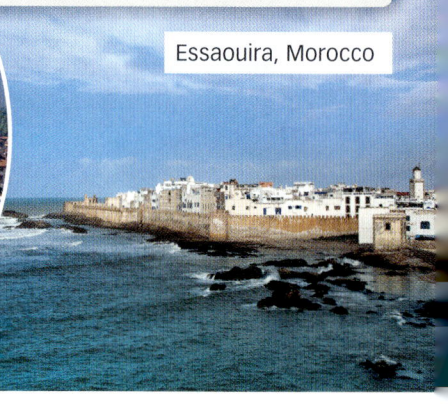

Essaouira, Morocco

b Which paragraph ...?

a describes places to eat

b describes what you can do there

c describes how the place looks

c Does the description make you want to go there? Why/Why not?

2 Read the information in the Language for writing box and answer the questions.

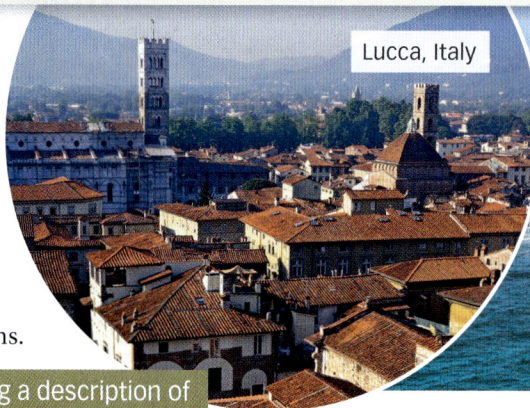

LANGUAGE FOR WRITING writing a description of a place

Make your descriptive writing more interesting by:

- referring to the <u>same thing</u> with different phrases and words
  ... surrounded by mountains and green <u>fields</u>. In spring the <u>meadows</u> are full of brightly coloured wild flowers.

- using a mixture of nouns and reference words
  ... walking around the top of the <u>medieval city walls</u>. Still in excellent condition, <u>they</u> provide a calm walkway, shaded by trees.

- addressing the reader directly, using imperatives and questions
  ... enjoy the sunshine ...
  Fancy a picnic?

- using a variety of adjectives
  narrow   ancient   tasty   fascinating

1 Find two other words in the description which have the same meaning as 'walking'.

2 Find another word in the last paragraph which has the same meaning as 'delicious'.

3 List at least five adjectives used to add interest to the description.

4 Find three examples of imperatives addressing the reader.

3a Read another description. Which place in the photos is being described this time?

The Traveller   ➕ @ ☸

_____ is known as 'the windy city'. The buildings are mostly painted white, and there is a red-brick wall around the city.

It is too windy at the beach to enjoy sunbathing, but the beach is very nice for surfers. The city is a relaxed place, and it is nice to walk around the streets. You can go shopping and buy nice things, such as boxes made from thuja wood.

You can eat nice food such as grilled sardines at Chez Sam. Chez Sam is at _____'s port.

---

b How could this description be improved? Discuss with a partner and write an improved version together.

4 Choose a place you know quite well and write a similar description, using the Language for writing box to help you.

Listening & Speaking enquiries

5   **4.12**》 When you travel, you often need to call people to make enquiries. Listen to someone making an enquiry and choose the correct situation.
   - Asking about opening hours
   - Asking about lost property
   - Asking about hotel facilities

6a How did the woman ask the waiter to check for her? Tell a partner.

   A Check for me.
   B Could you check for me?
   C I wonder if you could check for me.

b Work with a partner. Cross out the letters or words to make true statements.

   1 A / B / C is an instruction and the other two are polite enquiries.
   2 A / B / C is the most polite form.
   3 Polite forms in English often use *more* / *fewer* words and *conditional* / *imperative* forms.

7   Work with a partner. Ask politely, starting with *I wonder if, …*

   1 for a phone number.
   2 for some information.
   3 if someone can repeat what they said.

8a Put the conversation in the right order.

   a Yes, that's right. It's in the basement.   ___
   b Yes, just one last question. Do I need to take a towel with me, or are they provided?   ___
   c Thank you. Could you tell me the opening hours, please?   ___
   d Hello, I understand that the hotel has a gym?   ___
   e It's open from 7 a.m. until 9 p.m.   ___
   f Hello, how can I help you?   _1_
   g Thank you, that's great.   ___
   h Can I help you with anything else?   ___

b **4.13**》 Listen and check your answers.

c Work with a partner and role-play the conversation the customer then has with the manager.

9a **TASK** Do a role-play with a partner. On your own, choose one of these situations.

> You have to check out of your hotel room at 11 a.m., but you are not leaving the city until 4 p.m. You need somewhere to leave your luggage. Call the front desk of the hotel and ask for help.

> You work in a big company. You think you left your phone in the canteen at lunchtime. Call the main reception of the company and ask them to check.

> You have just started a course at your local college, but you now have a problem with the class time. You would prefer to study later or on a different day. Call the secretary and ask if you can change class.

b Take turns to make your enquiries. Use the Language for speaking box to help you.

LANGUAGE FOR SPEAKING making enquiries

When we make enquiries, we generally use polite forms in English.

Dealing with enquiries
How can I help you?
Could I just check some details?
Can I help you with anything else?

Making enquiries
Could you check this number for me?
I wonder if you could check this number for me.
Just one last question.

4.5 Video

Songdo

1 Work with a partner. Discuss the meaning of the phrases in bold. Find examples of some of these phrases in the photos.

In my town, …

a you can see a lot of large **property development projects** at the moment.

b many people use **environmentally friendly forms of transport** such as walking or cycling.

c designers are developing **cutting-edge technology** to help keep pollution levels low.

d there are **fast transport links** to the country's other main cities.

2 Tell your partner if you think the sentences in exercise **1** are true (T) or false (F) about your hometown. Why?

3 ▶ Watch the video. Answer the questions.

a Why did city planners decide to develop a new city?

b How is Songdo different to many other cities?

4 ▶ Watch again. Complete the summary with the words in the box.

> businesses university park space waste and rubbish
> land   pollution

City developers are building Songdo on **1**_____ which was underwater until some years ago. There are plenty of green spaces in the city, and there is a large **2**_____ in the centre with skyscrapers, all around it. Property developers have built 80,000 new homes as well as schools and a **3**_____. The city aims to watch **4**_____ levels carefully by using technology to measure energy use and car use. Designers are also planning a system which will soon use the population's **5**_____ to generate renewable energy. Families like living here because there is so much **6**_____. Planners also hope that they will soon see more **7**_____ in Songdo when transport links with Seoul are even faster.

Songdo is a city of the future, and it could become a model for many other cities around the world.

5a **TASK** Work with a partner. Student A lives in Songdo and loves it. Student B has a small business and young family, and is thinking of moving to Songdo. Discuss whether or not Student B should move to Songdo.

b Work with another pair and compare your ideas.

Review

1a Complete the replies with the correct form of *will* or *going to* and the verbs in brackets.

1 **A** I just can't do this maths problem.
   B Don't worry, I _____ (help) you.

2 **A** Can you lend me £20?
   B I suppose so.
   A Thanks, I promise I _____ (give) it back next week.

3 **A** I'm starting college next week.
   B Really? What _____ (study)?

4 **A** Have you got any plans for your birthday?
   B Yes, I _____ (have) a big party.

5 **A** Why have you got your coat on?
   B I _____ (get) a few groceries we need from the supermarket.

6 **A** You look tired.
   B Yes, you're right. I think I _____ (go) to bed now.

b Tell your partner about some plans you have already made about:
- holidays
- work or study
- celebrations

2a Choose the correct options to complete the sentences.

1 *I might / I'm not likely to* get a new car soon. My old one is 10 years old now.

2 *I'll probably / I'm going to* go out tonight, but I haven't quite decided yet.

3 *I'm definitely going to / I'm going definitely to* live abroad one day.

4 I *may / won't* move house soon, it's too expensive at the moment.

5 I will *likely / definitely* visit Bolivia one day.

6 I *probably won't / won't probably* move to another city. I like living here.

b Change three of the sentences so they are true for you. Discuss your sentences with a partner.

3a Choose the best words to complete the text.

In 1998 British artist Richart Sowa created his first artificial island. He filled nets with empty plastic bottles, covered them with wood and ¹_____, and then planted mangrove plants. The island had a two-storey house and three ²_____, where Sowa could relax and sunbathe. Unfortunately, the island was destroyed by a hurricane in 2005, but Sowa has now built an even better one, with two sea-water ³_____ and even a solar-powered ⁴_____. His house also has a washing machine powered by the ⁵_____. Sowa believes that ⁶_____ islands could be built on rivers, ⁷_____ and oceans all over the world, saving space, and meaning that people's homes would be safe when the level of the water rose.

1	a season	b sand	c sea
2	a peaks	b canals	c beaches
3	a pools	b rocks	c cliffs
4	a coast	b sand	c waterfall
5	a waves	b beaches	c forests
6	a fresh	b steep	c floating
7	a peaks	b lakes	c greenery

b Would you like to live on an island like this? Work with a partner and think of three advantages and three disadvantages of living there.

4a Read the conversation between a receptionist (R) and a guest (G) and complete each sentence with up to four words.

R Hello, Grand Hotel. ¹_____ you?

G Hello, I think I may have left my briefcase at reception this morning. I wonder ²_____ if it's been handed in?

R Certainly. Could I ³_____ some ⁴_____? What colour was it?

G It's black, and it has my initials on it, MHG, Miguel Hernandez Garcia.

R Thank you ... one moment ... Yes, we have it.

G That's great. I ⁵_____ I could come and pick it up this evening?

R Yes, any time. Can I help you with ⁶_____?

G No, that's all. Thank you for your help, though. I really ⁷_____.

b **4.14**))) Listen and check your answers.

c Have the conversation with a partner. Close your book and try to remember it.

Entertainment

5.1   Universally popular?

GOALS ■ Talk about different genres of films   ■ *-ing* form and infinitive with *to*

Vocabulary & Listening   going to the movies

1   What are your favourite kinds of films?
- action films
- comedies
- musicals
- thrillers
- science fiction
- animated films
- rom coms
- horror films

2   Work with a partner. Look at the film posters. What kind of film do you think each one is? Which film would you probably prefer to see? Why?

THE SECRET LIFE OF WALTER
MITTY
COMING SOON

3   **5.1**)) Listen to a review of both films and answer the questions.
1   Which genre/kind does the reviewer say each film is?
2   Which film does the reviewer prefer?
3   Which film has won a prize?

4a   Complete the sentences with the words/phrases in the box.

THE SECRET LIFE OF **WALTER MITTY**

action hero   actors   cast (n)   character   performance
plays (v)   remake (n)   scenes   special effects   stars (v)

1   Ben Stiller _____ in the film *The Secret Life of Walter Mitty*.
2   The film is a/an _____ of a film made in 1947.
3   He _____ the part of the main _____, Walter Mitty.
4   Mitty dreams of being a/an _____ who rescues people from dangers.
5   The _____ filmed in Iceland and the Himalayas have amazing _____, and show Mitty doing apparently impossible things.
6   Although there are several very good _____ in the _____, Stiller's _____ is the best.

b   Complete the sentences with the words/phrases in the box.

RIO 2096: A STORY OF LOVE AND FURY

animated   characters   plot (n)   set (v)   voiced

1   *Rio 2096: A Story of Love and Fury* is a/an _____ film, which is _____ in three different periods of Brazil's history.
2   The main _____ are _____ by Brazilian actors, Selton Mello and Camila Pitanga.
3   The _____ is quite difficult to follow if you don't know about Brazilian history.

c   Have you changed your mind about which film you would prefer to see? Why/Why not? Discuss your reasons with a partner.

Grammar & Speaking *-ing* form and infinitive with *to*

5a Look at the extracts from the review and choose the correct form of the verbs: *-ing* or infinitive with *to*. Some verbs can take both forms.

1 Walter Mitty is a quiet man who secretly dreams of *being / to be* an action hero.

2 Soon, however, his adventures start *becoming / to become* real.

3 He decides *setting out / to set out* on a journey to find a missing photographic negative.

4 At the start of the film, we meet the main character, a Tupinamba Indian in Brazil, attempting *saving / to save* his tribe.

5 After he fails *saving / to save* them and the woman he loves, he magically turns into a bird.

6 He hopes *being / to be* with Janaina, the woman he loves, once more.

7 We then see the couple living in 1825 and 1970 before *returning / to return* to the future in 2096.

8 It is a disturbing future where poor people can't afford *buying / to buy* water.

9 He and Janaina continue *fighting / to fight* against evil.

10 The story is told with such passion that you can't help *enjoying / to enjoy* it.

b Check your answers with a partner.

6 Read the information in the Grammar focus box and complete the rules with verbs from exercise **5** with a partner.

GRAMMAR FOCUS *-ing* and infinitive with *to*

-ing form
• After some verbs we use the *-ing form* of other verbs:
avoid, imagine, finish, miss, recommend, suggest, ¹_____

These include verbs expressing likes and dislikes:
can't stand, enjoy, feel like, hate, like, love, prefer

We also use the *-ing* form after prepositions:
about, after, at, by, in, on, ²_____, ³_____

infinitive with *to*
• After some verbs we use the infinitive with *to* of other verbs. These include:
afford, agree, aim, appear, expect, intend, manage, need, plan, seem, tend, want, would like, ⁴_____,
⁵_____, ⁶_____, ⁷_____, ⁸_____

both forms
• Some verbs can be followed by both *-ing* and infinitive with *to*, with little or no change in meaning (though note that we don't usually use two *-ing* forms next to each other):
begin, can't stand, hate, like (= enjoy), love, prefer,
⁹_____, ¹⁰_____

→ **Grammar Reference** page 144

7a Work with a partner. Complete the description of the plot of *Stepping on the Flying Grass*, a film from Indonesia, by choosing the correct form of the verb. In some sentences, both forms are possible.

Stepping on the Flying Grass

A beautiful film about the dreams of village school children in rural Indonesia, *Stepping on the Flying Grass* is both visually stunning and truly moving.

When their teacher asked them to write an essay about their dearest dreams and wishes, a group of village schoolchildren begin ¹_____ (think) seriously about what they plan ²_____ (do) with their lives.

Puji enjoys ³_____ (be) useful and just wants ⁴_____ (help) others. Mei fantasizes about ⁵_____ (become) an actress. She spends hours practising in front of the mirror, but does she really love ⁶_____ (act), or is it actually her mother's dream? Agus's family can't afford ⁷_____ (eat) any special food at home, but he really wants ⁸_____ (eat) at an authentic Padang restaurant in the city. When an opportunity arises to make some money, he decides ⁹_____ (make) his dream come true. As the film progresses, he gradually realizes that for dreams to come true you need ¹⁰_____ (work) at them.

b **5.2**))) Listen and check your answers.

8 **TASK** Complete the questions with the correct form of the verbs in brackets. Work with a partner. Ask and answer the questions.

1 Do you avoid _____ (watch) any particular genre of film? If so, which one? Why?

2 Are there any actors you really can't stand _____ (watch)? Why/Why not?

3 Do you like _____ (watch) films based on books that you have enjoyed _____ (read)? Why/Why not?

4 Have you ever enjoyed a film you didn't expect _____ (like)? Why did you change your mind?

5 What do you tend _____ (think) is the most important: the plot, the cast or the script? Why?

6 Are there any films you hope _____ (see) in the near future? Why do you want _____ (see) them?

▶ **VOX POPS VIDEO 5**

5.2 Mosquito smasher!

GOALS ■ Describe a video game ■ Use present perfect simple and past simple

Vocabulary & Reading   adjectives to describe a video game

1   Work with a partner or in small groups and discuss the questions.

- Do you play any games on your phone, computer or tablet?
- Which adjectives could you use to describe any of the games?

> amusing   disappointing   dull   enjoyable   entertaining
> intelligent   ordinary   original   predictable   silly
> surprising   unexciting   violent

PRONUNCIATION   word stress in longer words

In longer words with more than two syllables, it is important to put the stress on the correct syllable to be understood.

2a Put the adjectives in exercise **1** with more than two syllables into the columns according to the stress pattern.

●●●	●●●	●●●●	●●●●
amusing			

b 5.3 ⟩⟩⟩ Listen, check and repeat.

3   Read the article and answer the questions.

1   Why is the video games industry growing so fast in Nigeria?

2   What is special about the games produced by Maliyo Games?

3   Which adjectives does the writer use to describe video games?

NEWS 〉 TECHNOLOGY 〉 GAMES

Nigerian video games score highly

Meet Sharp Sule! He works hard to make a living by dashing through the streets of Lagos, Nigeria on his bike, avoiding cars, trucks and potholes, while collecting the coins he needs to realize his dream of owning a bigger transport business.

There are plenty of people just like Sharp Sule in Lagos, but he's actually a character in an original new video game, designed, as Hugo Obi, founder of Maliyo Games, says, 'to showcase African culture to the world, through games'.

[1] *Over the past few years, a growing middle class that is looking for entertainment has resulted in Nigerian movies and music sweeping across the continent*, as sub-Saharan Africa becomes increasingly connected online. Now game publishers hope to achieve the same success.
[2] *Last year Nigerians bought an astonishing 21.5 million mobile phones*, so more and more people are looking for entertaining apps and games.

The global video game industry is now worth $66 billion – more than Hollywood – but [3] *so far many of the games produced have been rather unexciting and predictable.* In contrast, Maliyo aims to produce something clever, amusing, and definitely African.

As well as Sharp Sule, [4] *Maliyo has also recently produced another highly enjoyable game, Mosquito Smasher.* Like many video games, it's quite violent – but the only things that get hurt are the mosquitos, a constant irritation in Lagos and in many other countries around the world.

In fact, the games do seem to have a worldwide appeal. [5] *European companies have already copied Mosquito Smasher* and [6] *Nigerian company Gamsole, which a few months ago became the first in the region to gain more than 1 million app downloads*, said most of its fans log in from Brazil, India and the US.

Grammar & Speaking　present perfect simple and past simple

4 Look at these extracts from the article. Which of the verbs in bold are about a specific, finished time in the past and which are about unfinished time?

1 Over the past few years, a growing middle class that is looking for entertainment **has resulted** in Nigerian movies and music sweeping across the continent, as sub-Saharan Africa is becoming increasingly connected online.

2 Last year Nigerians **bought** an astonishing 21.5 million mobile phones, so more and more people are looking for entertaining apps and games.

5 Read the Grammar focus box and choose the correct options to complete the rules.

> **GRAMMAR FOCUS** time expressions with present perfect and past simple
>
> We use the **present perfect** to talk about
> * ¹ **finished / unfinished time periods**
>   *So far many of the games produced have been rather unexciting …*
> * a past action with a ² **past / present result**
>   *European companies have copied Mosquito Smasher …*
>
> Other time expressions often used with the present perfect:
> *ever, for, just, never, since, yet*
>
> We use the **past simple** for ³ **finished / unfinished** time periods.
> *Last year Nigerians bought an astonishing 2.5 million mobile phones …*
>
> Other time expressions often used with the past simple:
> *last, in January, on Wednesday, recently, when, yesterday*
>
> → **Grammar Reference** page 145

6a The article on page 48 is about daily life in Lagos, Nigeria. Read a blog about living in New York and choose the correct form of the verbs.

> ABOUT　EVENTS　BLOG　　🔍 SEARCH　➕ @ ••
>
> ## BLOG ENTRY / 26 JULY
>
> ¹ *I've lived / I lived* in New York for about three years now. It's an exciting place to live, but there are quite a few annoying things about it, too. For a start, it's incredibly expensive.
>
> When ² *I've moved / I moved* into my flat three years ago, the rent was already quite high, but it ³ *has gone up / went up* three times since then.
>
> It can also be quite a violent place. ⁴ *I haven't been / I wasn't mugged* yet, but my best friend has. Luckily, she wasn't actually hurt; ⁵ *they've just taken / they just took* her bag.
>
> And the traffic – it's dreadful. It ⁶ *has taken / took* me more than an hour to get to work today, and nearly as long to get home.
>
> However, ⁷ *I've never lived / I never lived* anywhere where there is so much to do. Over the past month ⁸ *I've been / I went* to the theatre three times, as well as to a number of great art exhibitions. ⁹ *I've also just / I also just started* salsa classes. You can find everything from everywhere here.
>
> So, although living in New York has some bad points, on balance I don't think I want to live anywhere else in the world.

b 5.4))) Listen and check your answers.

7a **TASK** Work in small groups. Describe the positive or negative features of a video game you know that you would include in a video game like *Sharp Sule*. If you don't know a video game, make one up.

b Use the questions below to plan a video game and present your idea to other students.
* Who is/are the main character(s)? Give them some background.
* What do they have to do in the video game?
* What adjectives could you use to describe your video game and make it attractive to people?

c Describe the video game.

5.3 Vocabulary and skills development

GOALS ■ **Understand linkers** ■ **Use extreme adjectives**

Reading & Speaking understanding linkers

The Rise of the Second Screen

1 The kids are in bed, the house is quiet, and my wife and I turn on the TV. What's on? It doesn't really matter, because thirty seconds later, I'm working on my laptop. Meanwhile my wife is on Facebook on her phone. This is a typical evening in our house. And what's more, it's how many of us watch TV. The second screen is part of modern-day life, especially for young people.

2 A second screen can be a tablet, a smartphone, a laptop or a hand-held gaming unit used whilst watching TV. Smartphone and tablet owners in particular are very keen on second-screen viewing. People use second screens to look at things that are related to or totally different from what they are watching on TV.

Comments   Like · Comment · Share ∨

1 The more ways we have to interact with people the better – it's absolutely essential we are accessible all the time, *especially / what's more* with a job like mine, where customers email at all hours of the day and night.

2 If you ask me, it is extremely rude. Nobody talks to each other any more. My son plays games all day. *Meanwhile / As well* my daughter spends her days chatting online. It's absolutely infuriating.

3 *On the one hand / In addition*, I don't like the idea of constantly looking at screens, but on the other, I must admit that unless the programme is absolutely fascinating, I tend to check emails and messages while I watch.

1 Work in small groups and discuss the questions.
   - How much TV do you watch on average each day?
   - Do you do anything else while you are watching TV?

2a Look at the headline and the photo and discuss what you think the article is about.

 b Read paragraphs 1 and 2 and check your ideas.

3a Work with a partner and look at the highlighted expressions in paragraph 1. Which phrases are linkers for …?
   1 adding information
   2 emphasizing something
   3 saying two things happen at the same time
   4 giving both sides of the argument

 b Read the information in the Unlock the code box about linkers to check your answers.

🔓 UNLOCK THE CODE
linkers

We use linkers to organize information when we speak and write. They are like signposts and have different purposes:
- adding information: *as well, what's more*
- saying two things happen at the same time: *meanwhile*
- emphasizing: *above all, especially*
- giving both sides of the argument: *on the one hand*

 c Read the rest of the article. Add the highlighted phrases to the categories in exercise **3a**.

4 Read the three comments on the article above and choose the correct options.

5 Read the whole article and answer the questions. Check your answers with a partner.
   1 What two types of technology are used most for second-screen viewing?
   2 What kind of people like second-screen viewing?
   3 In which countries are second screens most popular? And least?
   4 What is the advantage of second-screen viewing?
   5 What is the main disadvantage of second-screen viewing?

Vocabulary & Speaking   extreme adjectives

6 Look at sentences 1–2 from the comments in exercise **4**. How does the writer feel? Which words does he/she use to express his/her feelings?

  1 It's absolutely infuriating.
  2 … the programme is absolutely fascinating …

3 A recent study carried out in Brazil, Germany, Russia, the UK, and the USA showed that viewers use second screens to chat (72%); to follow/like programmes (57%); to share posts (61%); to watch clips (61%); to find information (66%); and for gaming (49%). In addition, the study found that Brazilian viewers used second screens the most, while those in Germany used them the least.

4 Of course, second screens are both good and bad for TV companies. On the one hand, they can take our attention away from the TV. On the other hand, they can improve our viewing experience with interesting information and chat. One thing is for sure: with apps and social media on the rise, the second screen is here to stay.

Like · Comment · Share ∨

7a Match adjectives 1–7 to adjectives a–g which have a similar meaning.

  1 bad   a essential
  2 annoying   b terrifying
  3 good   c awful
  4 important   d infuriating
  5 interesting   e impossible
  6 difficult   f brilliant
  7 scary   g fascinating

  b Which adjectives are stronger?

  c Read the information in the Vocabulary focus box about extreme adjectives to check your answers.

VOCABULARY FOCUS extreme adjectives

- Use extreme adjectives when you want to make the meaning of the adjective much stronger:
  bad → awful; difficult → impossible; annoying → infuriating; important → essential; interesting → fascinating; scary → terrifying
- To make extreme adjectives sound even stronger, use *absolutely*:
  The game was **absolutely brilliant**.
- With non-extreme adjectives, use *very*, or *extremely*:
  The film was **extremely scary**.

8 Work with a partner. Here are some more extreme adjectives. Can you work out what the underlined adjectives mean?

  1 I can't walk any further. I'm absolutely <u>exhausted</u>. I'll have to sit down.
  2 She was absolutely <u>amazed</u> when she saw her sister standing at the front door. They hadn't seen each other for ten years.
  3 That smells absolutely <u>delicious</u>. I love the smell of garlic. What are you cooking?
  4 It's absolutely <u>astonishing</u>. This is the first time you haven't been late this year!
  5 I can't carry that. It's absolutely <u>enormous</u>. I'll need some help to get it up the stairs.
  6 Put the heater on. It's absolutely <u>freezing</u> in here.

PRONUNCIATION extreme adjectives

When we use extreme adjectives, we stress both the adverb and the adjective.

9a **5.5**⟩⟩ Listen to the sentences and underline the stressed syllables in the adverbs and adjectives in bold.

  1 I'm **absolutely exhausted**.
  2 She was **absolutely amazed**.
  3 That smells **absolutely delicious**.
  4 It's **absolutely astonishing**.
  5 It's **absolutely enormous**.
  6 It's **absolutely freezing** in here.

  b Practise the stress.

  c **5.6**⟩⟩ Now listen to the sentences in exercise **8** and practise them, stressing the extreme adverbs and adjectives.

10 **TASK** Work in small groups. What is your reaction in these situations? Why? Use some extreme adjectives to express how you feel.

- You are having a meal with a friend who keeps looking at his/her phone and sending messages.
- You settle down to watch your favourite TV programme and a friend calls you.
- A friend invites you to dinner, but leaves the TV on and keeps watching while you are eating.
- Your flatmate wants to play noisy video games, but you want to watch a TV documentary.

5.4 Speaking and writing

GOALS ■ Write a film review ■ Compare and recommend

Reading & Writing a film review

1a You are going to read a review of the classic American film, *The Shawshank Redemption*, based on a book by Stephen King. What information do you expect to find in the review?

b Compare your ideas with a–e below.
  a the writer's opinion
  b the plot/storyline
  c the name of the director
  d who stars in the film
  e whether the book is better than the film

2 Read the review and match the information from the review (a–e) to the paragraph it is in.

Paragraph 1 _____
Paragraph 2 _____
Paragraph 3 _____
Paragraph 4 _____

3a Read the information in the Language for writing box about contract linkers.

> **LANGUAGE FOR WRITING** contrast linkers
>
> We use the following linkers to show that things are different.
>
> **Although/Even though**
> *Although I don't like action films, I loved this one.*
>
> **Despite/In spite of**
> *Despite seeing the film twice, I still didn't understand the ending.*
>
> **However**
> *However, I loved the rest of the film.*

b Underline the linkers and what follows them in the review.

Home	What's On	Reviews	Film News	Book Tickets

TIM **ROBBINS**   MORGAN **FREEMAN**

The Best Film of All Time?

What is your favourite film of all time? We are inviting fans to post reviews this month. Then you can vote for your favourite.

1 *The Shawshank Redemption* was directed by Frank Darabont and is based on a novel by Stephen King. Starring Tim Robbins and Morgan Freeman, the film is surprisingly sad in places, but essentially, it is a positive story about friendship and hope. Despite failing at the box office when it was originally released in 1994, it has now become a modern classic.

2 The film is set in the late 1940s in the USA. Tim Robbins plays Andy Dufresne, a banker who is falsely sent to prison for killing his wife. At first, Andy finds prison life difficult. However, he soon makes friends with another prisoner, Ellis 'Red' Redding (Morgan Freeman), who is in for life. Andy gets a job in the prison library and helps with the prison's finances. This changes everything for Andy and allows him to spend years planning the surprising events at the end of the film.

3 Darabont makes few changes to King's original novel, and manages to make the end result even more exciting than the book. Thomas Newman's soundtrack creates an exciting atmosphere throughout the film.

4 *The Shawshank Redemption* is terrific entertainment. Freeman's performance is very moving, and Tim Robbins gives one of his best performances of his career. Although the film is a little slow in places, the end is absolutely brilliant and I highly recommend it to everyone.

The Shawshank Redemption
★★★★✫

Director: Frank Darabont
Cast: Tim Robbins, Morgan Freeman
Release date: 1994

4 Complete the extracts from a review of the film *One Day* with the correct contrast linkers. Then check with a partner.

One Day ★★★✩✩

One Day is a story about love and friendship based on David Nicholls' very successful novel. The two main characters, Emma and Dexter (Anne Hathaway and Jim Sturgess) meet at university and become friends ¹_____ they grow apart during the next few years. The story follows them on the same day every year …

Sturgess plays the upper-class Dexter with great skill. ²_____, Hathaway's performance is the best in the film, ³_____ her terrible English accent.

Nicholls' novel was a charming, clever romantic comedy about how the world has changed over the past twenty years. ⁴_____ it is not as brilliant as the novel, the film *One Day* is still funny, entertaining and worth seeing.

5a Think about a film you have recently enjoyed. Make notes on the film using the points from exercise **1b** and the language in the Language for writing box on page 52.

b Write a review of the film.

Listening & Speaking comparing and recommending

6 Work with a partner and discuss the questions.
1 When do you like to listen to music?
2 Is there one film you think everyone should see? Why?
3 What TV programmes do you never miss? Why?

7 **5.7**)) Listen to extracts from conversations about music and entertainment and answer the questions.

Conversation 1
Which statistic surprises one of the speakers?

Conversation 2
Do they both want to watch the programme about the environment?

Conversation 3
What doesn't the speaker recommend?

8 **5.7**)) Listen again and complete the sentences. Which phrases tell you what the speaker's opinion is?
1 The statistics look much _____.
2 That _____!
3 _____ *that* if you have to go to work the next day!

9 Complete the sentences with phrases from the Language for speaking box to express what you think about these topics, and finish the sentences so they are true for you.
1 _____ going to 3D versions of films …
2 _____ sitting through a whole opera …
3 _____ sure that I like jazz …
4 The first time I went to a live concert _____ …
5 Listening to recorded music is _____ …

LANGUAGE FOR SPEAKING
comparing and recommending

Comparing
It's nothing like as good as …
I expected it to be …, but it's not really.
It's more/less … than I thought it would be.

Recommending (or not)
I'd really recommend you see/hear/watch …
I wouldn't recommend it.
I'm not at all sure about that.
I'm pretty sure that I …
It's really/not worth + noun or + -ing
It sounds/looks … great/fantastic/awful/boring …

10a TASK Use the phrases in exercises **8** and **9** and the Language for speaking box to make notes for a short talk on one of these topics or one of your own.
• My favourite music
• A film/TV series I really enjoyed/really didn't enjoy
• A great video game

b Work in small groups. Talk for a minute on your topic.

c Listen to the person talking and ask questions to find out more information.

5.5 Video

Film studies

1a You are a film production student and you want to make a movie. When would you usually do each of these tasks? Put the tasks in the correct column.

> add music/special effects   direct the actors
> edit the scene   mix the sound   record the sound
> shoot the film   write the script

Before filming	During filming	After filming

b Which of these tasks can you see in the photos?

2 ▶ Watch the video. Complete the course details with the words in the box.

> jobs   places   process   semesters   stages   years

> **Name of course:** *Film production course*
> **Length of course:** 2 ¹_____
> **Number of** ²_____: 4
> **Number of** ³_____: 25
> **Aim of course:** during the course, you will be involved in all of the ⁴_____ of the film-making ⁵_____ and you will get valuable work experience doing many of the ⁶_____ you can find in the modern-day film industry.

3 ▶ Watch again. Choose the correct options to complete the sentences.

a These days it is common for people to *have / want* a job in the film industry.

b The City College of New York *is now / has always been* a free university for poorer students.

c Classes are *always fun / usually full* because there are just twenty-five places on each course.

d At the end of the course, students will *get a degree / begin to work* in film production.

4a **TASK** Work with a partner. You are going to create a general knowledge quiz about the film industry. First, write down the name of a famous …

- film   • actor   • director

b Write five questions using your ideas from exercise **4a**.

c Work with another pair. Read your general knowledge quiz to each other. Can you answer all the questions?

Review

1a Complete the statements with the correct form of the verbs in brackets.

1 I tend _____ (prefer) watching a film to reading a book.

2 I can't stand _____ (watch) horror films.

3 Once I've started a film I always carry on _____ (watch) it to the end, even if I don't like it.

4 When I see well-known actors are in a film, I always expect _____ (enjoy) watching it.

5 I never seem _____ (find) the time to watch many films.

6 If I got the chance, I'd like _____ (be) in a film.

b Which of these statements are true for you? Discuss with a partner.

2a Choose the correct options to complete the text.

Animated films for grown-ups

Animated films used to be clearly aimed at the under tens. But in the 1990s, Pixar, Dreamworks and other companies **1** *has started / started* to make films which **2** *has appealed / appealed* to both kids and adults. Take *Toy Story*, for example, which **3** *has become / became* a top-selling film as soon as it was released, and **4** *has made / made* $361 million since then.

A relatively new development, however, is animated films which are actually *for* adults. Hayao Miyazaki, for example, **5** *has become / became* world-famous in recent years for films such as *Spirited Away*. His latest film, *The Wind Rises*, **6** *has been / was* one of the Best Animated Feature Film nominees for the Oscars this year, alongside the more usual children's films.

b Do you enjoy animated films? Why/Why not? Discuss with a partner.

3 Complete the two texts with the words in each box. In each case there are two words you do not need.

action hero	animated	based on	character	plot
starring				

The Wind Rises is a/an **1**_____ film, **2**_____ a short story by Tatsuo Hori. The main **3**_____ is an aircraft designer, Jiro Horikoshi, and the **4**_____ is basically an account of his life.

actors	cast	plays	performances	scenes
special effects				

The **5**_____ of *The Best Exotic Marigold Hotel* are all very well-known **6**_____, and their **7**_____ have generally been highly praised, especially that of Judi Dench, who **8**_____ a recently widowed housewife.

4 Divide the adjectives in the box into those that have a positive meaning and those that have a negative one.

amusing clever disappointing dull enjoyable
entertaining ordinary original predictable silly
surprising unexciting violent

5a 5.8))) Listen to six sentences. Rewrite each sentence you hear to make it stronger. Either change the normal adjective to an extreme adjective, or use a modifier.

b Compare your sentences with a partner. Check that together you have at least two different ways of making each sentence stronger.

6a 5.9))) Listen to some negative opinions about a film and complete the sentences with up to three words.

1 It was _____ good as I expected it to be.

2 It's really not _____.

3 I _____ it.

4 I'm _____ you wouldn't like it.

5 It was much less interesting _____.

b Work with a partner. Change each phrase to make it positive.

c Tell your partner about a film or TV programme you have seen using some of the phrases (positive or negative). Talk for 1–2 minutes each. Try to use as many of the adjectives and opinion phrases as possible.

In control?

6.1 Man and machine

GOALS ■ Talk about machines in our lives ■ Use defining and non-defining relative clauses

Vocabulary & Reading machines

1 Do you prefer to be a passenger or the driver in a car. Why?

2a Complete paragraphs 1 and 2 in the online car magazine article with the words in the box.

> brake (v)   busy traffic   ~~driverless~~   lane   motorway
> park (v)   steering wheel

b Complete paragraphs 3 and 4 of the article with the words and phrases in the box.

> accidents   at speed   injured   junctions   overtake (v)
> speed limit   traffic lights   traffic jams

c 6.1))) Listen and check your answers.

d Which words and phrases are illustrated in the photos? What is happening at the junction?

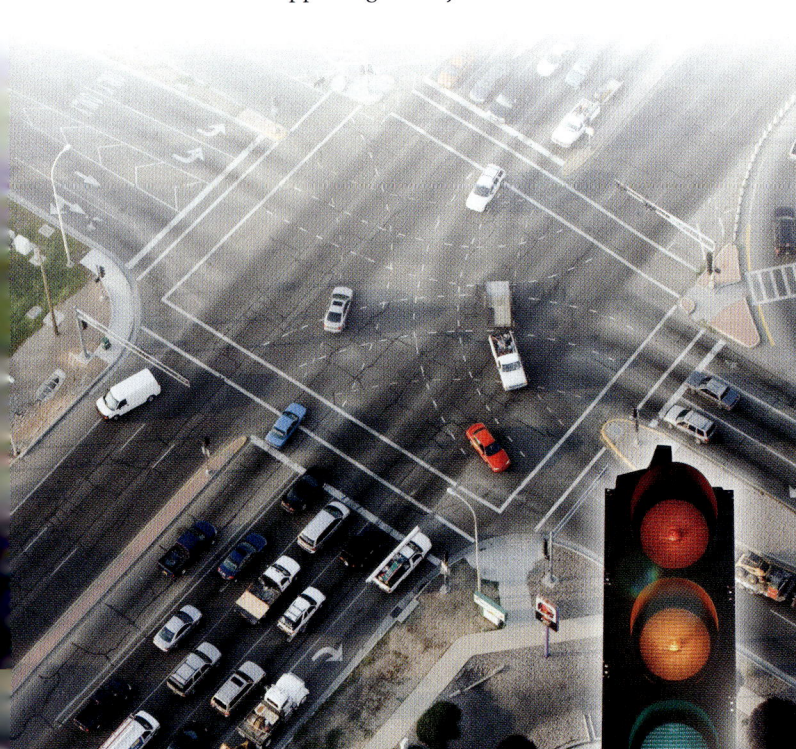

FEATURE

Your car is now in charge: ¹_driverless_ cars are already here.

1 Driving along the ²_____ in ³_____, the driver presses a button on the ⁴_____. The car is now driving itself.

2 This may sound like science fiction, but driverless cars are already on the roads in California. Many cars can already ⁵_____ themselves by the side of the road, ⁶_____ automatically when the car needs to slow down, and warn the driver if they are slipping out of the correct ⁷_____, so going driverless is just the next step.

3 Driverless cars come with fast broadband, allowing them to ⁸_____ other cars safely, and even communicate with ⁹_____ as they approach ¹⁰_____. Being stuck in ¹¹_____ could become a thing of the past, as driverless cars will be able to drive ¹²_____ much closer to each other.

4 More than fifty million people die or are ¹³_____ in road ¹⁴_____ every year, and 90% of these accidents are caused by human error. Google's driverless car sticks to the ¹⁵_____ and doesn't get tired. So wouldn't it be much safer if all cars were driverless?

3a Work with a partner. Answer the questions on advantages and disadvantages of driverless cars.

1 Would driverless cars actually reduce busy traffic or traffic jams? Why/Why not?
2 Would they reduce the number of people injured in accidents? Why/Why not?
3 Who might particularly benefit from not having to hold a steering wheel or use the pedals?
4 Would you trust the car's computer with your life?

b Work with another pair and compare your ideas.

Grammar & Speaking defining and non-defining relative clauses

4   Read comments a–c. Are they for or against driverless cars?

COMMENT

a
16 MAY Ecco254

I hate commuting to work – it's so stressful. **¹ Having a car** *that drives itself* would be wonderful for me, and **² anyone else** *who has to drive a lot,* but doesn't enjoy it. I must spend about 15 hours a week driving. **³ Think of all the extra time** *that I could use to check my emails or read a book.*

b
16 MAY Dobs

@Lucyloop – People were worried about seat belts too at one time! **⁴ My cousin,** *who has actually been in one of these cars,* said he felt perfectly safe, and so would I.

c
16 MAY Itsme22

Driverless cars would provide transport to people who can't drive themselves, such as blind people or those who are physically disabled. **⁵ My own physical disability,** *which I have had since birth,* means that I will never be able to drive a 'real' car, so a driverless car could really change my life. **⁶ It would** also be great for **people** *whose eyesight has got worse with age,* or who have simply lost confidence in their driving.

5a   Read the information in the Grammar focus box and match examples 1–6 in exercise **4** to a–f in the box.

GRAMMAR FOCUS defining and non-defining relative clauses

- We use defining relative clauses to identify who or what we are talking about.

  1 *Who* or *that* – for people   a _____
  2 *Which* or *that* – for things   b _____
  3 *Whose* – for possessions   c _____
  We can leave out the relative pronoun if it is the object of the verb.   d _____

- We use **non-defining relative clauses** to give extra information.
  It is already clear who or what we are talking about.

  1 *Who* (NOT ~~that~~) – for people   e _____
  2 *Which* – for things   f _____
  We use commas around the relative clause, to show that it is extra information.

→ **Grammar Reference** page 146

b   Look at the sentence *Think of all the extra time that I could use to check my emails or read a book*. What does 'that' refer to? Why can it be left out?

_____

_____

6a   **6.2** Complete the extract from a newspaper article with the correct relative pronouns. Sometimes no relative pronoun is necessary. Listen and check your answers.

NEWS > TECHNOLOGY

Intelligent machines **¹**_____ can serve us in supermarkets, give us directions and even drive for us are becoming part of all our lives. Some of the things **²**_____ machines can do now would have seemed impossible just a few years ago. And there's more to come. Amazon promises robot drones **³**_____ will deliver our packages, and Rolls-Royce says robo-ships, **⁴**_____ won't need any crew, will soon be sailing our seas.

But what will this mean for our workers? Some think that only people **⁵**_____ skills are better than the machines' abilities will have work. Those **⁶**_____ don't have high-level skills risk being unemployable, or will have to work for very low wages.

Amazon drone

b   Decide which examples in the article are defining relative clauses and which are non-defining.

c   Compare answers with a partner.

7a   **TASK** Work with a partner. Make two lists, one of arguments for and one of arguments against intelligent machines.

b   Work with another pair. One pair should argue in favour of intelligent machines, the other should argue against. Which arguments are most convincing?

6.2 Controlling the weather?

Vocabulary & Speaking climate and extreme weather

1a Look at the photos and use the words in the box to describe what you can see.

> climate change   crop damage   destroyed housing
> decrease/increase in rainfall   drought   fires   floods
> global warming   heatwave   high temperatures
> landslide   strong winds   tropical storms
> water shortages

b Do you think climate change and extreme weather events are caused by global warming?

c Put the rest of the words into the correct column.

Extreme weather events	Effects/Consequences of extreme weather events

PRONUNCIATION compound nouns

2a Look at the compound nouns in the box and divide them into two columns, according to which word carries the main stress: the first or the second.

> climate change   global warming   strong winds
> tropical storms   water shortages   crop damage

b **6.3**⟫ Listen and check your answers.

c Work with a partner. Think about what part of speech each word is, e.g. noun or adjective, and work out a rule.

3 Work in small groups. Discuss these questions.
1. Do you think the weather has been getting worse in recent years? Why/Why not?
2. Do you think anything can be done to control extreme weather? If yes, what?

Grammar & Listening present perfect simple and continuous

4a **6.4** Listen to the start of a radio interview. Why are scientists researching ways to control the weather?

b **6.5** Listen to the rest of the interview and answer the questions.
1 What is cloud seeding?
2 Why doesn't cloud seeding work well in drought areas?
3 How can cloud seeding help prevent hurricanes?
4 Why do people worry about using cloud seeding?
5 What solution have scientists in Geneva found?

5 Look at these extracts from the interview and answer the questions.

a
'… it seems that one group of scientists has found a solution.'

b
'Professor Jean-Pierre Wolf and Dr Jérôme Kasparian… have been experimenting with using lasers to control the weather.'

1 Which action began in the past and is still continuing?
2 Which action was completed at some point before now?

6a Add the two examples in exercise **5** to the correct place in the Grammar focus box.

GRAMMAR FOCUS present perfect simple and continuous

• We use the present perfect simple for completed actions which happened at some point before now and still have an influence on the present.
Subject + *have/has* + past participle
1 _____

• We use the present perfect continuous for unfinished actions which started in the past and continue up to now. It often answers the question *How long …?*
Subject + *have/has* + *been* + present participle
2 _____

We don't generally use present perfect continuous with state verbs, such as *be*, *have* and *know*.

→ Grammar Reference page 147

b Complete the sentences with the correct form of the verbs in brackets.
1 It now seems clear that temperatures _____ (rise) over the past decades, and the trend looks likely to continue.
2 Clearly if changes in weather patterns _____ (happen) as a result, we should be trying to prevent further warming.
3 Many scientists _____ (study) the effects of global warming on weather patterns and _____ (publish) the results of this research.

7a Complete the summary of the listening with the correct form of the verbs in brackets.

In recent years, there **1**_____ (be) a noticeable increase in extreme weather events. Many scientists now agree that climate change **2**_____ (cause) this increase. The science correspondent in the programme **3**_____ (just finish) researching ways in which scientists around the world **4**_____ (try) to artificially control or change weather patterns. These scientists **5**_____ (explore) various techniques, including cloud seeding, over the past few years. However, many people are worried about putting chemicals into the atmosphere. Recently one team of scientists in Geneva **6**_____ (discover) a way to use lasers to control the weather.

b **6.6** Listen and check your answers.

8 Read the news item and discuss with a partner. What kind of solutions might be possible?

world NEWS

| HOME | WORLD | BUSINESS | WEATHER | SPORTS |

World News > Thailand

Statistics from Thailand's Meteorological Department show that in the last four decades, average temperatures in the country's north-east region have steadily increased. In addition, the seasonal rains have been arriving later and later over the last ten years. Crops have died from water shortages.

However, although the problem is very serious, local people have begun to find new and imaginative solutions.

9 **TASK** Work with the same partner. Read about two different rice farmers from Thailand. Student A, turn to page 128. Student B, turn to page 133.

▶ **VOX POPS VIDEO 6**

6.3 Vocabulary and skills development

GOALS ☐ Recognize linkers in conversation ☐ Understand and use adjective suffixes

Listening & Speaking linkers in conversation

→ WHAT THINGS CAN'T YOU LIVE WITHOUT? ←
In a study of 2,000 people from the UK aged 18-65:

1 in 20 said they need a foreign holiday once a year

6 in 10 said the things they can't live without have changed as they have got older

For **WOMEN** chocolate, a best friend, and a cup of tea are of high importance

For **MEN** it is football and a cooked breakfast

33% said they could easily live without their smartphone, computer, and social networking, but **60%** said they would find it very difficult

77% say every item they own is replaceable

THE TOP TEN

1 Internet connection
2 Television
3 A best friend
4 Daily shower
5 Central heating
6 Cup of tea
7 A strong relationship
8 Car
9 Glasses
10 Coffee

1 In a recent survey in the UK, people talked about the items they couldn't live without. Look at the infographic and discuss the information with a partner.
  1 Do the results surprise you?
  2 Do you think the results would be different in your country?
  3 What do you think would be in the top ten?

2a 6.7)) Listen to someone being asked what she couldn't live without. What does she answer?

b 6.8)) Listen and complete the extracts.
  1 _____, somewhere where the weather is a bit more reliable.
  2 _____, I'm sure the challenge keeps you healthy.
  3 _____, we've just booked two weeks exploring the lakes and volcanoes of Nicaragua. I can't wait …

3a What do you think the meaning/use of each missing phrase is in exercise **2b**? Discuss with a partner.

b 6.9)) Read and listen to the information in the Unlock the code box about linkers in conversation to check your answers.

🔓 **UNLOCK THE CODE**
linkers in conversation

We use linkers to show how ideas are connected and to help listeners to follow the conversation. For example:
• to get someone's attention we may say *actually, in fact*
• to paraphrase we may say *in other words, to put it another way, what I mean is*
• to return to a previous topic we may say *as I was saying, anyway, anyhow*

4 Which sentence a–d follows 1–4 most logically?

1 I wear a lot of make-up to feel confident.
2 I also think it will cost too much money.
3 I think you should always try something new.
4 I hate waiting at bus stops or in train stations.

a What I mean is, I'm a bit impatient.
b In other words, don't stick with the same old things – you'll get old before you should.
c Actually, I never leave home without putting it on. I just don't want people to see me without it.
d Anyway, to get back to the point, I don't agree with the idea at all.

5a **6.10))** Listen to four more speakers. What items can't they live without?

b **6.10))** Listen again and complete the extracts.
Speaker 1: _____, I'm in charge.
Speaker 2: _____, I usually wear flat ones to get to the event.
Speaker 3: _____, where is it? I had it a moment ago, wait it must be …
Speaker 4: _____, I think the real reason I love it so much is …

6a Work in small groups. Discuss the things you feel you can't live without. Give your reasons, using the phrases in the Unlock the code box on page 60.

b Make a list of the top five things you can't live without.

Vocabulary & Speaking   adjective suffixes

7a Look at these sentences from the listening in exercise **5** and underline the adjectives.

1 Get nervous about catching the train.
2 I find it very stressful.
3 They're rather uncomfortable.
4 I only wear them to special events.
5 It reminds me of all the happy times I had …
6 I'd be helpless without it.

b How do you know they are adjectives? Read the Vocabulary focus box and check your answers.

VOCABULARY FOCUS   adjective suffixes

We can make adjectives from verbs and nouns by adding suffixes. Some of the most common adjective suffixes are:

-ful → careful, cheerful
-less → helpless, careless
-ous → dangerous, nervous
-able → washable, sociable, reliable
-al → musical, practical
-y → cloudy, dusty

8 Add the correct suffix to complete the adjectives in these sentences.

-al   -y   -ous   -able   -ful   -less

1 Eating chips is not very health_____.
2 Mobile phones used to be really enorm_____. Now they're much smaller and lighter.
3 Most of our possessions are replace_____. We could live comfortably with a lot less.
4 She's really music_____. She can play three different instruments, and sing.
5 This guidebook is completely use_____. All the information is out of date.
6 My shoes may not be fashion_____, but they are very comfort_____.
7 I think this cheese is off. It's very smell_____.
8 She loves wearing very colour_____ clothes.

9a Complete the sentences so they are true for you.

1 The one possession I own that is not replaceable is …
2 To be successful in life, I think you should …
3 I feel nervous when …
4 I'm/I'm not a practical person. I can/can't …
5 The most sociable person I know is …
6 At weddings, it's traditional to …
7 I think what I eat is healthy/unhealthy because …
8 I find it easy/difficult to be cheerful when …
9 I feel comfortable when …
10 I'm totally useless at …
11 I'd love to/hate to take part in dangerous sports because …
12 I think you need to be very careful when …

b Compare your answers in small groups.

helpless
careless   washable
cloudy dangerous
easy successful sociable
dusty useful
careful cheerful
difficult reliable practical
traditional nervous
replaceable

6.4 Speaking and writing

Reading & Writing writing a professional email

1 Read the email from a student to a professor. How do you think the professor reacted? Why?

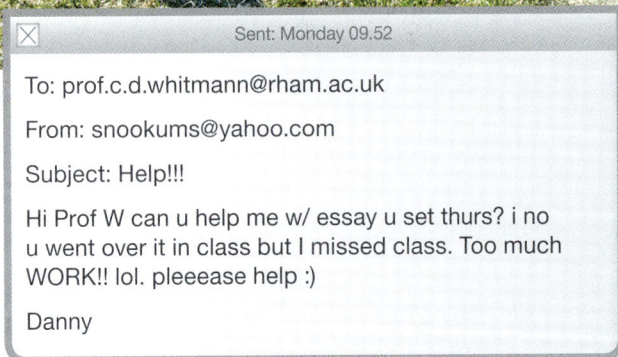

Sent: Monday 09.52

To: prof.c.d.whitmann@rham.ac.uk

From: snookums@yahoo.com

Subject: Help!!!

Hi Prof W can u help me w/ essay u set thurs? i no u went over it in class but I missed class. Too much WORK!! lol. pleeease help :)

Danny

---

2 Read the Language for writing box and find at least five examples of inappropriate language in the email in exercise 1.

LANGUAGE FOR WRITING
writing a professional email

Subject box

Put enough information in the subject box so that the recipient (the person receiving it) can see instantly who it is from and what it is about.
Subject: RE deadline for report

Addressing the recipient

Generally use the surname and title and 'Dear', not 'hi' or 'hello'.
Dear Dr Smart,

If you are on an equal level, you might use the first name.
Dear Chris,

Certain set phrases can be useful.
Thank you for your email.
I wonder if you could help me.
I would like to apologize for …
Unfortunately, I will not be able to …

Using abbreviations

The kinds of abbreviations you can use on social media are not appropriate.

Using too much punctuation

Avoid using exclamation marks (!) and emoticons, e.g. :)

Signing off

Always sign off with your name (full name if they might not know who you are) and one of the following.
Best wishes,
Many thanks,
Yours sincerely, (this is the most formal way)

3a Work with a partner. Rewrite the email in exercise 1 to make it appropriately professional.

b Swap your email with another pair. Compare what you wrote.

4 Your boss has set you a deadline for a piece of work. You have been ill and will miss the deadline. Write a professional email to your boss, apologizing and explaining what has happened.

Listening & Speaking   changing arrangements

5a **6.11**))) Listen to a phone conversation between two friends, Pedro and Sara, and answer the questions.

   1   Why can't Sara meet tomorrow lunchtime?

   2   Why can't Pedro meet after work?

   3   What has Sara arranged to do on Thursday?

  b   Check your answers with a partner.

6a   Complete extracts 1–6 from the phone conversation.

   1   There's been _____.

   2   I've got _____ tomorrow lunchtime.

   3   How _____ after work instead?

   4   I'm really sorry, but I _____ then.

   5   I'm _____ playing tennis with my sister.

   6   I'll speak to her, then _____ you.

  b   **6.12**))) Listen, check and repeat.

7   Replace three of the phrases in exercise **6** with these more formal alternatives, using the Language for speaking box to help you.

   1   I'll confirm it with you.

   2   I'm not available then.

   3   Would you be able to …?

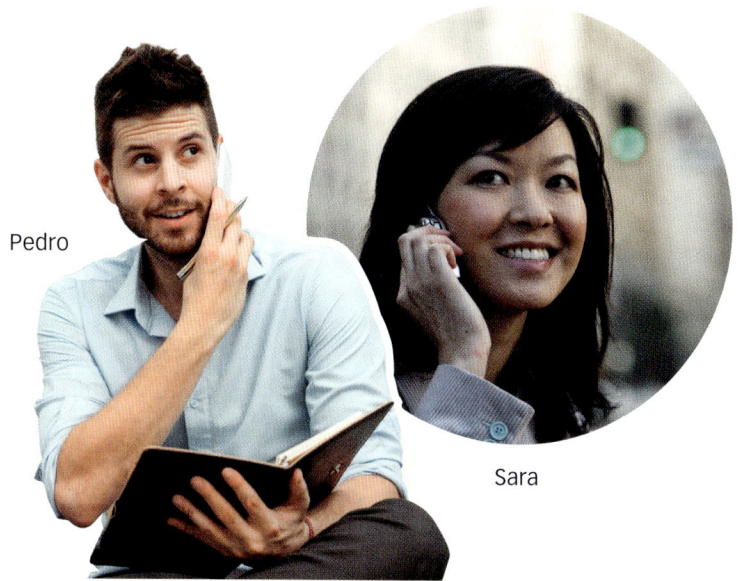

Pedro

Sara

LANGUAGE FOR SPEAKING
changing arrangements

Changing arrangements
I'm meant to …, but …
We had thought we'd …, but now …
How about getting together …?
Would you be able to meet on …?

Saying you are/aren't free
I'm (not) available then.
I can('t) make it then.
That's fine with me.

Confirming arrangements
I'll confirm it with you. I'll get back to you.

8a   **TASK**   Work with a partner. Choose one of these situations. You have arranged to …

- go to the cinema.
- have a lunchtime meeting in a restaurant.
- work on a presentation in the library.

  b   Take turns to have a phone conversation, using the prompts, the phrases in exercise **6a** and the Language for speaking box to help you.

A	B
Say hello and say who you are.	Say hello.
You need to change the time/place because of work/family/studies.	It's difficult for you to change it because you're busy at work/you have family problems/you are going on holiday.
Suggest a different time/place.	Say why you can't do that time.
Find a time you are both happy with and agree to meet.	
Say you'll check your diary and confirm later.	Say that's OK and finish call.

6.5 Video

Mist Catchers

1 Look at the photos, which show some mist catchers in the Atacama Desert. Match the words and phrases in the box to things in the photos.

> a container   a net   a pipe   drinking water   moisture   poles

2 Work with a partner. Answer the questions using some of the words from exercise **1**.

  a Why do you think people use mist catchers in the Atacama desert?

  b How do you think mist catchers work?

3 ▶ Watch the video. Check your ideas from exercise **2**. Were you right?

4 ▶ Watch again. Match the two halves of the sentences.

  1 There are a few areas in the desert which have had no rain

  2 The mist catchers in the Cerro Grande Reserve have been collecting rainwater

  3 The fog drifts over the land from

  4 Some water pipes carry water straight to

  5 Water conservationists may find this system useful in

  6 People in the Atacama Desert have been using water collection techniques

  a other dry regions around the world.

  b the Pacific Ocean.

  c the fields where crops are growing.

  d for hundreds of years.

  e for about six years.

  f since history began.

5a **TASK** Work in groups. Read the situation.

> There is a serious lack of fresh water in your country. Water shortages have become common. You can't live without water and so you need to save every drop!

  b Plan how to deal with these water shortages, at home or in your school. List your ideas under these two headings.

    • Saving water
    • Collecting water

  c Present your ideas to the class. Decide which ideas are the best and why.

Review

1a Work with a partner. How is the inside of this car different from a standard car? Who might want a car like this?

b Read the article and compare with your ideas.

Why should a car **1**_____ is self-driving look like an ordinary car? The Swiss company Rinspeed has designed a car **2**_____ transforms into a mobile office. This would allow the passengers, **3**_____ now don't have to drive, to use their time to work or relax.

The steering wheel would slide away and a desk, **4**_____ would be large enough for a laptop, could be pulled out instead. The driver, **5**_____ seat would be moveable, could turn to face the other passengers to chat, or just relax and watch the films **6**_____ would be available on four separate screens.

c Complete the article using *that, who, which* or *whose*. Use *that* where possible.

2a Complete the sentences with up to two words. The first letter of each is given.

1 You should keep both hands on the s_____ w_____ when you are driving.
2 Before you decide to o_____ a car, make sure the road ahead is completely clear.
3 Don't drive over the speed l_____.
4 If the t_____ l_____ are turning orange, you should stop rather than try and rush through.
5 Many people fall asleep while driving on the m_____, so take regular breaks.
6 Don't p_____ on the pavement, it can be dangerous for blind people.

b Check your answers with a partner. Decide together which are the three most important pieces of advice. Say why.

3a Match the two halves of each compound noun.

1 climate   a warming   5 land   e shortages
2 crop   b change   6 strong   f winds
3 global   c waves   7 tropical   g slides
4 heat   d damage   8 water   h storms

b 6.13))) Listen and check your answers. Practise the pronunciation with a partner.

4 Complete the questions using the present perfect simple or continuous form of the verbs in brackets. If both are possible, use the present perfect continuous.

1 Do you think that the weather _____ (get) worse in recent years? Why/Why not?
2 _____ you _____ (enjoy) the weather recently? Why/Why not?
3 What's the worst weather you _____ (experience)? What happened?
4 (Roughly) how many times _____ you _____ (see) snow? Is it common in your country?
5 _____ there _____ (be) any weather-related disasters in your country? What happened?
6 _____ you _____ (listen) to the weather forecasts recently? If so, why?

5a 6.14))) Write down each word you hear and then add the correct suffix to each root word you hear to make an adjective.

b Work with a partner. Think of at least two more adjectives with each suffix used in exercise **5a**.

6a Put the conversation in the right order.

a Ah, I'm meant to be meeting my brother and his wife for dinner next Saturday. But I'll talk to them and get back to you.
b Hi, Joanne.
c Hi, it's Joanne here. 1
d Oh dear. Sorry, but I'm not available then. How about next Saturday?
e OK, that's fine.
f You know we were supposed to be going to the cinema on Saturday? I'm really sorry, but there's been a change of plan. Can we go on Sunday instead?

b 6.15))) Listen and check your answers.

c Work with a partner. Write a similar conversation. Practise your conversation together.

Ambitions

7.1 Good prospects

Dublin

London

Milan

Lisbon

Buenos Aires

Luanda

Athens

Melbourne

Manila

GOALS ■ Talk about working conditions ■ Talk about finished habits and situations

Vocabulary & Reading working conditions

1 Work with a partner. Look at the cities on the map and discuss the questions.

1 What do you know about each city and/or the country?

2 If you had to choose one of these cities to live in, which one would you choose? Is there anywhere else you'd like to live and work?

2 Work with a partner. Read the extract from a magazine article and answer the questions.

1 Which countries do many of the young people moving to Argentina come from?

2 What reason for moving does each person give?

3 Is each person happy with their decision?

Young Europeans flock to Argentina for job opportunities

A mix of Italian, Spanish and English accents stand out in Buenos Aires neighbourhoods such as San Telmo, as the city welcomes a growing number of young professionals who have come here looking for jobs and a more relaxed lifestyle.

Two years ago, Hanson decided to change his occupation, leaving his job at a London financial services firm to teach English privately to business executives in Buenos Aires. 'The company was making people redundant,' he says. 'Sunny Buenos Aires is a welcome change from that stress. The climate is perfect, getting a job here was pretty easy and the people are great.'

For Chiara Boschiero, a 33-year-old film producer from Italy, Argentina has provided better career prospects. 'In Italy, it is very difficult for a director under 40 to make a film. But Argentina is young, and there are many directors and producers here younger than I am who are very successful.'

3 Underline any words from the box in the article. What do you think they mean?

> career prospects   job satisfaction   occupation
> promotion   qualification   (make) redundant
> rent-free accommodation   salary   sick/holiday pay
> unemployed   working conditions   working hours

4 Match the other words in the box in exercise **3** to the definitions.

1   the money a person receives for the work they have done
2   an exam you have passed or course you have completed
3   the pleasure you get from your work
4   a place to live that your employer pays for
5   a move to a higher position or more challenging job
6   money you get when you are temporarily not at work
7   when you are not able to find a job
8   the period of time when you are working
9   the situation you work in

5a Work in small groups. Decide the five most important reasons why someone might choose a job and put them in order of importance.

b What other reasons can you think of?

Grammar & Speaking   *used to* and *would*

6 **7.1**)) Listen to three people who moved abroad to work.

1   Which countries did each speaker moved to/from?
   • Dermot   • Maria   • Joaquim
2   What reasons do they give for their move?

7 Work with a partner. Look at the following statement about one of the speakers and answer the questions.

Dermot used to work in Dublin. He would spend a lot less time at work.

Was this true in the past? Is it true now? How do we know?

8 Read the information in the Grammar focus box and complete it with example sentences a–d.

a   Maria would spend all day calling people and getting nowhere.
b   Dermot didn't use to be a manager.
c   Maria designs gardens.
d   Joaquim used to live in Lisbon.

> ### GRAMMAR FOCUS *used to* and *would* for past habits and states
>
> • We use *used to/didn't use to* + infinitive for finished habits and states: things that were true but are not now.
>   1 _____
>   2 _____
>
> • We can also use *would* to talk about finished habits and typical past behaviour.
>   3 _____
>
> • However, note that we CANNOT use *would* to talk about past states, only actions and typical behaviour.
>   *Dermot used to live in Dublin.* NOT ~~Dermot would live in Dublin~~.
>
> • *used to/didn't use to* is only for past habits. For present habits we use the present simple.
>   4 _____
>
> → Grammar Reference page 148

9a Choose the correct options to complete the sentences. Use *used to* only or both *used to* or *would*.

1   I _____ like staying up very late, but now I'm in bed by 10.00 p.m. every night.
2   When I was a teenager, I _____ play a lot of sport, but now I just watch them on TV.
3   I _____ have very long hair when I was a teenager.
4   I _____ get very nervous before examinations when I was at university.
5   When I was a child, I _____ spend hours making model cars and planes.
6   I _____ think life would be easy when I became an adult – but that's not true at all.

b Make the sentences true for you and compare your answers with a partner.

10 **TASK** Work with a partner. Student A, turn to page 128. Student B, turn to page 134.

▶ **VOX POPS VIDEO 7**

7.2 Ask an expert

GOALS ■ **Talk about experts and high achievers** ■ **Use question forms**

Vocabulary & Reading high achievers

1 Work with a partner. The photos show three people who are well known as experts. What do you think they are expert at? Do you recognize any of them?

2 Read biographies 1–3 and check if your ideas were correct.

1 → Daniel Barenboim

Daniel Barenboim was born in 1942 in Buenos Aires, and moved to Israel in 1952. A talented musician, he began to learn the piano at five and gave his first public concert aged seven. As well as being an excellent musician and conductor, he is also well known for his work with young people. In 1999 he co-founded the West-Eastern Divan orchestra with Professor Edward Said to unite Israeli and Arab musicians. Barenboim has also set up a number of other projects to encourage young people to play music and has received various awards for his achievements.

2 → Jane Goodall

Jane Goodall was born in London in 1934. In her early twenties, she went to Tanzania, initially as a secretary to the anthropologist Louis Leakey. However, Jane was hard-working and ambitious, and soon became a researcher herself, studying the behaviour of wild apes and chimpanzees. Her discoveries changed many beliefs about ape behaviour, and she became an expert on the subject. In 1991 she set up Roots & Shoots, a global environmental and humanitarian youth education programme now based in more than 100 countries.

3 → Rebecca Adlington

Rebecca Adlington was born in Mansfield, UK, in 1989. At nineteen she suddenly became famous as a champion swimmer, after winning two gold medals at the Beijng Olympics, the first British swimmer for 100 years to achieve this. She also did well at the London Olympics, winning two bronze medals. In 2005, Adlington's sister became dangerously ill, with encephalitis*. She recovered, but Adlington has said that her sister's illness made her 'more determined' to succeed. In 2013 she retired from swimming, but uses her fame to raise money for an encephalitis charity.

- ■ **encephalitis** an infection or allergic reaction which causes the brain to swell

3a Work with a partner. Look at the highlighted words in the biographies and decide if each one is a noun, verb or adjective. Work out what they mean.

b Complete the sentences using a suitable word from the article. Compare your answers with a partner and give reasons for your choices.

1 Many _____ people never become really _____ because they are too shy.
2 He's very _____. He wants to become President one day.
3 She is _____ to _____ the highest mark in her class.
4 If you want to become a _____, you will need to train every day.
5 She never won any _____ for her _____, but her research changed the world.

4 **TASK** Work with a partner or in small groups and discuss the questions.

1 To become an expert at something, which is more important – hard work or talent?
2 Is being ambitious always a good thing? Why/Why not?

Grammar & Speaking question forms

5a The three experts all took part in an interview in a British newspaper. Look at the questions and answers and try to guess which person is answering. Discuss your answers with a partner.

b Based on their answers, which person would you most/least like to meet? Why?

1 ↓

1 **Which living person do you most admire, and why?**
My mum. She is the most thoughtful person that I've ever known.

2 **How would you like to be remembered?**
As someone who enjoyed life, was bubbly and worked hard.

3 **Would you mind telling us what you most dislike about your appearance?**
My big shoulders.

2 ↓

1 **Do you like giving interviews?**
No.

2 **When were you happiest?**
When I didn't have to give interviews.

3 **What would your super power be?**
To travel back in time – in order to spend a day with Mozart.

4 **What makes you unhappy?**
When I don't understand something.

3 ↓

1 **What is your most treasured possession?**
I don't like possessions.

2 **What is your earliest memory?**
When I was two, a dragonfly flew near me. A man knocked it to the ground and trod on it. I remember crying because I'd caused the dragonfly to be killed.

3 **How would you like to be remembered?**
As someone who helped to change attitudes towards animals.

6a Read the information about question forms in the Grammar focus box, then add an example for each type of question from the questions in exercise **5**.

GRAMMAR FOCUS questions

Direct questions
- In questions we normally put an auxiliary verb (*do, does, did*) before the subject.
  1 _____

- If the question word is the <u>subject</u> of the question, we don't use *do/does/did*.
  2 _____

Indirect questions
- We use indirect questions to make questions more polite. The word order doesn't change and we don't use *do/does/did*.
  Could you tell me which living person you most admire?
  3 _____

- Note that to make *yes/no* indirect questions we use *if*.
  Would you mind telling me if you think you are ambitious?
  I'd like to know if you think you are ambitious.

→ Grammar Reference page 149

b Look at the questions in exercise **5** and make them indirect.

7 Make interview questions using the prompts. Make at least two indirect questions.

1 Give an example of an embarrassing moment.
What / happen?
2 What / favourite smell?
3 Like / watch sport? Why/Why not?
4 Tell me about a time when you felt angry.
Who / make / angry and why?
5 How / relax?
6 What / think / greatest achievement?
7 Tell / favourite film?

8 **TASK** Work with a partner. Go to page 128 and prepare your questions.

7.3 Vocabulary and skills development

GOALS ■ Understand paraphrasing ■ Use collocations

Reading & Speaking understanding paraphrasing

1a Look at the statements. What do they mean? Do you agree with them? Discuss with a partner.

1 *I have not failed. I have simply found ten thousand ways that won't work.* (Thomas Edison)

2 *Failure is the key to success; each mistake teaches us something.* (Morihei Ueshiba)

b Look at the first statement in exercise **1a**. Which word or phrase is expressed in different words in the second statement?

2a Read the information in the Unlock the code box about paraphrasing.

> **🔓 UNLOCK THE CODE**
> understanding paraphrasing
>
> To avoid repetition, writers talk about the same thing in different ways. Writers use a synonym (either a word or phrase that means almost the same thing) to refer to the thing. Sometimes the new phrase has a different grammatical form.
>
> *People who do well in their jobs get promoted.*
>
> *My colleagues are pretty ambitious.*
> *Most people who work here want to get to the top.*

b Read paragraph **1** of the article. The underlined words or phrases are paraphrased later in the paragraph. Circle the phrases which are their near synonyms.

3a Think of two reasons why doing a task and failing could be good for you.

b Read the rest of the article. What reasons does the writer give for the value of failure?

The Festival of Errors

1 Some French education <u>specialists</u> recently put on a <u>festival</u> in Paris to encourage <u>children</u> to <u>make mistakes</u>. Yes, it's true! The experts were worried that young people in France were not <u>creative and innovative</u> enough for the modern world. Since they believe that a school system that concentrates on marks and grades will reduce the ability of the kids to produce new ideas, the activities in the week-long event showed the participants the wonder and pleasure of getting things wrong.

2 Most people believe in success. In sport, politics and business, success is king. Look at our education systems: they're based on the idea of encouraging people to be successful. We reward success in exams, for example, with entrance to university. We reward success at university with a good job. People who <u>do well</u> in their jobs get promoted to higher positions, and so on.

3 But there are reasons why we should value failure as well. The problem with the success model is that it tends to <u>give credit for</u> safe behaviour. We follow the procedures, obey the rules. More importantly, it encourages people to hang on to old ideas. On the other hand, people who like to take risks, think creatively, and come up with new, perhaps impossible, ideas, are told they are failures. In a very fast-changing world, this is not good practice.

4 Another point of view is provided by Dr Astro Teller who works for Google, a company famous for its incredible successes, and equally <u>unbelievable</u> failures. He says that if you criticize people for having good ideas, they will give up. His example is: imagine you send out a group of scouts* to a new land to find mountains to climb. They do their best to find one, but can't. If you <u>blame</u> them when they come back, those scouts will <u>quit</u>.

5 And what about learning a language? Sometimes you have to take risks, because otherwise it becomes difficult to communicate. If you're trying to <u>talk to</u> a person, and they don't understand you, then you have to find a completely different way of saying what you want to say! So making a mistake can mean you also make progress!

■ **scout** a person sent ahead to get information

4 The underlined words in paragraphs 2–5 are synonyms for words that come earlier in the article. Write the words they refer to.

Paragraph 2	do well	*be successful*
Paragraph 3	give credit for	
Paragraph 4	unbelievable blame quit	
Paragraph 5	talk to	

5 Answer the questions.

1 According to the article, how are successful people rewarded at work?
2 Why can failure be useful? What does it teach us?
3 What is the example of the scouts in paragraph 3 supposed to show?
4 What does the writer think you need to do to communicate in another language?

6 Work with a partner. What are the main ideas from the article that you both agree with?

Vocabulary & Speaking collocations

7 Find these collocations in the article in exercise **3**. In your own words, what do you think they mean?

Paragraph 2	1 a good job 2 get promoted 3 higher positions	
Paragraph 3	4 follow the procedures 5 obey the rules 6 think creatively 7 come up with ideas	
Paragraph 4	8 do their best	
Paragraph 5	9 take risks 10 completely different 11 make progress	

8 Read the information in the Vocabulary focus box about collocations.

VOCABULARY FOCUS collocations

There are several different types of collocations organized by word class, noun, verb, adjective, etc. The most common are:

- verb + noun → *obey the rules*
- adjective + noun → *a good job*
- verb + adverb or adverb + verb → *think creatively*
- adverb + adjective → *hugely important*

When you record collocations, it is essential to note down the grammar words like *a* or *my* as well. If you use the wrong grammar words, it will sound unnatural.

e.g. *I always try to do my best.* NOT ~~I always try to do the best~~.

9 Work with your partner. Write a summary of the article, using your ideas from exercise **6** and the collocations in exercise **7** to help you.

10a Complete the questions about work and study with collocations made from one word in column A and one word in column B.

Column A	Column B
job	job
take	employees
obey/follow	creatively
temporary	risks
supervise	satisfaction
think	the rules

1 Which is more important – a good salary or a/an/–_____?
2 At work, is it better to obey the rules, or to _____?
3 Have you ever had a _____? What was it? Did you want it to become permanent?
4 Have you ever had a job where you had to _____ other _____? Did you like the responsibility?
5 Would you like a job where you had to come up with new ideas, or one where you simply _____?
6 Do you find it easy to _____ and come up with new ideas? How do you do it?

b 7.2)) Listen and check your answers.

11a TASK Work with a partner or in small groups. Ask and answer the questions in exercise **10**. Give reasons for your answers.

b Report the two most interesting answers to the class.

7.4 Speaking and writing

GOALS ■ Write an application letter or email ■ Ask for and give clarification

Writing an application letter or email

1 Work with a partner. Read the adverts and answer the questions.

  1 Which advert needs people who are interested in learning about different cultures?

  2 Which needs people who have ideas about the latest trends?

  3 Which advert needs people with good group work skills?

  4 Which appeals to you most? And least? Why?

1

Team leaders needed for immediate start!

Want to get into management? Already got experience? We are looking for new and experienced leaders to manage our expanding group of coffee shops. We want excellent decision-makers who are good with people to organize and lead teams of up to ten employees in our new branches across the country. Opportunities for international travel.

Applications to Raj at admin@coffeehouse.com. No phone enquiries, please.

2

Study trips abroad

Have the experience of a lifetime: spend two months studying abroad. Trips available for studying science, sport, art, local culture or languages. Included in the trip:

• Overnight visits to places of local interest
• Short stays with local families

Applicants should have at least a school leaver's certificate, plus a strong interest in travel. Send applications to Carmen Ramos at studytrips@travelabroad.com or apply online.

3

Social bloggers wanted for online lifestyle magazine

Are you good with words and happy to write in your own language and/or English?

We are looking for writers with something to say about social media, fashion, food and entertainment. Our readers love to learn about what's new around the world. If you have great ideas and experiences to share with our magazine's online community, apply now to **Sam Fielding** at sam@wordcount.com. Interviews start next week (face-to-face or Skype).

2a Which of the three advertisements in exercise **1** is Asuncion applying to?

  [1] *Dear / To* _____,

  A [2] *This email is about / I am writing regarding* your advertisement for _____ posted on the Jobs & Training website this month.

  B [3] *As you will see from the attached CV, / Read the CV and you'll see that*, at present, I am working as an assistant manager in an international relocation office, helping companies set up abroad. In my present position, my main responsibility is organizing project teams to help companies find good locations in other countries, and I recently won a company award for this work.

  C With my work experience and skills, I believe I would be ideally suited to a management position in your company. I am highly organized, hard-working and positive. My business knowledge and IT skills are up to date, and I am also very active in the world of business networking. I am now ready for more challenges in my working life. [4] *I want to / I would like to* work for your company as it has a very good reputation for quality and customer care. [5] *You need to give me the chance to / I would like the opportunity to* use my skills to help your company grow.

  D [6] *Please invite me for / I would be happy to attend* an interview and I would be able to start work at the beginning of next month. [7] *If you need further information, please / Do you want to know more? Then* call me on 01422 44327, or email me at asuncion@email.com.

  E [8] *I look forward to hearing from you. / I am waiting for your call.*

  Yours sincerely,
  Asuncion Rico

b Read the information in the Language for writing box. Work with a partner to choose the correct phrases for 1–8 in Asuncion's email.

LANGUAGE FOR WRITING formal phrases

If we are applying for a job, we need to sound formal in the initial letter/email to make a good impression. We use fixed phrases like:

Formal	Neutral
I am writing regarding …	*I wanted to know …*
I would like to …	*I'd like to …*
I would be happy to attend …	*I'd like to come to …*
I look forward to hearing from you.	*Let me know.*

3 Here is a list of things people usually include in an application email or letter. Which paragraph was each in?

- Give the reason for writing   _A_
- Say you are sending your CV   _____
- Give information about your current situation   _____
- Give information about your skills   _____
- Say why you would be good for the job/company/course   _____
- Give extra contact details   _____
- Write a closing sentence asking the reader to reply   _____

4a Choose the advert you would most like to reply to and make notes for an application email using these headings.

- work experience   • reasons for applying
- job and personal skills

b Write the application email. Use your notes, the Language for writing box on page 72 and phrases from Asuncion's email to help.

Listening & Speaking   clarification

5 Look at the photo and imagine you are waiting for a job interview. Which person in the photo would you feel most like? Tell your partner why.

6a Read the interview questions. Which do you think is the most difficult to answer?

1 Where do you see yourself in five years' time?
2 What motivates you and what doesn't?
3 Why should we employ you?
4 When was the last time you had a disagreement at work, and how did you deal with it?
5 If you were a type of food, what would you be?

b Why do interviewers ask questions like these?

7a 7.3))) Listen to people in job interviews. Who answers each question from exercise 6a?

Li Yan _____   Marina _____
Parissa _____   Ken _____
Sophie _____

b 7.3))) Listen again and complete the phrases the people used.
Li Yan
1 Could _____ mean?
2 Well, _____, I spent three years working in a similar situation in …
Parissa
3 I'm not _____. _____ what job will I have?
4 Yes … in _____, what are your goals for the next few years?
Sophie
5 Could _____, please?
Marina
6 Let me _____ …
Ken
7 What _____, what makes you …?
8 Could _____ that?

PRONUNCIATION sounding polite

> In a situation like an interview, it is important to sound interested and polite.

8a 7.4))) Listen to the eight phrases in exercise **7**. Mark the intonation, the rise and fall, in each phrase.

Could you explain what you mean?

b 7.4))) Listen again and practise the phrases.

9a TASK Work in small groups. Read each other's application emails or letters. Together, choose four questions from exercise **6** and add two more.

b Interview each other. Use the phrases in the Language for speaking box to ask for and give clarification.

LANGUAGE FOR SPEAKING
asking for and giving clarification

Ask for clarification
Could you explain what you mean?
I'm not sure I understand. Do you mean …?

Give clarification
Let me give you a good example …   Well, for instance …

Get time to think
Let me see …   Let me think …   Now, what's the word again?

c Tell each other the two best answers each person gave and explain why.

7.5 Video

Moving abroad to work

1 Work with a partner. Guess the meaning of the phrases in bold.

   a I'm bored with my life here, so I'm going to **try my luck** somewhere else.

   b This job has good prospects, and I'll have the chance to **obtain** new skills, too.

   c I don't live in the same town as my job, so I'll need to **commute** to work by train.

   d It's exciting to **start anew** doing a different job in another country.

2 Look at the photos. What job do you think Zsuzsanna does? Where do you think she has lived?

3 ▶ Watch the video. Which of the following are mentioned?

   a her education in Hungary

   b reasons for moving abroad to work

   c the career benefits of moving abroad

   d finding new friends in the UK

   e the challenges of moving abroad

   f returning to Hungary

   g difficulties people might have when they go home

4 ▶ Watch again. Complete the table showing the differences between life in Hungary and the UK.

	Hungary	The UK
Cost of living		
A typical working day		
Travelling to work		

5a **TASK** Look at these reasons for moving to a new country for work. Why would you decide to move? Put these reasons in order of importance for you (1= most important).

- to challenge myself
- to find new friends
- to improve my career prospects
- to have an adventure
- to have a more relaxed lifestyle
- to learn a new language
- any other reason

   b Compare your ideas with a partner. Do you have similar reasons?

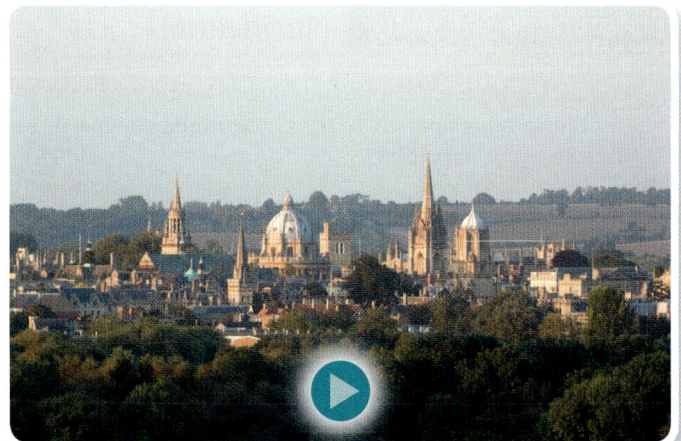

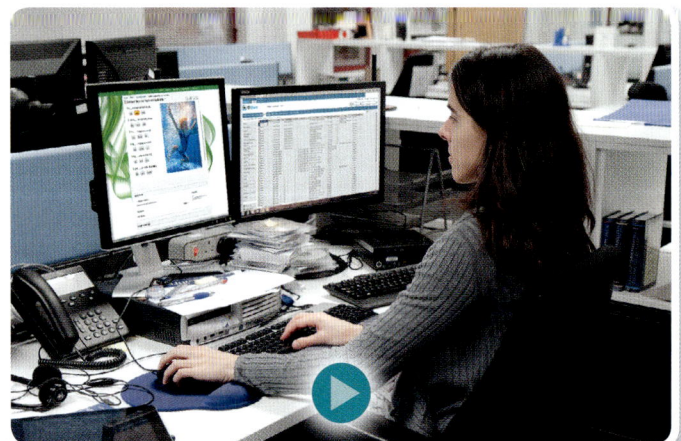

Review

1a Read the sentences and cross out the forms which are *not* possible. Sometimes both forms may be correct.

1 When I was little, I *used to / would* want to be a pop star when I grew up.

2 I *used to / would* practise in front of the mirror with a hairbrush as a microphone.

3 My mother *used to / would* laugh, but kindly.

4 She *used to / would* tell me that I could be anything I wanted.

5 But she *used to / would* warn me that it wouldn't be easy to be a pop star.

6 I really *used to / would* believe I could do it, but now I'm quite happy being a dentist!

b Talk to your partner. Tell them about the ambitions you had when you were a child, using *used to* and *would* where appropriate.

2a Make questions using the prompts.

1 What / being successful / mean to you?

2 Who / successful / in your family?

3 What / your biggest goal / in life?

4 What / one job / you wouldn't like to do?

5 Which / better – an indoor / outdoor job? Why?

6 What / your dream job?

b Make the questions indirect using *Would you mind telling me …* , *I'd like to know …* or another suitable starter. Then use the questions to interview your partner. Ask follow-up questions.

3a Read the text and complete it with one word in each space. The first letter is given.

According to a recent survey, about 20% of workers around the world work from home at least once a week, and nearly 10% work from home every day. There are obvious advantages. You can often fit in your **1** w_____ h_____ at any time that's convenient for you, and you don't have to spend some of your **2** s_____ on travelling to and from the office. The **3** w_____ c_____ might also be a lot better in the peace and comfort of your own home. However, many people also felt that if they weren't in the office, they were less likely to be given **4** p_____ as the boss might not notice their good work. Being out of the office could therefore damage their **5** c_____ p_____. Equally, they might be more likely to be made **6** r_____ if the company got into trouble, because they had not been able to build a relationship with the boss.

b Do you, or would you like to, work from home? Why/Why not? Discuss with a partner.

4a **7.5** Listen to the definitions and choose which word of each pair is being defined.

1 ambitious / famous

2 hard-working / determined

3 well-known / expert

4 talented / famous

5 hard-working / well-known

6 determined / talented

b Think of a person you could describe using all or some of the adjectives in exercise **4a**. Tell your partner about him/her.

5a **7.6** Listen and write down the words you hear.

b Work with a partner and put the words together to make six collocations. Then write a sentence using each collocation.

6a Put the words in the right order to make the sentences/questions.

1 repeat / you / please / that / could ?

2 you / mean / explain / you / could / what ?

3 me / example / give / let / you / good / a .

4 I / sure / understand / not / I'm .

5 word / the / what's / again ?

6 examples / that / some / you / could / of / give ?

b Work with a partner. Decide which of the expressions in exercise **6a** are a) ways of asking for clarification b) ways of giving clarification and c) ways of getting time to think.

Choices

8.1   World happiness report

Vocabulary & Listening   happiness factors

1   Work with a partner or in small groups. Put the words and phrases in the correct category in the table. Some words may fit into more than one category.

> balanced diet   childcare   cultural activities   healthcare
> high taxes   neighbours   physical activity   pollution
> poverty   strong economy   volunteer

Health	
Money	
Family/Society	
Leisure	

2a   Which factors are most important in order to have a good quality of life? With your partner or group put the four categories in order of importance.

b   Read an extract from a newspaper article about the UN *World Happiness Report*. According to the report, what makes a country a happy place to live in?

c   Discuss the questions together.
1   Are you surprised by any of the countries named in the list, or their position? If so, why?
2   What do you think is good about your country and how it does the things mentioned in exercise 1?

3a   8.1))) Listen to an extract from a podcast about Denmark, which was recently named the happiest country in the world. Number the ideas shown in the photos in the order in which they are discussed.

b   8.1))) Listen again. What do they say about each photo?

c   Do you think the same things are important? Why/Why not?

World Happiness

You might think that the happiest country in the world would have plenty of sunshine, but you'd be wrong. According to the recent United Nations *World Happiness Report*, nearly all of the top ten countries are well known for long, cold, dark winters. But what they do have is a strong economy, reliable government, and people who look after themselves and each other.

1	**Denmark**		6	Canada
2	Norway		7	Finland
3	Switzerland		8	Austria
4	Netherlands		9	Iceland
5	Sweden		10	Australia

b Match these sentences to a–c in the Grammar focus box.
- Money doesn't make you happy unless everyone has enough.
- If people work a thirty-seven hour week, they have quite a lot of leisure time.
- If you look a bit further down the list, you'll see that money isn't everything.

5a Choose the correct option in each sentence.
1 *If / Unless* people spend more than an hour travelling to work, they are generally less content.
2 *If / Unless* you have some close friendships, you will find it hard to be happy.
3 *If / Unless* you do regular exercise outdoors, you'll be able to work more efficiently.
4 People tend to be happier *if / unless* they are in a long-term relationship.
5 *If / Unless* people are active in work and free time, they'll probably be healthier.

b 8.2))) Listen and check your answers.

PRONUNCIATION intonation in *if* sentences

6a 8.2))) Listen again. Which clause rises in intonation? Which clause falls?

b 8.2))) Mark the rise and fall. Listen again and repeat.

7 Complete the sentences with the correct form of the verbs in brackets.
Use a modal verb where possible.
1 If they _____ (not have to) pay to visit museums, then people _____ (visit) them more often.
2 Extreme weather events _____ (happen) more often and _____ (be) more severe unless we _____ (do) something about climate change.
3 If parents _____ (be) allowed paid time off after the birth of a baby, they _____ (decide) how to share the time.
4 People _____ (tend) to have more job satisfaction if they _____ (work) reasonable hours and in pleasant conditions.
5 If there _____ (be) a cheap and reliable public transport system, people _____ (use) their cars less.
6 Doctors say that if you _____ (eat) lots of fresh fruit and vegetables and _____ (exercise) regularly, you _____ (probably live) longer.

8 **TASK** Work in groups of four. Take the roles of government ministers and discuss the budget. Turn to page 129.

▶ **VOX POPS VIDEO 8**

Grammar & Speaking   real conditionals

4a Look at the information in the Grammar focus box and choose the correct options 1–5.

> **GRAMMAR FOCUS** sentences with *if* – real conditionals
>
> *If*-sentences usually have two clauses: the *if*-clause and the result clause.
> - When we talk in general about things that can possibly happen, we use:
>   *If +* [1] present simple / *will*,   [2] present simple / *will*
>   *If people enjoy their job, they are happier in general.*
>   a _____
> - When we talk about specific situations in the future, and their possible results, we use:
>   *If +* [3] present simple / *will*,   [4] present simple / *will*
>   *If you eat a balanced diet, you'll feel healthier.*
>   b _____
> - We can use modal verbs, particularly *can* and *may*, in either clause.
>   *If you can cycle for thirty minutes a day, it may add one to two years to your life.*
> - *Unless* usually means *except if.*
>   c _____
>
> → **Grammar Reference** page 150

What makes a hero?

Vocabulary & Reading — personality and behaviour

1a Read the three short descriptions. Which of these people do you think are heroes? Why/Why not? Discuss with a partner or in small groups.

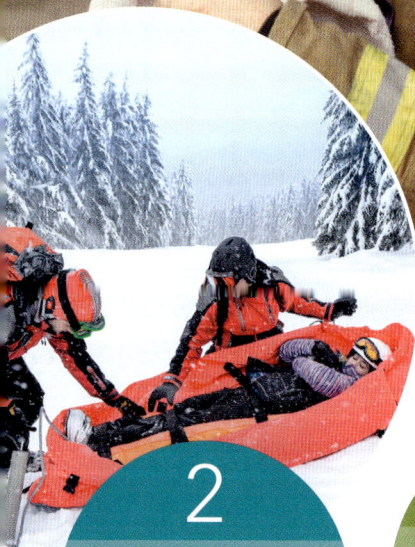

1
A firefighter who risks his/her life every day to save people from burning buildings.

2
A woman who risks her job by speaking out about something illegal happening at her place of work.

3
A boy who stops another child being attacked, even though he may get hurt himself.

2a Read the magazine article and compare your ideas with your partner.

What makes a hero?

Kerry Clark was sitting in the backyard of his farm when he saw a small plane crash in the nearby woods. He rushed over there immediately and started to rescue people, even though the plane was on fire and might explode any minute.

'Somebody needed to help,' Clark said afterwards. 'You do it because you have to.'

But if you saw a crash, would you risk your life to help? Was Clark crazy or unusually brave? Researchers at Berkeley University have spent the last five years studying what exactly makes people act heroically.

They have made some fascinating discoveries...

- One in five people has done something heroic, such as helping another person in a dangerous situation, or being honest when they find out about something unfair, even if it risks their safety or job.
- The more educated you are, the more likely you are to be a hero.
- Kind, generous people are more likely to be heroes. One third of the heroes in the study had also volunteered up to 5–9 hours a week.
- Men reported heroism more than women. However, this may be because women can be a bit embarrassed about their heroic actions.
- Having been lucky enough to survive a disaster yourself makes you three times more likely to be a hero and a volunteer.

The researchers believe that we are all capable of becoming heroes. It's about learning to make the right choices in a particular situation, about doing the right thing even if we are afraid. Everyone needs to realize that they are responsible for making the world a better place. They have created an online course, the Heroic Imagination Project, to train ordinary people to become less selfish and more heroic. For example, to stay calm in a difficult situation, so that we don't just automatically do what everyone else is doing.

b What other kinds of people or behaviour could be considered heroic?

b Did anything discovered through this research surprise you? Why/Why not?

3a Work with a partner as Student A and Student B. Find seven highlighted words in the article to match to your set of definitions.

Student A

1 thinking only about yourself and not of other people
2 not excited, worried or angry
3 having studied and learnt a lot
4 normal, not different from others
5 acting like a hero
6 caring about others
7 telling the truth

Student B

8 having good luck
9 happy to give more than is usually expected
10 ready to do things that are dangerous or difficult without showing fear
11 feeling fear
12 having the job of dealing with something
13 feeling uncomfortable because of something silly you have done
14 not sensible, not logical

b Test your partner on your set of words.

Grammar & Speaking   unreal conditionals

4a Work with a partner. Look at the following sentence from the text and answer the questions.

If you saw a crash, would you risk your life to help?

1 What form is the verb after *if*? Is this talking about something that happened in the past, present or future? Is this situation real or imaginary?
2 Which word in the second clause tells us we are talking about an imaginary situation?

b Look at the following sentence and answer the questions.

If I saw someone in trouble, I might/could/would help.

1 Which two modal verbs express possibility?
2 Which modal verb means *would be able to*?

c Read the information in the Grammar focus box and check your answers to exercise **4**.

GRAMMAR FOCUS   unreal conditionals

- We use *If* + past tense, *would* + infinitive without *to* to talk about a hypothetical/unreal situation in the present or future and its imaginary result.
  If I saw someone in trouble, I would (I'd) go and help.
- The clauses can be in any order, but we don't use a comma if the *would* clause comes first.
- After *if* we use *were* instead of *was*.
  1 in certain fixed phrases:
     If I were you, I'd keep quiet.
  2 in a more formal style:
     If I were stronger, I would stop that bully!
- When we are not sure about the result, we can use *might* or *could* instead of *would*.
  If you tried to help, you could/might hurt yourself.
- We can also use *could* to mean *would be able to*.
  If someone had an accident, I could help him because I know first aid.

→ **Grammar Reference** page 151

5a Complete the sentences using the correct form of the verbs in brackets. Use modal verbs where possible to express uncertainty or ability.

1 If I _____ (be) braver, I _____ (be) a firefighter.
2 We _____ (volunteer) more if we _____ (have) more time.
3 What _____ you _____ (do) if you _____ (see) someone being robbed?
4 If we _____ (win) the lottery, we _____ (give) some money to charity.
5 I _____ (not do) a job if it _____ (be) risky or dangerous.
6 He _____ (be) so embarrassed if he _____ (know) people were talking about his heroism.

b **8.3**》 Listen and check your answers.

c Work with a partner. How does using *would*, *could* or *might* change the meaning of each sentence?

6 **TASK** Work in small groups. Go to page 129, discuss the scenarios and complete the other tasks.

8.3 Vocabulary and skills development

GOALS ■ Recognize changing sounds in linked words ■ Use prefixes

Listening & Speaking sound changes

1 Work with a partner. Look at the photos of Icelandic culture and answer the questions.

1 What do you think each photo tells us about Iceland?
2 Would you see the same things in your country?

Iceland

2 **8.4**))) Read and listen to the information in the Unlock the code box.

🔓 **UNLOCK THE CODE**
changing sounds when we link words

Speaking at natural speed, we often change the last sound of a word to make it easier to say the words together, for example, when one word ends in sounds *t* or *d* and the next word starts with sounds such as *b, p, k, g, m.* Listening to natural speech, these changes can make groups of words more difficult to understand.

written form	→	natural speed
woul**d** move	→	/wʊ(b)muːv/
tha**t** place	→	/ðæpleɪs/

3 **8.5**))) Listen to the phrases. Underline the sound that changes.

1 red pram _____
2 could be _____
3 white coffee _____
4 mild coffee _____
5 should go _____
6 cold metal _____
7 hot pepper _____
8 hot milk _____

4a **8.6))** Listen to the first part of a podcast and complete the text with two words in each gap with two missing words.

> If you **1** _____ anywhere in the world to live, where would you go? **2** _____ not be the most obvious choice, but I don't **3** _____ here. I came to study earth science at the University of Iceland. Iceland has volcanoes, glaciers and earthquakes. **4** _____ you see here? I came to study the natural world, but I stayed in Iceland because I love the way of life.

b **8.7))** Listen to the rest of the podcast and answer the questions.

1 Why do Icelanders leave their babies outside to sleep?
2 What Icelandic habit used to make Julia feel annoyed?
3 What did Julia discover Icelandic people don't worry about?
4 What skill do 10% of Icelanders have?
5 Why does Julia now enjoy Icelandic food?

5 Work in small groups and discuss the questions.

1 How do you think life in Iceland would be different from life in your country?
2 Do you think you would enjoy living in Iceland? Why/Why not?

Vocabulary   prefixes

6 Read an online article about culture shock. What four different stages can you identify? What stage do you think Julia is at?

> ### BLOG ENTRY / 5 JUNE   🔍 SEARCH
> ABOUT EVENTS BLOG
>
> When you first arrive in a foreign culture, often your first reaction is completely positive. Everything seems exciting, different and fascinating. It's an adventure. If you're just on a short holiday, you'll probably never leave this phase, but if you stay longer, your attitude can start to change.
>
> As you start to realize how little you really understand the new culture, life can get frustrating. People misunderstand what you're trying to say, or they may laugh at you for saying something incorrectly. Even simple things, like posting a letter, can seem impossibly difficult, and you are likely to overreact by getting angry or upset when things go wrong.
>
> With time, though, you start to adjust, to become more comfortable with the differences and better able to handle frustrating situations. Your sense of humour reappears. Finally, you reach the stage of feeling able to be enthusiastic about the culture once again, enjoy living in it, and maybe even prefer certain aspects of the culture to your own.

7 Look at the highlighted words in the article and match the meanings of each prefix to the definitions below.

1 badly   3 too (much)
2 again   4 not

> ### VOCABULARY FOCUS prefixes
>
> Prefixes are groups of letters that added to the beginning of a word change the meaning of the word:
> mis- (= do badly) **mis**judge, **mis**behave
> re- (= do again) **re**place, **re**arrange
> in- (= not) **in**active, **in**convenient
> over- (= too much) **over**priced, **over**spend

8 Use the prefixes re-, under-, over- or mis- and the words in brackets to complete the sentences. Check your answers with a partner.

1 In the summer, north of the Arctic Circle, it stays light twenty-four hours a day. The stars stop coming out at night and don't _____ (appear) until August.
2 If you move to a very different culture, people may easily _____ (understand) your behaviour.
3 I haven't got a lot of money this month, so I'll have to be careful I don't _____ (spend).
4 I used to wear very smart suits to the office, but people here are much more _____ (formal) and even wear jeans to work.
5 The flight had to be _____ (schedule) due to the bad weather. We arrived back a day late.
6 Parents can be very embarrassed if their children _____ (behave) in public.

9a **TASK** Think about an interesting place you have been to. Use the questions below to prepare a short talk about it. Use at least **three** words with prefixes.

• What is interesting about the place?
• What facts do you know about the place?
• Why might you choose to move there?
• What things about the culture might be very different from your own?

b Talk for about two minutes about the place. Listen to your partner's talk and ask at least two questions about the place.

8.4 Speaking and writing

GOALS ■ Take notes while listening ■ Prepare and give a short talk from notes

Writing & Listening taking notes

1 Make a list of at least five decisions you have made today.

 1 Put the decisions in order of importance.

 2 Tell a partner about one of the more important decisions on your list. Did you make it quickly, or think about it for a long time? Did you discuss it with anyone else?

2 **8.8**))) Listen to the beginning of a lecture about making decisions and tick the topic the speaker mentions.
- Types of decisions we make
- Why we all make bad decisions
- The number of decisions we make

3a **8.8**))) Look at the note a student took during the lecture. Listen again and complete the note.

> Intro: Av. person – approx. _____ decisions/day!

 b Look at the abbreviations. What do you think the full words are?

4a Read the information in the Language for writing box and check your answers.

> **LANGUAGE FOR WRITING** taking notes
>
> When taking notes, to write quickly and save time:
> - write only the key information; leave out prepositions and articles:
>   ***Av.** person – the average person*
> - use abbreviations (often the beginning of the word):
>   ***intro** – introduction*
>   ***av** – average*
>   ***approx**. – approximately*

 b Work with a partner and look at the abbreviations. What do you think they are short for?

pers _____	poss _____
info _____	probs _____
neg _____	abt _____
adv _____	imp _____
disadv _____	no. _____

5 **8.9**))) Listen to the next part of the lecture. Complete the notes using abbreviations. Compare your answers with a partner.

> ### Factors affecting decision-making
> - 1_____ of decisions we make – too many decisions make brain tired.
> - To make ?_____ decisions, do it early.
> - Also consider how much 3_____ you need. Poss to have too much.
> - Stress can make you think more 4_____ positive results than 5_____.

6a **8.10**))) Listen to the last part of the lecture and take notes on the main points, using abbreviations where you can.
- _____
- _____
- _____
- _____

 b Compare your answers with a partner.

8a Prepare and give a two-minute talk. Choose a topic and make notes for the introduction, the main body and the conclusion. Use the Language for speaking box to help you.

Social: A difficult decision I have made.
        The country I would most like to move to.

Work: A job I would like to do.
        How to be a successful manager/other job.

Study: The course I would most like to study.
        How to pass exams.

LANGUAGE FOR SPEAKING giving a talk

Introduction
- introducing yourself/your topic:
  Hello, everyone. I'm _____ and I'm here to talk to you about …, I'm going to talk about …
- talking about the structure of your talk:
  firstly, …, then …, and finally …

Main body
- sequencing your points:
  the first point I'd like to talk about is …, our next (factor) is …, the third and last (factor) … is …
- starting a new section:
  Let's move on now to look at …

Conclusion
- starting the conclusion:
  So we've looked at … Now I'd like to finish with …
- inviting questions:
  Does anyone have any questions? Are there any questions?

Speaking giving a talk

7a Look at some of the phrases from the lecture. Match each group a–f to a category (1–6).

a I'm going to talk about … / firstly, … / then … / and finally …	b Does anyone have any questions? Are there any questions?
c the first one I'd like to talk about is … / our next (factor) is … / the third and last (factor) … is …	d Hello, everyone. I'm _____ and I'm here to talk to you about … / I'm going to talk about …
e So we've looked at … Now I'd like to finish with …	f Let's move on now to look at …

1 introducing yourself/your topic
2 talking about the structure of your talk
3 sequencing your points
4 starting a new section
5 starting the conclusion
6 inviting questions

b Check your answers with a partner. Use the Language for speaking box to help you.

b Work with a partner. Practise the talk you have prepared.

c Give your talk to the class or to your group. As you listen to other talks, decide what the most interesting piece of information in each talk is. Compare your choice with a partner.

9 After you have given your talk, complete the self-assessment of your performance by circling a number at the end of each sentence.

1 = needs improvement, 2 = OK, 3 = excellent

I spoke slowly and clearly.	1 2 3	I made appropriate eye contact with the audience.	1 2 3
I was happy with my use of grammar.	1 2 3	I used positive body language (e.g. I looked confident and smiled).	1 2 3
I used a range of phrases from the key language box.	1 2 3	I was happy with my use of vocabulary.	1 2 3

10 **TASK** Work with a partner. Talk about the assessment in exercise **9** and together choose **two** things that were good about your talks and **two** ways you could improve in the future.

8.5 Video

Happiness in Mexico

1 Look at the photos. Which photos show …

  1 a strong bond between close friends?

  2 a close-knit community?

  3 two generations spending time together?

2 Work with a partner. Match the factors used for measuring happiness to statements a–e.

  1 Health

  2 Wealth

  3 Social support

  4 Freedom to make choices

  5 Political satisfaction

  a 'If I have a problem, my friends, family and neighbours are all ready to help.'

  b 'I can rely on my government to keep our country safe and secure.'

  c ' I feel I can do anything I want in my life'.

  d 'I earn enough money to live quite comfortably.'

  e 'I am usually well, and I don't suffer from stress.'

3 ▶ Watch the video. Which of the reasons below make Mexico a happy country?

- Increasing wealth
- A friendly society
- Green spaces
- Good weather
- A healthy lifestyle

4 ▶ Watch again. Decide if sentences a–f are true (T), false (F) or if the video doesn't say (DS). Correct the false sentences.

The UN World Happiness Report says …

  a health and wealth are the two most important factors when measuring a population's happiness.

  b Denmark was higher on the list than all the other northern European countries.

  c most people expected Mexico to be higher on the list than the USA.

In Mexico, …

  d people know that their families will usually help them when life gets difficult.

  e it is normal for people to meet up with their neighbours.

  f the fine weather is the main reason for the population's happiness.

5a **TASK** Which activities increase or decrease your happiness?

  b Work with a partner. Compare your answers and say why each activity increases or decreases your happiness. Do you and your partner have a lot in common?

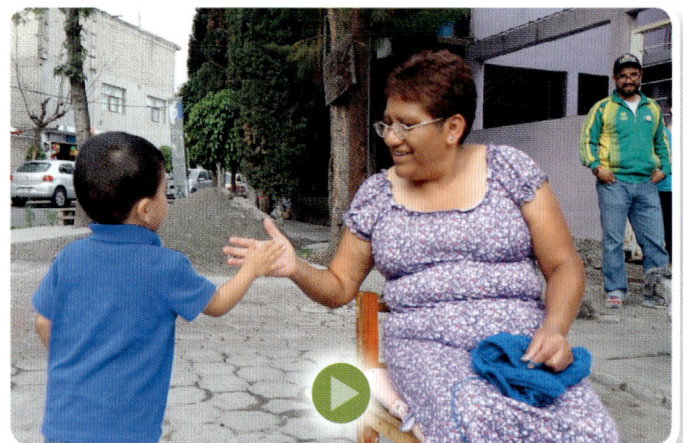

Review

1a Choose the correct option to complete the sentences.

Can money buy happiness?

1 If you spend it on the right things, money *must / can / has to* buy happiness.
2 Most people will be happier *unless / if / whether* you spend time with them rather than spend money on them.
3 If you're going on holiday, you *should / would / will* be happier if you pay for it straightaway.
4 People should buy experiences rather than things, especially if they *are / will be / are going to be* older.
5 People don't enjoy things as much unless they *will have to / have to / have* work hard for them.

b **8.11** ⟩⟩ Mark in exercise **1a** whether the intonation rises or falls at the end of each clause. Then listen and check.

c Which sentences do you agree or disagree with? Discuss with a partner.

2a **8.12** ⟩⟩ Listen to the beginning of six sentences. Write down what you hear and complete the sentence in any way you like.

b Compare your sentences with a partner and explain what you wrote.

3a Rewrite each sentence, using one of the words or phrases in the box to replace the underlined words.

> a balanced diet   childcare   cultural activities   healthcare
> high taxes   leisure time   neighbours   physical activity
> pollution   poverty   a strong economy   volunteer

1 <u>The people who live in your street</u> can help you if you have a problem.
2 <u>Being poor</u> can definitely make you unhappy.
3 At the weekends I <u>work for nothing</u> at a charity.
4 It's important to eat <u>healthily</u>.
5 There are plenty of opportunities to enjoy <u>the arts</u> in my town.
6 <u>Exercise</u> really helps me to stay fit and healthy.

b Work with a partner. Choose three of the other words and write sentences using them.

c Compare your ideas with another pair.

4a Divide the following adjectives into positive and negative (some may be both).

> afraid   brave   crazy   calm   educated   embarrassed
> generous   heroic   honest   kind   lucky   ordinary
> responsible   selfish

b Compare your answers with a partner. Explain the reasons for your choices.

5a Complete each sentence with a prefix and word from the box.

> mis-
> re-
> super-
> under-
> | appear   arrange   behave   ground   heat
> human   married   model   pronounced
> store   water

1 A _____ is a kind of really large shop.
2 The London _____ railway is often called the 'Tube'.
3 Diving equipment allows you to breathe _____.
4 If my coffee goes cold, I just _____ it in the microwave.
5 I didn't understand what she said because she _____ one of the words.
6 After her husband died, she never _____.

b Choose another word and prefix. Define it, giving clues to help your partner guess it.

6a Match phrases a–f to the correct section of the talk 1–3.

1 Introduction _____
2 The main body _____
3 The conclusion _____
a The third and last point is …
b Now I'd like to finish with …
c I'm going to talk about …
d Let's move on now to talk about …
e Hello, everyone. I'm …
f Does anyone have any questions?

b Plan a 1–2 minute talk about a good decision you made. Make sure you use some of the phrases to signpost each section of your talk.

c Take turns to listen to your partner's talk. Which phrases did your partner use?

9 Appearances

9.1 Real beauty?

GOALS ■ Describe appearances ■ Make comparisons

Vocabulary & Reading describing physical appearance

1a Work in small groups. Make a list of five things that make a person attractive – not just physical appearance.

b Look at photos 1–6. Which words from the box can you use to describe the people?

> blond(e) clean-shaven curly double chin dyed
> elderly fringe going bald grey in good shape
> twenties large forehead long eyelashes middle-aged
> moustache overweight large jaw round face
> shoulder-length slim spiky stubble thick eyebrows
> well-built

c Work with a partner. Put the words in exercise 1b in the correct category in the table.

Age	
Build	
Facial features	
Hair	

2a 9.1))) Listen to three descriptions. For each description, say which person in exercise 1b is being described.

b 9.1))) Listen again and note which words and expressions you hear from exercise 1b to describe the people.

3a Read the first two paragraphs to a magazine article. What do you think the beauty company was trying to prove through their experiment? Discuss with a partner.

b Now read the rest of the article and check if your ideas were correct.

BEAUTY
FASHION BEAUTY PEOPLE

BEAUTY NEWS WHAT TO WEAR STYLE FILES SHOWS & TRENDS

As other people see you?

1 Dove, the beauty company famous for its campaigns to make people feel better about themselves, have created the most interesting film they've ever done.

2 For the film Dove, *Real Beauty Sketches*, they asked a group of women to turn up to a place they hadn't been to before, and then make friends with another woman there. They were later asked to go into a room and describe their own faces, honestly, to a complete stranger who was hidden behind a curtain: police artist, Gil Zamora. All the women were very negative about their appearance. They used phrases like 'round face' and 'big forehead'. Once the sketch was done, Zamora thanked them and they left.

3 Next, each woman was asked back into the room to describe to Zamora the face of the woman they had made friends with. Already, you get the idea of what Dove was trying to prove; the descriptions were so much more positive. A 'protruding jaw', for example, was described as a 'nice and thin chin'.

4 Work with a partner and discuss the following questions.

1 Do you think it's true that women tend to believe they are less attractive than they really are? Why/Why not?

2 Are men equally self-critical? Why/Why not?

3 Does it depend on age? Do you become more or less self-confident as you get older?

Grammar & Speaking comparison

5a Look at the highlighted forms in the article in exercise **4**, and add examples from the article to the Grammar focus box.

GRAMMAR FOCUS comparison

1 We use **comparatives** to compare people and things with each other.
round → rounder; attractive → more attractive
a _____

2 To make a negative comparison use *less* + adjective.
Many women thought they were less attractive than they actually were.
b _____

3 We use a modifier when you want to give more detail about the degree of difference between things.
a bit   a little   a lot   far   much   very much

4 To say something is the same use (*just*) *as … as*; to say something is not the same, we use *not as/so … as*.

5 We use **superlatives** to compare a person or thing with all the other people or things in their group.
c _____

→ **Grammar Reference** page 152

---

b Look at the highlighted forms in the article. Which use a modifier?

1 _____
2 _____
3 _____

c Look at 3 in the Grammar focus box.

1 Which modifiers make the difference between the things being compared bigger/stronger?
a _____   b _____   c _____   d _____

2 Which make the difference smaller/weaker?
a _____   b _____

6 Complete the sentences using a comparative form of the adjectives in brackets and a modifier where possible.

1 Why is the campaign only about women? Are men _____ (confident) women?

2 Actually, I think men can be _____ (insecure) as women, can't they?

3 The campaign is not _____ (supportive) of women as it says. Why is it important to be beautiful anyway?

4 Surely, there are _____ (valuable) things _____ being beautiful.

5 The _____ (big) problem I have with the advert is that it's made by a beauty products company.

6 Although the campaign is selling beauty, I still think the advert is _____ (good) adverts that make women feel bad about themselves.

7 Which of the statements in exercise **6** do you agree or disagree with? Why? Discuss with a partner.

PRONUNCIATION changing stress

8a **9.2**)) Listen to the sentences and mark which word in each sentence carries the most stress.

1 The descriptions were more positive.
2 The descriptions were much more positive.
3 The descriptions were far more positive.
4 The descriptions were a bit more positive.
5 Their descriptions weren't as positive as their friends'.

b Compare your answers with your partner. What do you notice about the changing stress?

c **9.2**)) Listen again and repeat.

9 **TASK** Work with a partner. Go to page 130.

▶ **VOX POPS VIDEO 9**

---

4 When the two sketches were done, Zamora put them side by side and asked the women back in to take a look at both pictures, revealing the sketches from the women's descriptions of themselves, and the sketches the strangers had helped him to draw.

5 The difference between the two sketches in every case is incredible. Looking at her self-described portrait, one woman described her face as 'a lot more closed off and fatter, sadder, too,' while her second one 'looks much friendlier and happier.'

6 'We spend a lot of time as women trying to fix the things that aren't quite right, and we should spend more time appreciating the things we do like,' she goes on. 'We seem to feel less beautiful than other people think we are.'

7 'Do you think you're more beautiful than you say?' Zamora asks one woman. 'Yes,' she admits.

8 This is one campaign that will make you think, and hopefully, feel far more beautiful.

9.2 Paintings

Vocabulary & Listening
describing paintings

1 Look at the paintings. Which painting is
a) abstract, b) a landscape, c) a portrait?
Which painting do you like best? Do
you normally like this kind of painting?
Discuss with a partner or in small groups.

2 Work with a partner or in small groups.
Which of these words and phrases could
you use to describe each of the paintings?

> bright   colourful   curves   detailed
> historical   looks   modern   mysterious
> old-fashioned   seems   soft colours
> straight lines   tells a story   traditional
> warm

3a 9.3))) Listen to two speakers talking about
the paintings. Which paintings are they
talking about?

b Did they choose any of the same words
and phrases as you?

4   **9.3**))) Listen again and complete sentences 1–5 to describe which part of the painting each speaker is talking about.

1   In _the bottom left-hand corner_ there are some men with dogs.

2   Just _____
there's a group of women.

3   There's lots of snow on the ground and on the mountains in _____ .

4   People are skating on it in the valley towards the _____ of the picture.

5   The woman is in the _____ of the picture, but the _____ is also really detailed.

5a   Complete sentences 1–5 about painting 2, using the phrases in exercise **4**.

1   _____
there are some sharp, snowy mountain peaks.

2   _____
there are four or five tall black trees, with no leaves.

3   _____
there are some houses.

4   _____
someone is walking over a snowy bridge.

5   The people _____
look very small.

b   **9.4**))) Listen and check.

Grammar & Speaking   deduction and speculation

6   Look at these extracts from the listening. Which phrase is used when you are *sure* about something (S), and which when you are *not sure* about something (NS)? Write down S or NS with each phrase.

1   ... it **must be** either an old painting or a painting of a historical scene. ____

2   ... they **might be** going out to hunt. ____

3   They **could be** cooking something. ____

4   It **can't be** a window.   ____

5   It **looks** cold.   ____

---

7   Read the information in the Grammar focus box. Complete rules 1–4.

GRAMMAR FOCUS   deduction and speculation

We use the following modals to tell the listener how sure we are about something.

- *must* – when you are very sure something **¹ is / is not** true:
  It must be either an old painting or a painting of a historical scene.
- *can't* – when you are very sure something **² is / is not** true:
  It can't be a window…
- *might / could* – when you are not sure, but you think something **³ is / is not** possible:
  They might be going out to hunt.
  They could be cooking something.

We use *look* + adjective – when something **⁴ is / appears to be** …
It looks cold.

→ **Grammar Reference**   page 153

8a   Complete sentences 1–10 about the paintings in exercise **1** with suitable modal verbs. Sometimes more than one answer is possible.

Speaker 1

1   The river _____ be frozen over, because they're skating on it in the valley.

2   It _____ be summer; it _____ too cold.

3   The hunters _____ be coming back from the hunt because one has something on his back.

4   The painting _____ be a few hundred years old, I suppose.

Speaker 2

5   It _____ be a picture of an old story or something.

6   It _____ be a modern painting; it looks too old-fashioned.

7   It _____ be a mirror; I can see the reflection of her face.

Speaker 3

8   The abstract painting _____ be very modern. I don't think it was painted a long time ago.

9   It _____ be older than you think. People started painting abstracts more than one hundred years ago.

10   It _____ be a portrait of a mandrill. I can't see a mandrill in the painting at all!

b   **9.5**))) Listen and check your answers.

PRONUNCIATION   sentence stress – speculating

9a   **9.5**))) Listen again to the sentences in exercise **8a**. Which verb is stressed more, the modal verb or the main verb?

b   **9.5**))) Listen again and repeat.

10   **TASK**   Work with a partner. Student A, turn to page 130. Student B, turn to page 134.

9.3 Vocabulary and skills development

GOALS ■ Question a text ■ Use phrasal verbs

Reading questioning a text

1 Look at the title and photos from a recent blog, and in one sentence answer the question:
What do you think the text is about?

2 Look at some of the key words from the blog in the box below, and change your sentence from exercise **1** if you need to.

> faces houses laugh meaning museum scientists
> teapots website

3 Read paragraph 1 of the blog and think about the question:
What do you want to find out from the text?

Use the photos, key words and the start of the blog to write a question you want the text to answer. For example:
Which 'silly things' will the text talk about?

4 Read paragraphs 2–4 of the blog and see if you are able to answer your question.

5 Read the information in the Unlock the code box about questioning a text.

> 🔓 **UNLOCK THE CODE**
> questioning a text
>
> If you ask questions about a text before and while you read it, you will be more likely to understand it.
>
> Sometimes the questions will be quite general:
> *Do I want to read this text?*
> *What is the text about?*
> *Is the text going to give me useful information for my job/study/ research?*
>
> At other times, they will be more specific:
> *What is the author writing about?*
> *What is the main point he/she is making?*
> *Where is the museum/gallery/city …?*

6a Look at paragraphs 5–6 of the blog. Which of questions 1–4 do you expect to be answered?

1 Which other websites has the writer visited?
2 How does the human eye work?
3 Why do humans like to see faces where they don't actually exist?
4 How do websites attract visitors?

b Discuss with a partner. How did you choose? Write two more questions you would like the text to answer.

c Read the paragraphs and check if your questions have been answered.

---

myblog

POSTS ABOUT FOLLOW ARCHIVE

Seeing faces   🔍 SEARCH

1 Nowadays, all aspects of human behaviour are the subject of scientific research and enquiry. And sometimes we can learn about ourselves from even the seemingly silliest things.

2 One example comes to mind from my recent surfing on the internet. I'm an architect, and like most people, I often use the internet for professional research. The other day, I was looking for pictures of interesting houses for an article that a magazine had asked me to write, and I came across a website called 'Houses that look like Faces'.

3 The website interested me, (and really made me laugh) not only because the houses looked like faces, as you might expect, but because they seemed to express emotions as well. Some looked happy, some looked a bit irritated, and several looked really sad! I noticed that the website had a huge number of visitors, and I wondered why this might be.

4 I talked to some of my colleagues about this, and found out that, in fact, there are websites devoted to all kinds of objects that resemble faces. Taps, teapots, tape recorders – it seems as if we can't help making out faces where there aren't any. And once we have seen them, it is impossible 'not' to see them.

5 Of course, in some cases, the photos are fakes, but they started me thinking about why this happens. I did some research and found out that this phenomenon is called pareidolia[1]. Scientists have come up with various ideas to explain it. One is that humans are 'programmed' to see faces, perhaps because it helped us to survive many thousands of years ago, or because we simply try to find meaning and patterns in chance lines, blobs, and colours. Another idea is that we want to see faces, so we do.

6 The study of pareidolia is a serious business. A German design studio is making a database of such faces. And interestingly, images of some of these houses were put up on a wall at Exploratorium, a museum of 'science, art and human perception' in San Francisco as an example of how we find patterns in everyday objects.

[1] – **pronounced** /ˌpærɪˈdoʊliə/   ⊕ @ ☺

---

7 Work with a partner and answer these questions.

1 Did any part of the blog answer your questions?

2 Do you think asking questions before and while you read helped you to understand the text better?

Vocabulary & Speaking   phrasal verbs

8 Match the phrasal verbs in bold from the blog to their meanings.

1 I **came across** a website ...
2 we can't help **making out** faces where there aren't any ...
3 they started me **thinking about** why this happens ...
4 Scientists have **come up with** various ideas to explain it.
5 images were **put up** on a wall ...

a consider
b fix and display
c find an answer
d find by chance
e manage to see

9a True (T) or false (F)? Discuss the rules with a partner.

1 Phrasal verbs contain a main verb and one or two particles (like *up* or *out*).
2 They are very rare.
3 Some phrasal verbs can be separated by another word or words.

b Check your answers in the Vocabulary focus box. Make a note of whether a phrasal verb is separable or inseparable when you learn a new one.

> **VOCABULARY FOCUS** phrasal verbs
>
> - There are many common phrasal verbs in English. The meaning is often very different from the two separate words.
>   They contain a main verb and one or two particles (prepositions or adverbs).
>   *The plane **took off** at 6.30 a.m.*
>   *I'm **looking forward to** the party.*
> - These verbs are often separable. An object pronoun like *it, her* or *us* must come between the verb and the particle.
>   *We **looked up** the word.* OR *We **looked** the word **up** ...*
>   But
>   *We **looked it up** in the dictionary.* NOT ~~We looked up it~~ ...
> - With an inseparable verb, the object always comes after the particle.
>   *We **looked after** the baby. We **looked after** him.*

10a 9.6))) It is important to be able to hear phrasal verbs. Listen to the eight sentences and write down the phrasal verbs.

1 _____ on _____
2 give _____ _____
3 _____ _____
4 _____ _____
5 _____ _____ _____
6 _____ _____
7 _____ _____
8 _____ _____

b 9.6))) Listen to the sentences again and decide what the phrasal verbs mean. Check your answers with a partner.

c When could you use the verbs in exercise **10a**? Match them to the situations.

When you want to ...

1 invite somebody to your house. _____
2 talk about a future event that you are excited about. _____
3 talk about somebody starting a new hobby. _____
4 describe your relationship to somebody older in your family. _____
5 move an event until a later time. _____
6 talk about your relationship with somebody. _____
7 say that something is continuing. _____
8 talk about something you had to stop doing because it was too difficult. _____

11 **TASK** Write four questions using a phrasal verb from exercise **10a**. They must be real questions! Ask your partner the questions. Tell the class the most interesting thing you found out.

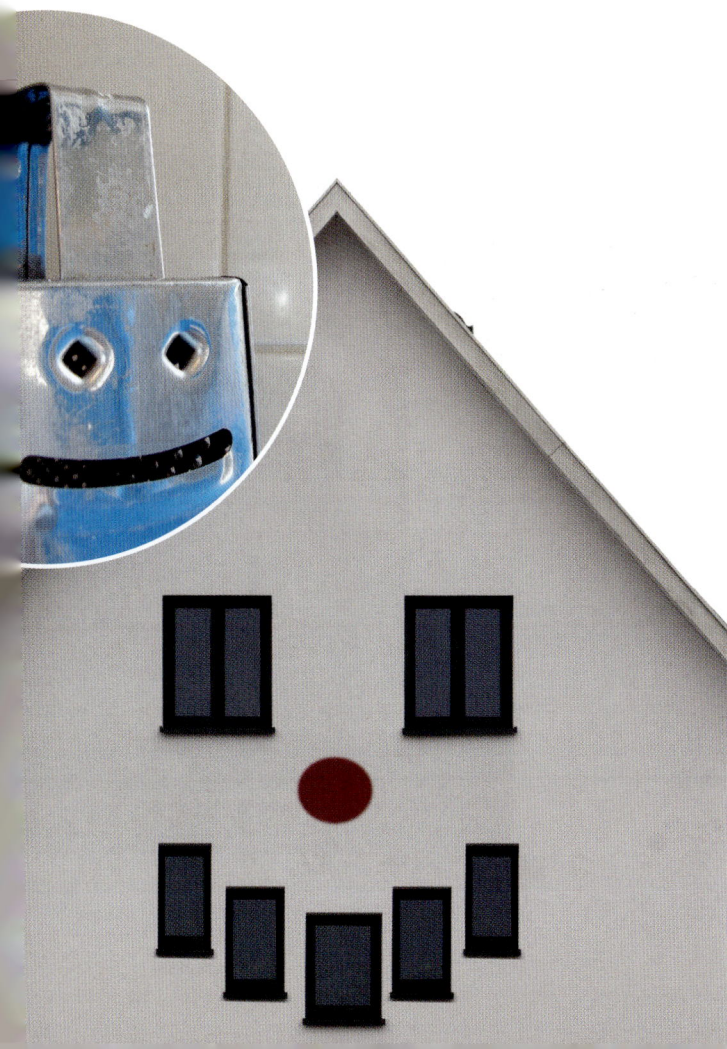

9.4 Speaking and writing

Reading & Writing taking part in online discussions

1 Look at the photos. Do you think the people are dressed appropriately for work? Why/Why not? Discuss your ideas with a partner.

2 Read the question in an online discussion forum. How would you answer it? Check with a partner.

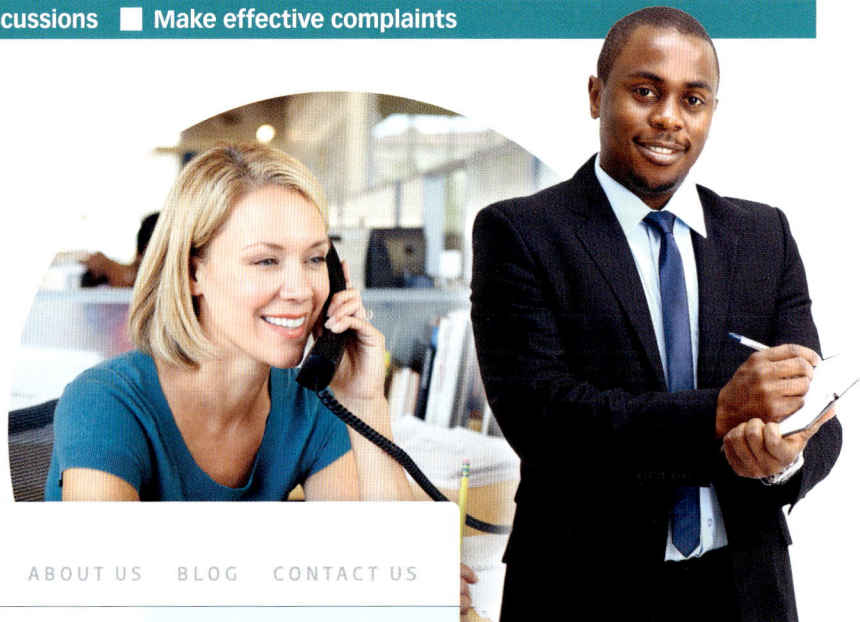

Forum.

HOME   ABOUT US   BLOG   CONTACT US

Problem solved?

I just don't know how to dress for work any more. I see colleagues wearing jeans, shorts, flip flops ... how do I know if what I'm wearing is appropriate? And does it even matter these days?

2 replies
Reply • Favourite • Forward

RECENT COMMENTS

Jay Cape Town

That's a great question. Thanks for posting it! Rules about what we wear have changed so much in the last few years, and not everyone likes this. However, in my opinion, these changes are good, especially in the office. I don't think appearance should be important there. People should judge us on the work we do, not the clothes we wear.

24
OCTOBER
7:21 PM

Reply • Favourite • Forward

Chiara Turin

I read your comment with interest. As you say, things have changed a lot. Many people, young and old, are not as formal at work now. I believe, though, that how we look still matters a lot. The issue is not really about dressing in a formal or informal style, but it is more about matching or 'fitting in' with our colleagues. In other words, we need to dress to suit where we work.

25
OCTOBER
11:37 AM

Reply • Favourite • Forward

3 Read the two comments on the question asked in the discussion forum. Which comment do you agree with most? Why?

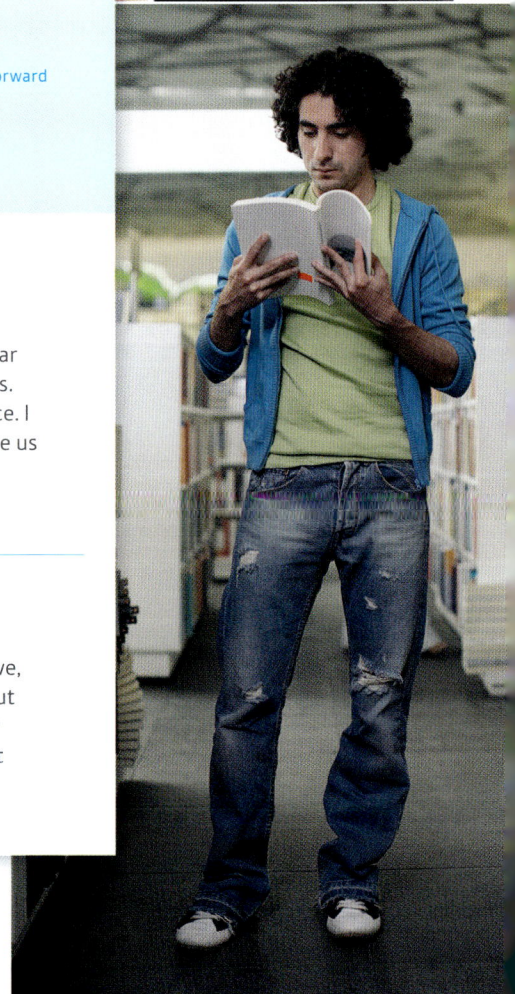

4a Read the information in the Language for writing box.

> **LANGUAGE FOR WRITING** taking part in discussion board posts
>
> To add a post to a discussion board, make connections with what other people have written.
> *That's a very important/great question.*
> *Thanks for commenting on/posting …*
> *I read your post/comments with interest.*
> *As you say, …*
> *You make some good/interesting points.*
> *As previously commented, …*

b Choose the best comment to come next. Explain your choice to a partner.

26
OCTOBER
12:06 PM

Post A

No one cares what people look like nowadays. You can make your own rules and you shouldn't worry about what other people think.

Reply • Favourite • Forward

26
OCTOBER
15:56 PM

Post B

You make some good points, Chiara. As previously commented, people should judge us on the work we do. It seems, however, that very often they don't, and research shows this.

Reply • Favourite • Forward

c Underline six *making connections* phrases in the three comments posted in the forum.

5 Work in small groups. Take part in written discussions.

1 On your own, choose one of the questions.
   Write it at the top of your piece of paper.
   - Is it right to judge people by how they dress?
   - Is getting work experience more important than having qualifications?
   - Is it OK to use office equipment to print or copy things for your personal use?

2 Write a post under your question to start the discussion.

3 Exchange with someone in your group. Read the question and the first post, and add your post to the discussion.

4 Exchange with a different student. Read and then add your post. Continue until you have added a post for each question.

Listening & Speaking   making complaints

6 What you wear at work could cause problems. Think of other situations that might cause problems at work.

7a 9.7))) Listen to the start of two conversations.
   1 What is the problem in each one?
   2 Which conversations are between friends, and which between a boss and an employee? How do you know?

b 9.8))) What would be a good result for each conversation? Discuss the question with a partner, and then listen to check what actually happened.

8a Match 1–5 to a–e to complete extracts from the conversations.
   1 I'm sorry to have to say this,
   2 Look, it's a bit awkward, but
   3 I'd like to apologize
   4 It would really help
   5 Would you mind

   a for being so annoying.
   b if you could just clear up your stuff.
   c but I need to talk to you about something.
   d taking the calls in your own time?
   e I'm afraid there's something I'm not happy about.

b 9.9))) Listen, check and practise.

9 **TASK** Work with a partner. Read the information in the Language for speaking box. Go to page 131 and choose one of the tasks.

> **LANGUAGE FOR SPEAKING**
> complaining effectively
>
> **Introducing the complaint**
> *Sorry to bother you, but …*
> *I'm afraid there's a problem with …*
> *There's something I'm not happy about …*
> *Can I have a word?*
> *It's a bit awkward, but …*
>
> **Explaining the problem**
> *To be honest, …*
> *The problem's been going on for …*
> *They keep … -ing …*
> *I think it's unfair that …*
> *We're getting a bit fed up with it.*
>
> **Proposing a solution**
> *Do you think you could …?*
>
> **Apologizing**
> *I'm sorry about that. I didn't mean to …*
> *I'll make sure …*
>
> We often get more formal when we are making a complaint, especially if we feel uncomfortable about it.

9.5 Video

The selfie

1 Complete the sentences with words from the box.

> bust selfies self-portrait portrait

a Do you like the stone _____ of Beethoven sitting on top of the piano?

b In Van Gogh's _____, we see that he painted himself wearing a bandage over one ear.

c Many celebrities post _____ of themselves on social media so everyone can see their latest image.

d I sat for two days while the artist painted my _____.

2 Work with a partner. Describe the photos, using some of the words in exercise **1** to help you. Which of these art forms would you choose to see in an art exhibition?

3 ▶ Watch the video. Complete the statement with the best option.

Modern-day selfies …

a are completely different to the portraits in the National Portrait Gallery.

b are very similar to the portraits in the National Portrait Gallery.

c share a few similarities with the portraits in the National Portrait Gallery.

4 ▶ Watch again and answer the questions.

a What did Oxford Dictionaries do in 2013?

b Why have artists been creating portraits of people for hundreds of years?

c What negative opinions of selfies does the presenter mention?

d What is the value of selfies?

e What can great portraits show us that selfies might not be able to?

5a **TASK** Choose a question, A–D. Go around the class, ask your question and note down the answers people give you.

> A Do you take selfies? Why/Why not?
> B Do you like looking at other people's selfies?
> C What do you do with selfies you have taken?
> D What do you think of selfies?

b Work in groups, with a Student A, B, C and D in each group. Report your answers. Does your group think selfies are a good thing or not?

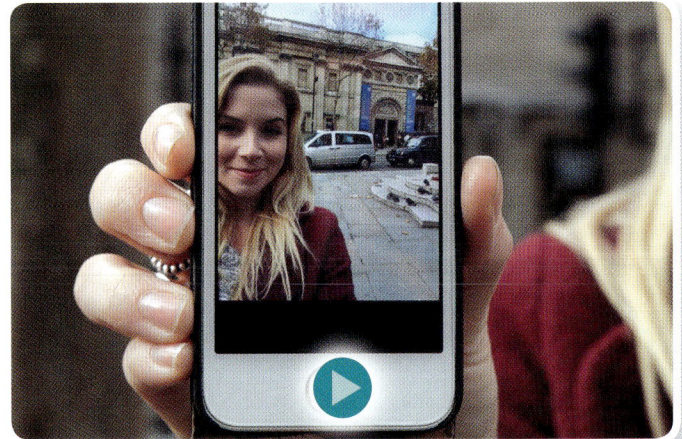

Review

1 Work with a partner. Describe the people in the photos. Give as much detail as possible.

2a Write five sentences comparing the two people in the photos, using modifiers and at least one *(not) as … as* construction.

b Compare your sentences with a partner. Do you agree?

3a **9.10**)) Listen to each sentence and write a conclusion, using *might*, *must* or *can't* and the word in brackets.

She's wearing a uniform. (police officer)
<u>She might be a police officer</u>

1 (curly) _____

2 (very old) _____

3 (in good shape) _____

4 (clean-shaven) _____

5 (going bald) _____

b Work with a partner. Describe someone in the class. After each sentence, say what your conclusion is.

A *He's got blond hair.*

B *It can't be Marek because he's dark.*

4 Complete the sentences with the most suitable words or phrases from the box.

> bright colourful curves detailed historical looks
> modern mysterious old-fashioned seems soft colours
> straight lines tells a story traditional warm

1 The painting uses a lot of _____, with very few curves.

2 Although it was painted nearly 100 years ago, it still feels quite _____.

3 It _____ as if it was painted outside.

4 It's very bright and _____, with reds, blues, yellows and black and white.

5 The picture obviously _____; you can see exactly what's going to happen next.

6 The man in the foreground seems _____ because we can't see his face.

5a **9.11**)) Listen and write down as much of the text as you can.

b Work with a partner. Try to reconstruct the text.

c **9.11**)) Listen again to check. How many phrasal verbs can you find?

6a Put the conversation in the right order.

a Do you have the receipt?

b Do you think you could get the manager? He might remember selling it to me.

c Er, no I don't, actually.

d I only bought it a few weeks ago, but it keeps turning itself off.

e Oh, I'm sorry to hear that. What seems to be the problem?

f Sorry to bother you, but I've got a bit of a problem with this tablet. *1*

g Well, I'm afraid I can't help you, then.

b **9.12**)) Listen and check your answers.

c With a partner, role-play the conversation the customer then has with the manager.

Compete and cooperate

10.1 Crowd-funding

Vocabulary & Reading business

1 Work with a partner. Look at the photo. What kind of company do you think Kickstarter might be? Discuss your ideas in pairs. Do you think it is ...?
   a a company that helps entrepreneurs find investors
   b a company that lends money to entrepreneurs
   c a company that arranges bank loans for entrepreneurs

2a Read the article about Kickstarter and check your predictions.

 b Work with a partner. Answer questions 1–3.
   1 What first gave Perry Chen the idea for Kickstarter?
   2 What is the minimum amount anyone can invest?
   3 What does Kickstarter not guarantee?

3a Choose the correct option to make a business phrase.
   1 raise *money / in value*
   2 share *an investor / the risk*
   3 set up *money / a business*
   4 present *an idea / a bank loan*
   5 back *a project / money*
   6 become *a guarantee / an investor*
   7 find yourself *short of cash / the risk*
   8 get *funding / a profit*
   9 take out *a project / a bank loan*
   10 increase *in value / an idea*
   11 give *a guarantee / a project*
   12 make *a profit / a bank loan*

 b Check your answers in the article.

4a Choose six phrases in exercise **3a**. Write a sentence/ definition for each and read it to a partner. Can they guess which one it is?

 b Work with a partner. Use the phrases above to write a list of advantages and disadvantages of crowd-funding for entrepreneurs or investors.
   Crowd-funding is an easy way to become an investor.

 c Compare your ideas with another pair.

The 21st-century way to start a business?

When Perry Chen, a musician, had to cancel a concert because he couldn't raise the $20,000 he needed to put it on, he started to think about ways he could share the risk with others. Together with Yancey Strickler and Charles Adler, he started up Kickstarter, a crowd-funding website. Anyone who wants to set up a business can present their idea on the website, setting out exactly how much money they are looking for, and anyone who wants to back their projects can become an investor, sometimes for as little as $1. For entrepreneurs who find themselves short of cash, it's a great way to get funding without having to take out a bank loan. For investors, it's fun and there's always the possibility that their investment will increase in value – although Kickstarter won't give any guarantees that the new businesses will make a profit.

Grammar & Speaking passives

5 Work with a partner. Read the article *Travel in comfort*. Answer questions 1–5.

1 What is the product or service?
2 Who was the product or service aimed at?
3 How many investors backed the idea?
4 How much funding did the entrepreneur get?
5 Has the business been successful? Why/Why not?

7 Add one missing word to each sentence.

1 The Ostrich Pillow company is co-owned *by* Ali Ganjavian.
2 The pillow invented in Ganjavian's studio.
3 The Ostrich Pillow been well designed.
4 You are protected from all sides a soft cushion.
5 There are two holes which located near your ears so you can put in earplugs.
6 It arrived safely and it packed well.

Travel in comfort

1,846 backers

$195,094 $70,000 goal

[Back This Project!]

A surprise Kickstarter hit has been the 'Ostrich Pillow', a kind of padded hat that people can pull over their heads to take a nap. It has been backed by 1,846 people who have pledged $195,094. Ali Ganjavian, who co-owns the studio where the pillow was invented, admitted that they had no idea it would be this popular. 'We thought that it would appeal to travellers,' Ganjavian said, 'but we've had lots of emails from people in all different kinds of fields saying that they have found it useful, like a firefighter who spends a lot of time waiting on call.' Five thousand pillows were sold in the first three months and shipped to fifty-two different countries. More are currently being manufactured.

6a Read the information in the Grammar focus box and choose the correct options.

> ## GRAMMAR FOCUS active and passive forms
>
> - We use active verbs to describe **¹ what someone or something does / what happens to someone or something.**
>   *Ali Ganjavian co-owns the design studio.*
>   a _____
>
> - We use passive verbs to describe **² what someone or something does / what happens to someone or something**. If we want to say who or what does the action, we use *by*.
>   *The design studio is owned by Ali Ganjavian.*
>   b _____
>
> - Often the person or thing that does the action is **³ known / not known**, obvious or **⁴ important / unimportant**.
>   *… how the beans were roasted.*
>   b _____
>
> - We also choose **⁵ active / passive** to continue talking about the same thing or person.
>   *A surprise Kickstarter hit has been the 'Ostrich Pillow' …*
>   *It has been backed by 1,846 people …*
>   c _____
>
> → **Grammar Reference** page 154

b Complete the explanations in the box with sentences from the article in exercise **5**.

8a Complete the sentences with the correct form (passive or active) of the verbs in brackets.

1 Ali Ganjavian noticed that people who _____ (travel) a lot often get very tired.
2 The Ostrich Pillow _____ (invent) to help long-distance travellers.
3 It is a kind of hat that _____ (pull) over the head in order to take a nap.
4 So far, over $195,000 _____ (pledge) by its backers.
5 In the first three months of production, Ganjavian's company _____ (ship) five thousand pillows to fifty-two countries.

b **10.1**))) Listen and check your answers.

PRONUNCIATION passives

9a **10.2**))) Listen to sentences 1–5 in exercise **8a** again. Mark the main stress. Which is stronger, the main verb or the auxiliary verb?

b **10.2**))) Listen again and repeat.

10 **TASK** Work in small groups. Student A, turn to page 131. Student B, page 134.

10.2 Competitive sport

GOALS ■ Talk about competition ■ Use articles

Vocabulary competitive sport

1 Look at the photos. Work with a partner and discuss the questions.
   - Which of the sports and activities do you consider to be competitive or non-competitive?
   - Which did you (not) enjoy at school, or do you (not) enjoy now?

2a Read the article about what the government thinks of competitive sports. Do you agree with the government's point of view?

SPORT ▷ OLYMPICS

SPORTING COMPETITION?

As figures show that more and more children are overweight, the government has announced that highly ¹_____ sports days and ²_____ are to be re-introduced at schools. Under the new plans, schools will play ³_____ each other in an Olympics-style event, with sports such as football, athletics, rugby, swimming, tennis and cycling. Winning teams will ⁴_____ in sixty county competitions before going on to a national ⁵_____.

For too long, schools have been avoiding competitive sports, introducing activities such as yoga, trampolining, cheerleading and dancing instead. They seem to believe that losing a ⁶_____ will make people feel bad about themselves. We have to realize that taking ⁷_____ in competitive sport is not bad for people's self-esteem. Whether you ⁸_____ or ⁹_____, competitive sport teaches people to work in a ¹⁰_____ and to try hard to be the best that they can be. These are skills which are just as important in the workplace as they are in school.

It is also hoped that the new plans will help Britain to ¹¹_____ records in future Olympic Games.

---

b Complete the article using the words in the box.

> against   break   compete   competitive   final   lose
> part   race   team   tournaments   win

c 10.3 ⟩⟩ Listen and check your answers.

3 Choose the correct options to complete the sentences.
   1 A prize was given to the *win* / *winner* of the race.
   2 There were several different types of sports in a *race* / *tournament*.
   3 Next week my football team will *play against* / *take part in* the current champion.
   4 As well as winning a gold medal, she also *broke* / *competed* the world record.
   5 He's so competitive – he hates *losing* / *taking part*.
   6 We won the first few matches, but lost in the *race* / *final*.

4a 10.4 ⟩⟩ Listen to six different opinions on competitive sports and tick the box you think is closest to each opinion.

Speaker	1	2	3	4	5	6
Against						
In favour of						
Has a different idea						

b 10.4 ⟩⟩ Listen again. Make notes about what each speaker says and the reasons they give. Discuss your answers with a partner.

7a Complete the text with *a/an, the* or – (no article).

> Almost unheard of in Europe, sepak takraw is
> ^{1}_____ extremely popular sport throughout
> East Asia, and is growing in popularity in countries like
> the United States, Switzerland and Canada. Roughly
> translated as 'kickball' it is ^{2}_____ thrilling mixture
> of soccer, volleyball and gymnastics. ^{3}_____
> game is played with ^{4}_____ net and ball, but
> ^{5}_____ players are only allowed to use their feet
> to get ^{6}_____ ball over ^{7}_____ net. Each team
> has three players and ^{8}_____ first team to score
> 21 wins. Usually introduced to sepak takraw at
> ^{9}_____ school, players have to be very fit and
> practise daily to achieve ^{10}_____ almost
> super-hero skills needed to win ^{11}_____
> international matches.

sepak takraw

Grammar & Speaking using articles:
a/an, the, – (no article)

5a Complete the extracts from the listening with *a/an, the* or – (no article).

1 It's just unrealistic for children to be told that everyone can win; ^{1}_____ life is competitive.

2 If you lose ^{2}_____ race, then you should just try harder.

3 That's what I learnt when I was at ^{3}_____ school.

4 I don't think more competition is ^{4}_____ answer.

5 The school used to hold sports days in ^{5}_____ public park, so everyone in ^{6}_____ park could watch.

b **10.5**)) Listen and check your answers.

6 Match answers 1–6 in exercise **5a** to rules a–f in the Grammar focus box.

GRAMMAR FOCUS *a/an, the,* – (no article)

- We use *a/an* (indefinite article):
  a when something is one of many _____
  b when we mention something for the first time _____
- We use *the* (definite article):
  c when it is the only one of something, or the only one in a place _____
  d when we have talked about the things before _____
- We use no article:
  e when we talk about plural and uncountable nouns in general. _____
  f in some common phrases after a preposition _____

→ Grammar Reference page 155

---

b Match 1–11 to rules a–f in the Grammar focus box.

8a **TASK** Work with a partner. Which quote do you agree with most? Give your reasons.

> *'Whoever said, "It's not whether you win or lose that counts," probably lost.'*
> Martina Navratilova (tennis player)

> *'Just play. Have fun. Enjoy the game.'*
> Michael Jordan (basketball player)

> *'You have to fight to reach your dream. You have to sacrifice and work hard for it.'*
> Lionel Messi (soccer player)

b Listen to another pair who have a different view. Discuss the different views together.

c Decide together who had the best arguments. Why?

▶ **VOX POPS VIDEO 10**

10.3 Vocabulary and skills development

Listening & Speaking unstressed words

1a Work with a partner. Look at the photo and make guesses about what you think it shows.

b **10.6**))) Listen to another clue. Does this help you to guess?

2a **10.7**))) Listen to the first part of a radio programme and check your ideas.

b Do you think this is a good idea? Why/Why not? Discuss with a partner.

3a Look at the following extract from the listening. Underline the three words which carry the main meaning and stress.

> 'The robots can cheer on their team.'

b **10.8**))) Listen and check if you underlined the correct words.

c What happens to the other words in the extract?

4a Mark the main stresses in this extract in the same way.

> 'Then the robots can also cheer on their own team.'

b **10.9**))) Listen to both sentences and check your answers. What do you notice about the unstressed words in both sentences?

c **10.10**))) Listen and read the information in the Unlock the code box about unstressed words and check your ideas.

🔓 UNLOCK THE CODE
unstressed words

Words which carry the main meaning of a sentence are usually stressed; the other words, which are 'grammar' words, are generally unstressed. The following kinds of 'grammar' words are usually unstressed:

- the verb *to be*
- auxiliary verbs: *do, did, will*
- pronouns: *he, it, they*
- articles: *a, an, the*
- conjunctions: *and, so, when*
- prepositions: *to, from, at, with*

There may be two or three unstressed words between two stressed words. However, the length of time between the two stressed words remains about the same, no matter how many unstressed words there are between the two stressed words. This can make it harder to hear the unstressed words.

5a **10.11**))) Listen to the sentences and write down how many words there are in each.

1 _____
2 _____
3 _____
4 _____
5 _____

b **10.11**))) Check your answers with a partner. Listen again if necessary.

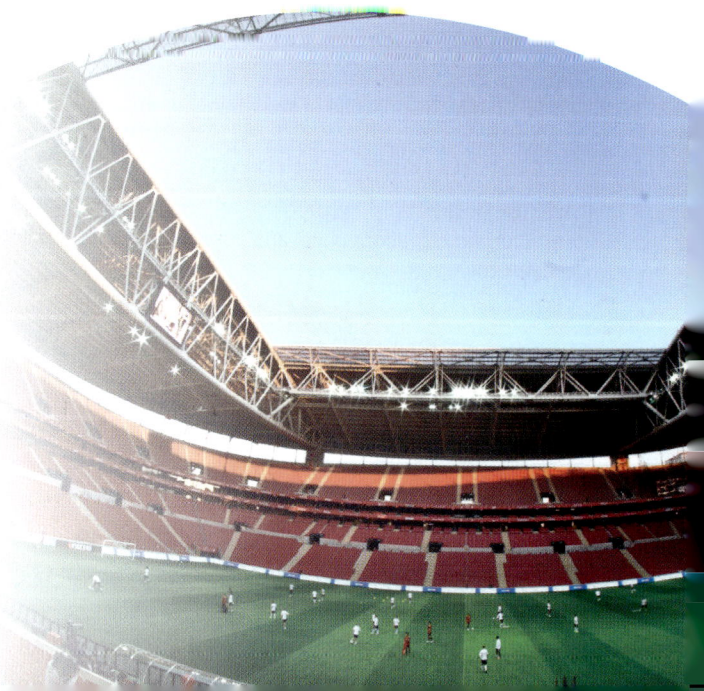

6 **10.12)))** Listen to the rest of the radio programme and answer the questions.

1 What percentage of games do teams playing at their home stadium usually win?
2 What is it about Galatasaray's stadium that makes it particularly noisy?
3 What effect can the crowd have on the referees of a game?
4 What kinds of sport benefit from a noisy crowd?
5 What effect might a crowd have on an athlete who needs to focus and concentrate?

7a Work with a partner. Do either of the following.

a Make a list of at least five reasons why going to see a live game or another sporting event live is better than watching it at home on the TV or internet.
b Make a list of at least five reasons why watching a game or another sporting event on the TV or internet is better than going to see it live.

b Join with a pair who made the opposite list to yours and compare your ideas. Which pair has the best arguments?

Vocabulary & Speaking phrases with *take* and *have*

8a Complete the extracts from the listening with *take* or *have*. Compare your answers with a partner.

1 Don't the fans _____ a responsibility to turn up and encourage their team?
2 … the home team really does _____ an advantage.
3 … there are certain football stadiums … which seem to be designed to _____ advantage of the noise fans make.
4 … they can learn to _____ no notice of whatever the other team's fans might be shouting.
5 … referees, or match officials, who have to _____ decisions about whether to allow goals and so on.
6 … noise from the crowd might cause them to _____ unnecessary risks and make a mistake.

b **10.13)))** Listen and check your answers.

9 Work with a partner. Read the information in the Vocabulary focus box and match six of the phrases in the box to the definitions below.

1 be aware of something, but not certain about it
2 try to do something
3 be irrelevant or unrelated to something
4 believe that something is important
5 find that doing something is not easy
6 expect someone or something to be always there for you, even when you aren't grateful

VOCABULARY FOCUS
phrases with *take* and *have*

take and *have* are two of the most common verbs in English phrases. For example:

- *have difficulty in doing something*
- *have a go at doing something*
- *have a feeling that …*
- *have a responsibility to do something*
- *have nothing to do with something/someone*

- *take something seriously*
- *take advantage of*
- *take (no) notice of …*
- *take something for granted*
- *take risks*
- *take a decision*

Note that in these phrases the main meaning is not in the verb *take* or *have*, but in the whole expression.

10 Rewrite sentences 1–7, replacing the underlined words or phrases with one of the phrases in the Vocabulary focus box.

1 Don't <u>do anything dangerous</u> – it's not worth it.
2 He <u>used</u> his friend's kindness to borrow a lot of money he couldn't pay back.
3 Just <u>ignore</u> him – he's being silly.
4 I <u>know my studies are very important</u>.
5 It's very important to <u>make the right choice</u> about which degree to do.
6 It's a bit difficult at first, but just <u>try doing it</u>.
7 I <u>somehow think that</u> this holiday will be a mistake … I don't know why.

11 **TASK** Choose three or four of the following situations and tell each other about them. Work with a partner. Ask questions to find out more information.

A time when you …
- had difficulty in doing something.
- had a go at something new.
- had a feeling that something was wrong.
- took advantage of a situation or person (or a time when you were taken advantage of).
- took a risk.
- took an important decision.

10.4 Speaking and writing

Reading & Writing changes and differences

1 Work with a partner. Look at the photos of Istanbul, Liverpool and Riga and answer the questions.

   1 What do you know about these cities?

   2 What do you think they might have in common?

Istanbul

Liverpool

Riga

2a **10.14**))) Listen to an extract from a radio programme and check your ideas.

b Which city in your country would you recommend for this competition? Why? Tell your partner.

3a Read the article about Istanbul and make notes about past and present Istanbul with the headings.

	Past	Present
The Ortaköy area		
Istanbul Modern		

b Check your answers with a partner.

TRAVEL › ISTANBUL THE NEW ISTANBUL

Istanbul has long been recognized as one of the world's great cities. However, whereas in the past it was famous for its magnificent ancient sights, today Istanbul is becoming just as well known for its modern galleries, designer shops and fashionable restaurants.

In the past decades, development has dramatically changed many parts of the city. Whereas before, the skyline was dominated by historic buildings and monuments, now it is starting to resemble Manhattan in some districts where modern skyscrapers are rapidly being built. In preparation for the city becoming European Capital of Culture in 2010, the run-down buildings in many areas were renovated and turned into boutique hotels and trendy cafés. The neighbourhood of Ortaköy is now home to sophisticated nightclubs and restaurants, in contrast to the small fishing village that was once there.

Compared to twenty years ago, the city's list of must-see attractions has also changed. In the past, most visitors explored the city's abundance of historic buildings, but today there is also a wide choice of exciting new art galleries and museums. One of the most talked about is the stunning Istanbul Modern – a former empty warehouse that is now a state-of-the-art gallery with a stylish restaurant that offers excellent views of the old city.

In 2014 the city was voted the world's top destination in TripAdvisor's Travellers' Choice Awards, and there's no doubt that Istanbul is now one of Europe's most popular and vibrant cities.

4a Look at the article again and underline five words or phrases used for comparing things. What is being compared?

b Check your answers in the Language for writing box.

LANGUAGE FOR WRITING writing about changes and differences

When writing about changes and differences we use phrases like:

before … now …
whereas in the past … today …
whereas before … , now …
in contrast to …
compared to …
one of the most important changes …
another important change …

5 Complete the text about the city of Liverpool in the UK. Use the information in the Language for writing box to help you.

> A city which has changed its image a great deal since it was named European Capital of Culture in 2008 is Liverpool. ¹_____ before, people in the UK thought of Liverpool as a city of high unemployment and poverty, now they are more likely to link it with positive cultural events such as art exhibitions and music concerts.
>
> ²_____ has been the Liverpool One development in the city centre, which opened in 2008. ³_____ the old, often empty buildings that were there before, this fashionable shopping, living and leisure area now attracts millions of visitors a year and is the biggest open-air shopping centre in the UK.
>
> ⁴_____ can be seen in the Albert Dock area. ⁵_____ in the early 1980s it lay empty and forgotten, it is now Liverpool's most popular tourist attraction, with more than four million people a year visiting its shops, museums, galleries and street festivals.

6a Think about a city or town you know that has changed. Make notes about at least five changes to the city.

b Write a paragraph about the city or town. Use the language from the Language for writing box to describe the changes.

Listening & Speaking making recommendations

7a **10.15** ⟩⟩ Listen to some people talking about different cities.
1 Which cities are they talking about?
2 What do they recommend doing?

Cities	Recommendation
1	
2	
3	
4	

b Compare answers with a partner.

8a **10.16** ⟩⟩ Listen and complete the expressions.
1 You _____ learning flamenco …
2 OK, I'll _____.
3 If you like skiing, I'd _____ Portillo or Valle Nevado, both world class ski resorts.
4 Is there anything _____?
5 Where _____ I stay?
6 Well, _____ trying a traditional Japanese inn?
7 They're the _____ in luxury and relaxation.
8 That _____. I'll definitely try it.

b Which expressions:
a ask for a recommendation: _____ _____
b recommend something: _____ _____ _____ _____
c respond to a recommendation: _____ _____

9 Choose two cities you know and make a list of 3–5 things you would recommend to someone who is going to visit the cities for work, study or social purposes.

10 **TASK** Work with a partner (A and B). Use the expressions in exercise **8a**, the Language for speaking box and the prompts below to have a conversation about cities to visit. Then change roles.

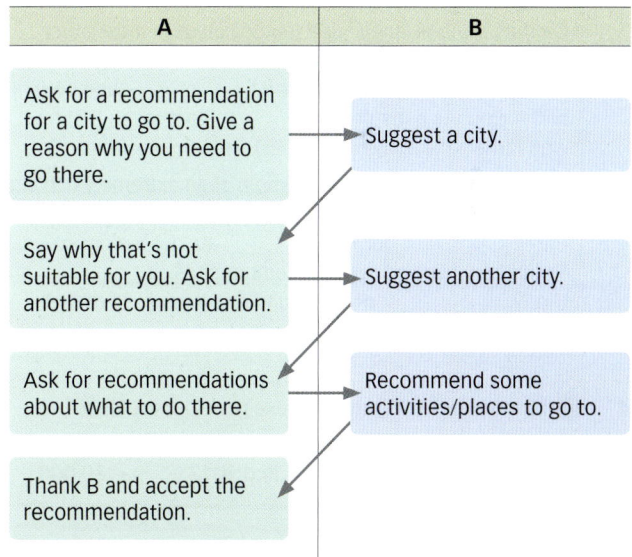

A	B
Ask for a recommendation for a city to go to. Give a reason why you need to go there.	Suggest a city.
Say why that's not suitable for you. Ask for another recommendation.	Suggest another city.
Ask for recommendations about what to do there.	Recommend some activities/places to go to.
Thank B and accept the recommendation.	

LANGUAGE FOR SPEAKING
making recommendations

Ask for a recommendation
Could you recommend (a) …?

Recommend something
I'd definitely recommend …
… it might be a good idea to …
Don't miss …

Respond to a recommendation
Thank you, that's a great suggestion, but …
That's a good idea, (but) …

10.5 Video

Borussia Dortmund

1 Look at the phrases in the box and choose which you would not connect with international football.

> affordable tickets   big business   loyal fans
> wealthy investors

2a Work with a partner. In one minute, list some more words or phrases on the topic of international football. Use the photos to help you.

b Compare your ideas with another pair.

3 ▶ Watch the video. Complete the information about modern football.

> countries   decisions   fans   investors   matches   people
> players   projects   teams   tickets

> There is one big difference between [1]_____ in the German football league and football clubs in most other [2]_____ around the world. Instead of being controlled by rich [3]_____, it is the [4]_____ who own most of the club. As a result, [5]_____ are taken that help the club rather than making its investors even wealthier.
>
> Borussia Dortmund is one example of an extremely rich club. It has some top-level [6]_____, and it is very successful. But [7]_____ for [8]_____ are not terribly expensive. The club is involved in many community [9]_____, and the [10]_____ of Dortmund are very proud of their local team.

4 ▶ Watch again. What do these numbers refer to?
- 3 billion
- 13–63
- 1909
- 500
- 2011 and 2012
- 100
- 4
- 80,000

5a **TASK** Work in small groups. Read the situation.

> You are on the board of directors of a big football club. The directors need to discuss some ideas for some community projects in your city, e.g. organizing a charity football match to raise money for a local children's hospital.

b In your group, write down three ideas for community projects.

c Share your ideas with the class. Make a list of everyone's ideas. Take a vote. Which idea is the most popular?

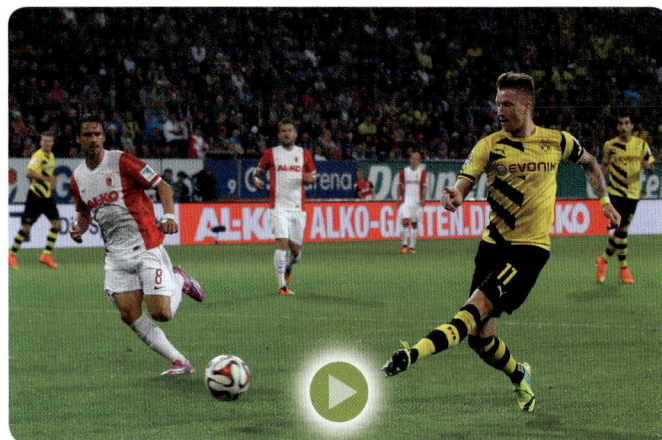

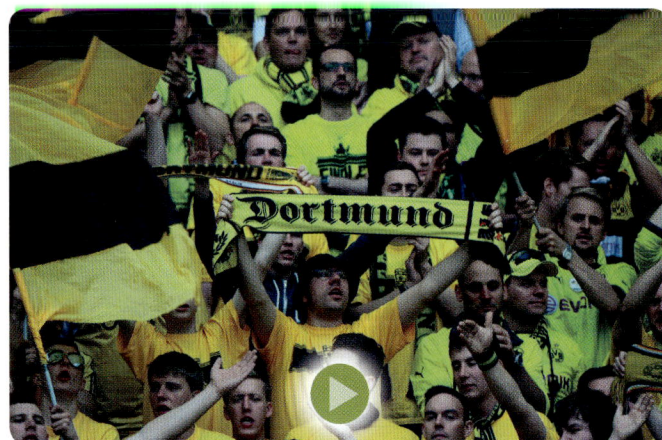

Review

1a Choose the correct options to complete the text.

> Havaianas ¹ *were developed / developed* in Brazil in the late 1950s. They ² *were based / based* on the sandals which ³ *wear / were worn* by Brazilian-Japanese immigrants, but these sandals soon ⁴ *became / were become* a hit with everyone. Being cheap but exotic, tourists ⁵ *were packed / packed* them in their baggage and their fame spread all over the world. In the mid-1990s the flip-flops ⁶ *were redesigned / redesigned*. New colours and an improved style ⁷ *caused / was caused* an explosion in sales. Nowadays around 22 million pairs ⁸ *export / are exported* annually to 80 markets.

b What are some of the typical products from your country? How are they made or grown? Who are they bought or used by? Discuss with a partner.

2a Complete the text using *a/an*, *the* or – (no article).

> With its tropical weather and snow-free mountains, ¹_____ Jamaica may not seem like ²_____ obvious country to send competitors to ³_____ Winter Olympics. But ⁴_____ Jamaican bobsled team were determined to make it to the Games. They qualified but needed to find $80,000. So Lincoln Wheeler, ⁵_____ fan of the Winter Games, set up ⁶_____ campaign on the crowd-funding site, Crowdtilt in 2014. Within days ⁷_____ campaign had raised more than $115,000. 'This is ⁸_____ internet coming together,' said James Beshara, the Crowdtilt CEO. 'It couldn't have been done five years ago.'

b Work with a partner and discuss the following questions.
1 Do you watch the Winter or Summer Olympics? Why/Why not?
2 What are your (least) favourite events? Why?

3a Choose the correct verb to complete each phrase.
a *make / get* an idea
b *set up / make* a profit
c *increase / become* an investor
d *get / make* funding
e *become / give* a guarantee
f *support / find* yourself short of cash

b **10.17**))) Listen to six definitions. Match each definition to a phrase in exercise **3a**.

4a Divide the words in the box into nouns, verbs and adjectives; two words can be in more than one of the categories.

> break a record compete competitive final lose
> play against race take part team tournaments
> win winner

b Compare your answers with a partner.

c Write five sentences together using any of the words from the box.

5a Cross out the word or phrase that *doesn't* go with the verb in the first column.
1 **take**   advantage of something
               a feeling that …
               care of someone
2 **have**   something seriously
               a word with
               not … a clue about something
3 **take**   someone's word for it
               nothing to do with someone
               turns
4 **have**   notice of
               difficulty in doing something
               something to do with

b Choose one of the completed verb phrases and tell your partner about a time when you did this, or this happened to you.

6a Put the conversation in the right order.
A I'd really like to get a bit fitter. What sport or activity would you recommend? *1*
A Thank you, that's a good idea. I'll give it a go.
A That's a good idea, but I have some problems with my knees. Could you recommend something a bit gentler?
B Have you thought of swimming? It's really good for you.
B I strongly recommend running; you'll get fit very fast.

b **10.18**))) Listen and check your answers.

c Role-play with a partner. You have moved to a new city and have been working very hard in your new job. Now you would like your partner to recommend a sport that will …
• help you meet new people.
• get you outside in the fresh air.

Change roles once you have heard your partner's suggestions.

Consequences

11.1 Outlaws

GOALS ■ Talk about crime ■ Talk about unreal situations in the past

Vocabulary & Reading crime

1a Work with a partner. Look at the title of the news article. What do you think a 'barefoot bandit' is?

b Read the article and compare it with your ideas.

NewsOnline

'Barefoot bandit' Colton Harris-Moore sentenced to 7 years in prison

Suspected of more than 100 thefts in the United States and Canada, including bicycles, cars and planes, the police had been trying to capture 19-year-old Colton Harris-Moore for nearly two years. Known as 'the barefoot bandit', Harris-Moore often carried out his robberies with no shoes on leaving his footprints behind. After this, he drew chalk footprints on the floor of a grocery store that he robbed.

Although none of his victims were actually injured, his burglaries terrified local residents, as no one knew where he might turn up next. Nevertheless, the outlaw became an internet sensation, with a Facebook fan page collecting thousands of 'likes'.

As the police came close to arresting him, he escaped by flying a stolen plane all the way from Indiana to the Bahamas. He had reportedly taught himself to fly, using information he found on the internet – though that didn't stop him from crash-landing in the sea. He then attempted to escape from local police officers using a stolen motorboat, but the police managed to stop the boat and arrested him.

■ **bandit** a thief, sometimes violent

2 Why do you think he became a 'Facebook sensation'? Give 2–3 possible reasons.

3a Match the highlighted words in the article to the following definitions.

1 crimes involving entering a building illegally in order to steal
2 thought to be guilty of a crime
3 people who are killed or hurt by someone else
4 catch someone you have been following or looking for
5 a building where criminals are kept as a punishment
6 taken without permission
7 crimes involving stealing from a place or person, especially using violence
8 given a punishment (of)
9 got away
10 making someone a prisoner
11 crimes involving stealing something
12 a person who has done something illegal and is hiding to avoid being caught

b Check your answers with a partner, then work together to complete the table.

Noun (person)	Noun (action)	Verb
thief	¹ *theft*	
2	burglary	
robber	3	4
	stealing	5

4 Choose the correct words to complete the text.

> A ¹ *burglar / victim* was ² *caught / escaped* on Friday night, after getting stuck in a bathroom window. The man who lived in the house found him when he went to the bathroom in the middle of the night. He called the police, who came and ³ *arrested / sentenced* the burglar. Police ⁴ *suspect / escape* that the man had already carried out several ⁵ *thieves / thefts* in the local area.

5a Look at the list of reasons why outlaws sometimes become popular with the public. Which reasons could apply to Harris-Moore? Discuss with a partner.

1 The police or authorities are unfair.
2 The outlaw is kind to ordinary people.
3 People admire the outlaw's bravery.
4 The outlaw is defending something he/she believes in.

b **11.1**))) Listen to a radio programme where two people are discussing popular outlaws and complete the texts.

Colton Harris-Moore

Known as ¹_____.

People found his story very ²_____ and loved the fact he taught himself to ³_____.

Ned Kelly

Arrested for ⁴_____, but claimed he was innocent. He and three friends then started ⁵_____, but they were ⁶_____ to the people who worked there.

Ned claimed the police were unfair to him because ⁷_____.

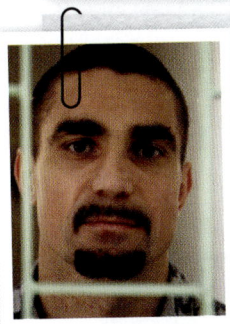

Attila Ambrus

His crime was also ⁸_____. He was polite to the bank workers and even ⁹_____. People supported him because they felt ¹⁰_____.

c Compare your answers with a partner's.

Grammar & Speaking unreal past conditional

6a Look at the following extract from the listening and answer the questions.

> 'If he had crashed the plane in a town, he would probably have killed someone.'

1 Did Colton crash the plane in a town?
2 Did he kill anyone?

b Read the example sentences in the Grammar focus box and choose the correct options to complete the information.

> **GRAMMAR FOCUS** unreal past conditional
>
> • If + past perfect, *would/might/could have* + past participle
>   *If he had crashed the plane in a town, he would probably have killed someone.*
>   *He would probably have killed someone if he had crashed the plane in a town.*
>
> • We use the unreal past conditional to talk about ¹ **real /** **unreal** situations in the ² **past / present** – things that are *different* from what actually happened.
>
> • If the meaning is clear, the clauses can be in any order, but we ³ **don't use / use** a comma if the result clause comes first.
>
> → **Grammar Reference** page 156

7 Complete the unreal past conditional sentences about the three outlaws, using the verbs in brackets.

1 If Colton _____ (not steal) a plane, he _____ (might/not become) so famous.
2 They _____ (not make) a film about Colton if he _____ (not have) so many Facebook fans.
3 Ned Kelly thought that if he _____ (not be) Irish, he _____ (not get) into trouble with the police.
4 If the police _____ (not arrest) Ned for murder, he _____ (not rob) any banks.
5 If Attila _____ (give) the money away, he _____ (might/be) even more popular.
6 If Attila _____ (not have) any bed sheets, he _____ (could/not escape).

8a Write one sentence about each of the outlaws, Colton Harris-Moore, Ned Kelly and Attila Ambrus, using an unreal past conditional form and your own ideas.

b Compare your sentences with a partner, and explain your ideas.

9 TASK Work with a partner. Student A, turn to page 132. Student B, turn to page 135.

▶ **VOX POPS VIDEO 11**

I should never have clicked 'send'!

Vocabulary & Reading   behaviour on social media

1   Work in small groups and discuss the questions.

   1   What differences are there between communicating online and face-to-face?
   2   Look at the headline of the article. Why do you think one in four people regrets sending their messages?

2a   Read the article and compare your ideas with the survey findings.

b   Read the article again and match statements 1–3 to the percentages of the two thousand people who agreed.

   26%   36%   55%

   1   People nowadays communicate more online than face-to-face. _____
   2   I have said something online which I wouldn't say in real life. _____
   3   I have seen online bullying or been a victim of it myself. _____

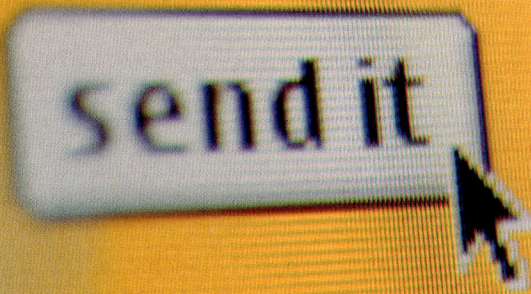

One in four regrets messages on social networking sites

More than a quarter of all users of Twitter and other social networking sites send messages they later **regret**, according to research.

The fact that the communication is not face-to-face makes people online more likely to **criticize** and **insult** each other, a survey of 2,000 people has found.

While social media websites are becoming places for people to **stand up for what they believe in**, people can also often feel they shouldn't have pressed the 'send' button so quickly.

More than half (55%) of the 2,000 people surveyed said that they felt social media had replaced face-to-face interaction; and nearly two in five (39%) people said they used social media to **speak up about** something they **felt passionate** about. Of these 39%, nearly half (44%) believed what they said had **made a real difference** because it led to **people blogging or tweeting about the issue**, or actual changes being made.

However, social media does have some problems. More than a quarter (26%) admitted they have said something nasty on a social media website they would **never say to someone's face**.

Some 44% of those regretted it because what they said had been **rude**, while 27% regretted it because they thought it had upset someone.

The research also revealed that online bullying was a serious problem, with more than a third (36%) having seen someone become **a victim of online bullying** or been one themselves.

Professor Adrian Dunbar said: 'Our research has shown that people are more likely to say something on social media that they later regret, because in these digital environments we don't receive the immediate feedback that we get during face-to-face interactions. This can therefore result in a **careless** or unpleasant tweet, or at worst, **cyberbullying**.'

c Work with a partner and discuss the questions.

1 Which findings would you agree with?

2 How accurate do you think this survey is? Give reasons.

3a Work with a partner. Read the article again. Student A, work out the meaning of the words or phrases in groups 1–4. Student B, work out the meaning of the words or phrases in groups 5–8. Work out how the words and phrases are different in each group.

> **Student A**
> 1 criticize/insult
> 2 rude/nasty
> 3 communicate face-to-face/say something to someone's face
> 4 stand up for what you believe in/speak up about something you feel passionate about

> **Student B**
> 5 have a positive effect/make a real difference
> 6 be sorry you did something/regret doing something
> 7 not thinking enough about what you are doing/being careless
> 8 blog or tweet about an issue/(be a victim of) cyberbullying

b Explain any differences in meaning in each pair of words or phrases to your partner. Give examples to show the differences.

4 Work with a partner or in small groups. Which of the following statements do you agree with more? Give your reasons.

1 People are more likely to say something rude or nasty online that they would never say to someone's face.

2 Online communication is essential for our lives. Its benefits are much more important than any possible drawbacks.

Grammar *should/shouldn't have*

5 Read the information in the Grammar focus box and choose the correct options to complete the rules.

> **GRAMMAR FOCUS** *should/shouldn't have*
>
> We use *should have* + past participle to talk about and criticize things we did and didn't do in the past.
> *They should have thought more carefully before putting something on a social media site.*
> They **1 did / didn't** think carefully – that was a **2 good / bad** idea.
> *They shouldn't have pressed the 'send' button so quickly.*
> They **3 did / didn't** press the send button – that was a **4 good / bad** idea.
>
> → **Grammar Reference** page 157

6a **11.2** ⟩⟩ Listen to two people talking about mistakes they made with social media and complete the sentences with *should/shouldn't have* + the correct form of the verbs in brackets.

1 She _____ (be) more careful when she posted the video.

2 She _____ (accept) her boss as a 'friend' online.

3 She _____ (behave) badly at the party.

4 She _____ (post) any videos online.

5 He _____ (think) before pressing *send*.

6 He _____ (say) anything negative about the interviewer online.

7 He _____ (wait) until he was offered the job.

8 They _____ (give) him the job anyway if he was the best candidate.

b **11.3** ⟩⟩ Listen and check.

c Do you agree with all the statements? Discuss your ideas with a partner.

PRONUNCIATION *should/shouldn't have*

7a **11.4** ⟩⟩ Listen to two sentences from exercise **6**. What do you notice about the pronunciation of *have*?

She should have been more careful.
She shouldn't have behaved badly.

b **11.4** ⟩⟩ Listen again and repeat.

8 **TASK** **11.5** ⟩⟩ Listen to two more people talking about their mistakes. After each one, discuss what happened with a partner, using *should/shouldn't have*. Do you agree with each other? And with the class?

11.3 Vocabulary and skills development

Listening hearing modal verbs

1 Look at the pictures. What is happening in each photo?

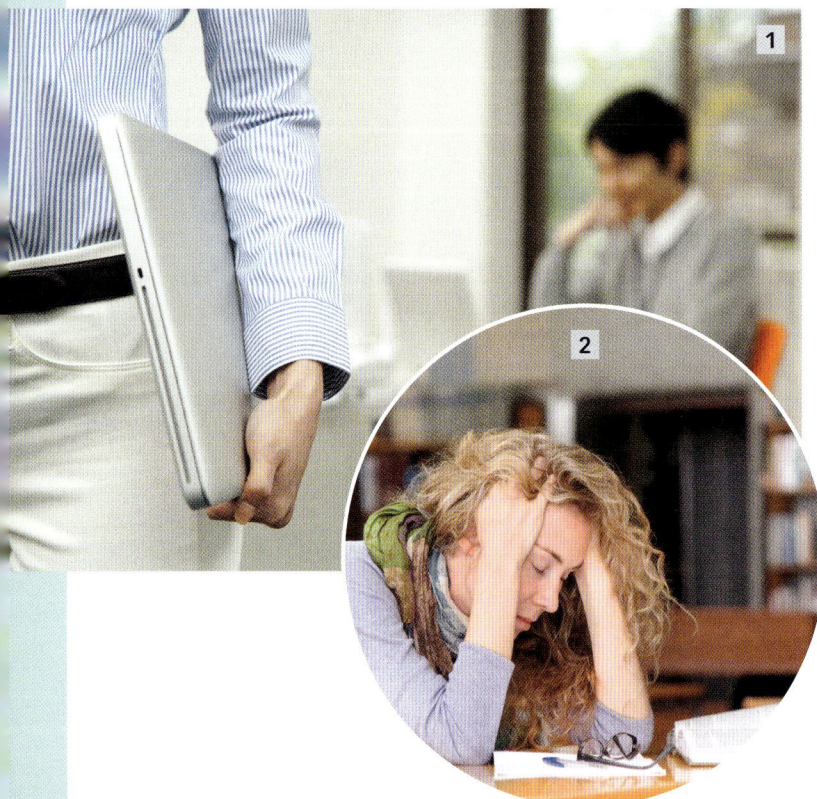

2 **11.6**))) Listen to the conversation related to each photo. For each conversation, answer the questions.

1 What did the person in the photo do?
2 What did they want to happen?
3 What actually happened?

3 **11.6**))) Listen again and complete the sentences from the conversations. What kind of verbs do all the spaces contain?

Conversation 1

1 I decided to borrow a laptop from the office so _____ it at home ...
2 We _____ permission ...
3 Anyway, I _____ into work on the Tuesday ...

Conversation 2

1 I _____ Professor Dudley ...
2 I thought _____ a better grade in my exams.

4 **11.7**))) Read and listen to the information in the Unlock the code box about hearing modal verbs.

> 🔓 **UNLOCK THE CODE**
> hearing modal verbs
>
> Modal verbs such as *must, may* and *could* are very important for the meaning of a sentence, but they are often difficult to hear. We sometimes form the past using a different verb.
>
> For example:
> We **must** get permission.   I **had** to help.
>
> When you are listening, use the context to decide if the speaker used a modal verb, and which one suits the context best.

5a Read the definition of 'unintended consequences'. Can you think how the photos could relate to the definition? Discuss with a partner.

> The idea of unintended consequences is an important one in politics and economics, but it is also common in everyday life. It means that the consequence or result of an action is sometimes very different from our intention. This can be a good or a bad consequence.

b **11.8**))) Listen to a radio programme about the unintended consequences of a law about crash helmets for cyclists. Were your ideas the same as the example in the programme?

c Answer the questions about the crash helmet law example.

1 What does the law say?
2 What is the intention behind the law?
3 What's the young person's reaction to the crash helmets?
4 What are the consequences of this reaction?

d **11.8**))) Compare your answers with your partner. Which modal verbs did you hear in the answers? Listen again and check.

6 **TASK** What might be the unintended consequences of these actions? Choose one to discuss with a partner. Report your answers to the class.

1 A doctor makes patients pay a fine if they are late for an appointment.
2 In order to improve his performance in an exam, a student drinks three large cups of coffee ten minutes before the exam starts.
3 To stop customers eating a meal and then leaving without paying, a restaurant makes them pay for the meal at the same time as they order the food.

Vocabulary & Speaking words with multiple meanings

7a Look at the pairs of sentences. For each pair, choose one word from the box that goes in both sentences.

> bank   fine   jam   performance   wave

1   a   The doctor made the patients pay a _____ if they missed an appointment.
    b   It was a _____, sunny day as they left for the picnic.
2   a   The _____ starts at 7.30, so don't be late!
    b   Over the last ten years, China's economic _____ has been very strong.
3   a   They stopped at the _____ to get some money.
    b   We pulled the fish out of the river and put it on the _____.
4   a   My mother gave me a final _____ goodbye as the train left the station.
    b   The boat was sunk by an enormous _____.
5   a   There was a terrible traffic _____ on the way to the airport.
    b   For breakfast, they gave us toast and _____.

b   All of the words in the box have two meanings. Match the words to the pairs of meanings.

> change   key   light   match   rock   square

1   large stone
    type of loud music
2   shape with four equal sides
    area of a town with four sides and buildings all around
3   thing for locking a door
    answer to a problem
4   game between two teams
    piece of wood for lighting something
5   the energy that comes from the sun
    something you turn on when it's dark
6   money which is coins (not notes)
    something different from before

8a   Read the Vocabulary focus box.

> **VOCABULARY FOCUS**
> words with multiple meanings
>
> There are many pairs of words in English which have the same spelling and pronunciation but different meanings. Sometimes these are the same parts of speech (e.g. both nouns).
> a traffic **jam** vs bread and **jam**
>
> Sometimes they are different word classes.
> pay a **fine**/feel **fine** (a noun and an adjective)
>
> Use the context to decide which meaning is correct.

b   Finish the sentences in **two** different ways to show the two meanings of each word.

1   The **square** was …
    a   *drawn on a piece of paper.*
    b   *full of people shouting.*
2   I couldn't find the **key** because …
    a   _____
    b   _____
3   It's important that the **change** …
    a   _____
    b   _____
4   I saw a **match** which …
    a   _____
    b   _____
5   We had to stop playing because the **light** …
    a   _____
    b   _____
6   We saw the rock …
    a   _____
    b   _____

9   **TASK**   Work with a partner. Write four sentences each using words from exercises **7** and **8**. Put a space where the word you have chosen goes. Then swap sentences with your partner and complete them.

The small boy threw a _____ and broke the window.
OR
I'm not keen on _____ music – I prefer salsa.
Answer: *rock*

rock
light change
key wave
match
square

11.4 Speaking and writing

Listening & Speaking decisions

> 'What are the three most important factors in choosing where to live? – Location, location, location.'

1a Do you agree with the quotation above? What are the most important factors for you? Make a list with a partner.

b What are the consequences of (not) having each factor? For example: If it's in a good area, it may be very expensive.

2 **11.9**))) Listen to a group of friends talking about moving to a different apartment. Which of the factors you listed in exercise **1** do they mention?

3a **11.10**))) Listen and complete the expressions.
  1 Let's _____ extras like that _____.
  2 _____ a balcony is essential ...?
  3 Well, another _____ to go for a ground-floor apartment ...
  4 So, _____ a three-bedroomed apartment ...

b Work with a partner and match the four phrases in exercise **3a** to categories a–d.
  a Arriving at a decision   c Making a point stronger
  b Discussing options   d Controlling the time

c Practise saying the expressions.

4a Read the information in the Language for speaking box.

LANGUAGE FOR SPEAKING making decisions

Controlling the time
Could we move on?
Let's leave that for now. We're running out of time.

Discussing options
Are there any other suggestions?
What would happen if ...?

Making your point stronger
I'm convinced that ...
You must admit that ...

Arriving at a decision
So, what we're saying we've decided is ...
That's settled, then.

b **TASK** Work in small groups. Look at the descriptions on page 132 and decide together which home would be best for a couple with a girl aged nine and a boy aged eleven.

Present your ideas to another group and compare your decisions and the reasons you gave for them.

Reading & Writing apologizing

5 Work in small groups. Have you ever done any of these things? What were the consequences?

- missed an important deadline at work or college
- left someone out of an important decision
- forgotten to thank someone for helping
- sent a special invitation to the wrong friend

6 Work with a partner. Read the three messages and match each to a situation in exercise **5**.

1

Sent: Tuesday 10.16

Hi Tomoe,

I'm so sorry for sending you that email by mistake. I can understand that you were a bit upset when you spoke to Susie. I had actually meant to send that email to her – she really likes the theatre, so I thought it would be good to offer her my spare ticket.

I really hope you understand! Why don't we get together soon anyway? Do you fancy a coffee next week?

Apologies again,

Tania

2

Sorry for not getting in touch sooner. Please forgive me! I just wanted to say thanks so much for the other day – I really appreciated the help!

08:19

3

Sent: Friday 15.25

Dear Dr Phillips,

Please accept my apologies for the late submission of this term's work. I have had some problems completing work in the last month due to family issues. I can see now it would have been better to ask for an extension earlier. If I face similar problems in the future, I will make sure I discuss them with you.

I apologize for the inconvenience.

Best wishes,

Raul

7 Find phrases in the messages with similar meanings to phrases 1–4. Write them here.

1 Sorry for the trouble this causes.

_____

2 I apologize for the delay in replying.

_____

3 I hope you will be able to forgive me.

_____

4 I apologize once again.

_____

8 Decide which phrase in each pair in exercise **7** is more formal (MF) and which is less formal (LF). Then read the information in the Language for writing box to check your answers.

LANGUAGE FOR WRITING apologizing

It is important to get the tone right when you apologize. We can say the same thing in more or less formal ways, depending on the words we choose to use.

apologize – say you are sorry
inconvenience – trouble

More formal (MF) English uses complete sentences. Less formal (LF) English can miss out words.

Formal	Informal
Apologizing	
I apologize for the delay in replying.	Sorry for not getting in touch sooner.
Please accept my apologies for …	Apologies for …/Sorry for …
I apologize for the inconvenience.	Sorry for the trouble this causes.
I hope you will be able to forgive me.	Please forgive me.
I hope you understand. I can see now it would have been better to …	I can understand that you …
Accepting an apology	
I understand completely.	It's perfectly all right.
There's no need to apologize.	That's OK/fine.

9a Read Dimitri's email apologizing to a customer. What is the problem with the tone? How do you think the customer will react when he receives the email?

Sent: Saturday 18.57

Hi there, Mr Carter,

Sorry for not writing sooner – I have been a bit busy. Apologies for the problem you had in our shop last Tuesday. It was a very busy day and some staff were off sick. Please forgive us!

Dimitri

Customer Services

b Rewrite the email with the correct tone.

10 **TASK** Write an email to apologize.

a Work with a partner. Choose one of the situations in exercise **5**, or think of your own and discuss the details.

b On your own, write an email to apologize.

c Read your partner's email. Is the tone and style right?

11.5 Video

Cyber crime

1 Work with a partner. Complete the sentences with words in the box. Discuss the meaning of the verbs in bold.

> malware   Web   application   criminals/hackers

a As I was **browsing** the _____, I was redirected to a different site.

b This website has been **hacked** by _____ in order to infect your machine.

c My computer has **become infected** with _____.

d Please **download** this _____ and **install** it to protect your system.

2 Work with a partner. What do you know about Sophos? Use the photos and the words in exercise **1** to help you talk about what they do.

3 ▶ Watch the video. Choose the best summary of the information given in this interview.

a This video summarizes of the internet security firm Sophos's latest product which can protect systems against most cyber attacks. An employee offers advice on how we can protect our computers and other electronic devices these days.

b The video describes the challenges for users and internet security firms these days. An employee from Sophos explains that the threat of cyber crime is growing because there are so many different ways in which data can now be stored.

4 ▶ Watch again. Decide if these statements are true (T) or false (F). Correct the false sentences.

a Fraser Howard sells internet security products.

b Fraser Howard gives an example of how a cyber attack could take place.

c 'Security Shield' is a software which protects computers against cyber attacks.

d In this example, the servers which host the hackers' activities are in Canada.

5a TASK Work in groups. List five threats from computer hackers. Put them in order of the highest to the lowest threat.

b Compare your ideas with another group. Were any of your ideas the same? Have any of these things happened to you?

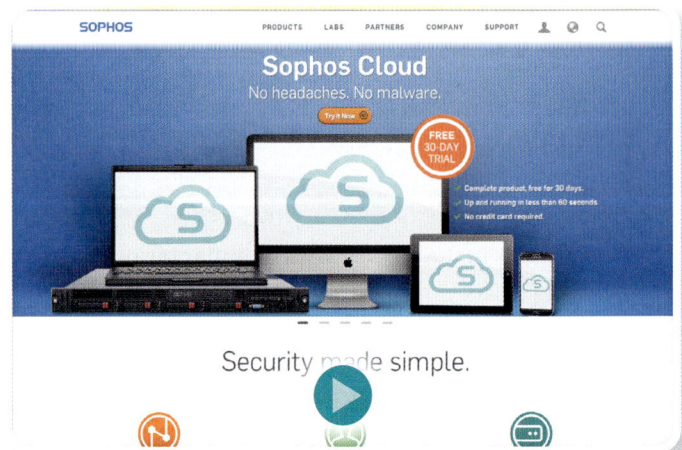

Review

1a Complete the sentences below each situation.

1 Anna was burgled while she was on holiday. She left a window open.

   a She should _____ (lock) the window.

   b She shouldn't _____ (leave) the window open.

   c If she _____ (leave) the window open, she _____ (be) burgled.

2 Thieves broke into my car and stole my handbag.

   a I should _____ (hide) my handbag in the boot.

   b I shouldn't _____ (leave) my handbag in the car.

   c If I _____ (leave) my handbag in the car, they _____ (break) in.

b Work with a partner. Talk about the following situations using *should/shouldn't have* and a past unreal conditional.

1 Nick made an insulting comment on a friend's social networking page. He was only joking, but his friend was very upset.

2 I was in a hurry to catch my train, so I didn't buy a ticket. The ticket inspector fined me a lot of money.

3 Lucy responded angrily to a comment on her blog. Now the person who made the comment keeps posting more and more angry comments.

2a Read the biography of 'the Gentleman Bandit' and complete the text with the correct form of the words in the box.

arrest   escape   prison   robbery   steal   thief   victim

The Gentleman Bandit

Ezra Allen Miner, known as 'Bill Miner', was nicknamed 'the Gentleman Bandit' because he was polite and considerate as he ¹_____ from stagecoaches and trains in the Old West. Many people believe he was the first ²_____ to say, 'Hands up!' Miner became a folk hero in Canada after he was ³_____ for the ⁴_____ of a Canadian Pacific Railway train in 1906. The company was very unpopular at the time and hundreds of Canadians cheered Miner as the police took him to ⁵_____. Miner never actually hurt any of his ⁶_____, but he spent most of his adult life in prison, apart from a couple of exciting but short-lived ⁷_____.

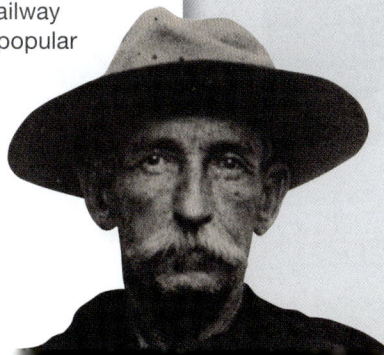

b Why do you think Miner became a folk hero? Discuss with a partner.

3a Match the first part of the phrase to the correct second part.

1	be a victim of	a	a real difference
2	make	b	about something
3	feel	c	what you believe in
4	stand up for	d	online bullying
5	speak up	e	someone
6	upset	f	passionate about something

b Tell your partner about something you feel passionately about. Try to use at least three of the phrases in exercise **3a**.

4a 11.11))) Listen to the beginning of six sentences. Write them down and complete them in any way that makes sense.

b Compare your sentences with a partner's. Is the meaning of the noun in each sentence the same or different?

5a Put the phrases in the right order.

1 running / time / of / we're / out .

2 suggestions / are / any / there / other ?

3 settled / then / that's .

4 for / let's / that / now / leave .

5 must / that's / true / admit / you .

6 would / option / another / be / that .

7 that / convinced / I'm .

8 saying / we're / what / so / is .

b 11.12))) Listen and check your answers.

c Work with a partner. Decide if the phrases in exercise **5a** are a) controlling the time, b) discussing options, c) making your point stronger or d) arriving at a decision.

12 Influence

12.1 Advertising

GOALS ■ Talk about advertising ■ Understand and use reported speech

Vocabulary & Listening advertising

1 Work with a partner. Look at the photos and discuss which advertisement you think makes the biggest impact and why.

FOOTBALL.
WE KNOW HOW YOU FEEL ABOUT IT,
BECAUSE WE FEEL THE SAME.

JCDecaux

2a Work with a partner. Find examples of the words in the box in the photos in exercise 1.

advert   billboard   brand   logo   poster   product   slogan

b Match the adjectives in the box to definitions 1–7.

amusing   clever   confusing   effective   memorable
persuasive   unpleasant

1 able to make someone do or believe something
2 causing you to laugh or smile
3 successfully producing the effect that you want
4 difficult to understand
5 not nice or enjoyable
6 worth remembering or easy to remember
7 showing skill or intelligence

c Which adjectives could you use to describe each of the photos in exercise 1?

3 12.1))) Listen to three people talking about a memorable advertisement. Match speakers 1–3 to photos a–c.

a _____   b _____   c _____

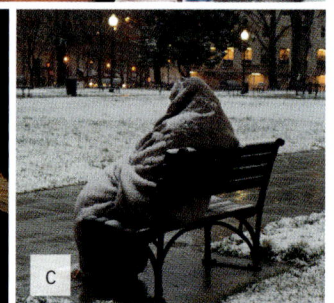

4 **12.1**))) Listen again and write the number of the speaker next to the statement which most closely matches what they say. There is one extra statement you do not need to use.

a People dislike being told they aren't allowed to do something. ____

b I was really upset when I saw this advert. ____

c Adverts can make people aware of social issues. ____

d Funny adverts can be a good way to influence people.
____

Grammar & Speaking   reported speech

5 Look at sentences a–b about the listening in exercise **3** and answer the questions.

a *The man said that it was just one light and wouldn't make any difference.*

b *She said (that) the point of the advert had been to persuade people not to send texts while driving.*

1 What do you think the original words in each advert were?

2 What is the difference between the tense used in the original words and in the reported speech?

6 Read the information in the Grammar focus box on tense changes in reported speech and complete the examples.

GRAMMAR FOCUS   reported speech

Tense changes

- We use reported speech to tell people what someone said. Tenses usually move one tense back, for example *go → went, did/have done → had done, will → would*, to show that the words were spoken in the past, and the pronoun can also change (e.g. from *I → he*).

Direct speech	Reported speech
'It**'s** really memorable.'	He said (that) it **1**_____ really memorable.
'The ad **has won** an award.'	She said (that) the ad **2**_____ an award.
'It **was** really moving.'	He said it **3**_____ really moving.
'They **are hoping** more countries **will do** it next year.	He said they **4**_____ more countries **5**_____ do it the following year.

- We often use *say* or *tell*. Note that *tell* must have a personal object: we tell somebody something. *Say* doesn't have a personal object: we say something (to somebody).

  He said it was really amusing.
  *He **told us** it was really amusing.*

→ **Grammar Reference** page 158

7 Use the information in the Grammar focus box to report these statements.

1 The best ad I've seen had a serious point.
He said _____

2 Earth Hour is about saving energy.
He told us that _____

3 They asked homeless people to present the weather forecast on TV.
She said that _____

4 In future people will think before they text.
She told us that _____

5 I don't like being told what to do.
He said that _____

6 There were lots of silly little accidents.
He told us _____

PRONUNCIATION   linking

8a **12.2**))) Listen to these extracts from the listening and listen to how the words in **bold** are linked.

1 The **best ad** I've seen **had a** serious point.

2 Earth Hour **is about** saving energy.

3 I saw **an amazing ad** ...

4 **Lots of** them were offered help.

5 The instructor told them **that a** new law had been passed.

6 There were **lots of** silly little accidents.

b Work with a partner. Look again at the words in bold and circle all the vowel sounds (sounds, not letters) and underline all the consonant sounds.

c Look at how each pair of words in bold are linked. What happens when a consonant sound ends one word and a vowel sound starts the next word?

d Practise linking with the extracts.

9a **TASK** Work with a partner. Use questions 1–5 to tell your partner about a memorable advert you have seen.

1 Was the advert for a brand or was it a public service announcement?

2 What happened in the advert (if a film), or what could you see (if a picture)?

3 What was it trying to persuade people to do or buy?

4 Did it use a slogan or a logo? Was that effective? Why/Why not?

5 What adjectives would you use to describe it?

b Find a new partner and report to them what your partner from exercise **9a** said.

Juan told me about an advert he'd seen that ...

▶ **VOX POPS VIDEO 12**

Vocabulary & Reading persuading people

1 Look at the advertisement for a book. What kind of book is it?

Books

How to Persuade and Influence People

by Philip Hesketh | ★ ★ ★ ★ ★

Do you want to be able to persuade and influence people?

Wouldn't it be great if you could always get people to see things your way? Now you can. You won't be successful in business if you can't bring people round to your way of thinking. Some people find it easy; the rest of us just need a little help.

This second edition contains plenty of practical exercises to help you …

- Find the perfect way to win people over
- Become an amazing negotiator
- Understand the other person's point of view
- Know why people buy what they buy
- Make sure people remember you and what you want
- Overcome objections

Philip Hesketh is a full-time international business speaker on the psychology of persuasion. Thousands of people have benefited from his advice. In his book, he gives the reader plenty of simple and memorable persuasion techniques that can be used to deal with many of life's challenges.

It's up to you to use them.

2a Read the advertisement for the book. What would you expect to read in the book?

b What kind of person might want or feel they need to read this book? Would you read it? Why/Why not?

3a The two phrases on the list mean *to persuade or influence someone*. Find four more phrases in the information in the advertisement that mean the same thing and add them to the list.

- *get your own way*
- *convince someone you're right*
- _____
- _____
- _____
- _____

b Complete the questions with the six phrases in exercise **3a**.

1 How important is it for you to get _____ own _____?

2 If someone doesn't like you at first, do you try to win _____ ? Why/Why not?

3 If someone disagrees with you, are you usually able to see things _____?

4 If you argue with a friend, will they usually bring _____ their way of thinking, or will you _____ them you are right?

5 What do you think is the best way to overcome someone's _____ to an idea?

c Work with a partner. Ask and answer the questions.

4a Read this short extract from the book. What different things could the assistant do to make a sale? Discuss with a partner.

> I was in town recently in a menswear store. A smartly dressed man came in and the owner asked, 'Can I help you?' The man smiled, and said, in a very polite way, 'I'm looking for a BOSS suit. I like the brand BOSS. Do you sell BOSS?'
>
> The shop didn't sell BOSS. So what would you do if you were the assistant?

b Work with a partner. Look at suggestions 1–3 from the book and choose the best option. What would be the benefits or drawbacks of this solution?

1 Tell the customer that you don't sell BOSS, but you know where he could find it.

2 Say that you agree that BOSS is a fine brand and although you don't sell it yourself, you have something similar.

3 Say that you agree BOSS is a fine brand and ask him what in particular he likes about it.

c Work with two pairs who have looked at different options and compare your ideas. Look at the author's solution on page 135.

Grammar & Listening reported questions

5a 12.3))) Listen to a review of the book on a radio programme. Is the review positive or negative?

b 12.3))) Listen again and write down the seven questions that the presenter asks.

6a Read the information in the Grammar focus box.

GRAMMAR FOCUS reported questions

- Reported questions also usually move one tense back to show that the words were said in the past.

- As a reported question is no longer a direct question:

a The word order is the same as in statements.
  Where **is he** going? – She asked where **he was** going.

b We do not use auxiliaries.
  Where **do** you live? – He asked where I lived.

  1 *When did you arrive?*
  He asked _____

  2 *Where will you go?*
  _____

  Yes/No questions use *if* or *whether*.
  Do you like reading? – He asked **if**/**whether** she liked reading.
  He asked if she had enjoyed it.

  3 *Have you been to France?*
  _____

  4 *Can I leave early?*
  _____

→ **Grammar Reference** page 159

b Rewrite the seven questions in exercise **5b** as reported questions.
Did you enjoy it? – He asked if she had enjoyed it.

7a 12.3))) Listen again and make notes about the answers to the questions in exercise **5b**.

b Take turns to report the questions and answers to a partner.

8a In the interview Tania says:

> 'But probably the most important thing is to really listen to people and to ask questions to find out what's really important to them …'

Write five questions that could help you to understand someone else better – for example, about their family, their hobbies, etc.

- Who do you get on best with?
- How do you like to relax?
- What's the most dangerous sport you have tried?

b Work with a partner. Take turns to ask and answer your questions.

9 **TASK** Work with a new partner and tell them about your conversation. Use reported speech and reported questions.

I asked Maria what she usually did to relax. She said she enjoyed jogging and thought it was really good for getting rid of stress.

12.3 Vocabulary and skills development

Reading & Speaking — complex noun phrases (2)

1a Look at the sentences about soft power. What do you think soft power is? Do you think it's important? Why?

1 What's interesting is that soft power has little to do with politics.

2 According to a 2013 survey Germany is the country that currently has the most soft power, followed by the UK, the US, France and Japan.

3 Italy's strength is its reputation for great food, fashion and art.

4 The Olympic Games can increase a country's soft power. By hosting the 2020 Games Japan has something big to aim for in the coming years.

5 The 226 Alliance Françaises throughout the world and France 24 online provide an alternative to the English-language dominated news agenda, i.e. news from a different perspective.

b Circle the subject (who does the action) and the verb and underline the object (what they do) in sentences 4 and 5 in exercise **1a**.

c Read the Unlock the code box. Check your answers.

> **🔓 UNLOCK THE CODE**
> recognizing complex noun phrases (2)
>
> Objects, like subjects, often consist of more than one word, and are sometimes quite complex. Here are some common kinds of more complex objects.
> By hosting the 2020 Games Japan has something big to aim for in the coming years.
> The 226 Alliance Françaises throughout the world and France 24 online provide an alternative to the English-language dominated news agenda, i.e. news from a different perspective.

2a Before you read the article about soft power in South Korea, discuss the questions with a partner.

1 What aspects of South Korean culture are shown in the photos?

2 How do you think these aspects make South Korea a more important or successful country? Give reasons for your answer.

b Read the article and compare what it says to your answers.

3 Look at the highlighted verbs in the article. Underline the object of each of the verbs.

4 Read the article again. Work with a partner and answer questions 1–4. What does it say about …?

1 South Korean TV shows and pop music.

2 Iranian TV viewers.

3 *Monocle* magazine.

4 social media.

5a Discuss with a partner. Which other countries do you think have soft power? Why? Use the ideas in the box to help you.

> architecture   businesses   cinema   famous people
> fashion   music   sport

b Work with another pair. Compare your ideas.

South Korea's 'soft power' – a global success

Something has been changing in South Korea in recent years, and the world has definitely noticed. What has changed is its 'soft power'.

Since the 1990s, a new wave of South Korean culture called Hallyu, or Korean Wave (한류), has changed the country's image abroad.

TV shows such as Jumong and Dong Yi, and K-pop (Korean pop) singers like Kim Jae Joong and Kim Hyun-Joong have made an incredible difference to the country's image. In fact, many think they have done more than the government. Even the popularity of South Korean food has increased.

Jumong, a historical drama, was sold to ten Asian countries and proved extremely popular. In fact, in Iran, 80% of TV viewers watched it. And who could forget Psy's Gangnam Style video, which broke all records for YouTube views?

Vocabulary & Speaking   dependent prepositions

6   What prepositions go in 1–3?

- They don't rely ¹_____ radio stations to tell them what music they should listen ²_____ any more.
- One thing is for sure – South Korea's influence is growing. Who knows what it will lead ³_____?

VOCABULARY FOCUS   dependent prepositions

- With some verbs, we have to put a preposition before the object (noun or verb + -ing).
  *She **works for** an international company.*
  *You can't **rely on** the weather in England, even in the summer.*
- Some *adjectives* also have dependent *prepositions*.
  *He's **good at** communicating.*
  *They are **interested in** South Korean films.*

All this has increased the country's soft power, its ability to make a positive impression through things like culture, architecture, sport and popular brands.

The international magazine *Monocle* recently published a report about the countries with the most soft power. Tyler Brule, the magazine's editor-in-chief, said soft power was more important than ever before. He said it is now fashionable for countries to use culture rather than force or even politics to increase their influence abroad.

Interestingly, Hallyu has largely attracted attention through social media. People all over the world are watching K-pop videos on the internet. They don't rely on radio stations to tell them what music they should listen to any more.

One thing is for sure – South Korea's influence is growing. Who knows what it will lead to?

7a   **12.4**))) Listen to three people talking about soft power and business. What does each person say about the subject?

1   _____
2   _____
3   _____

b   **12.4**))) Listen again. Complete these extracts with the missing prepositions.

1   Countries no longer depend _____ force or politics to increase their influence abroad.
2   We're not afraid _____ being more open in the workplace any more. Of course, we have women to thank _____ a lot of these changes.
3   We want to work in a group and deal _____ problems effectively, …

8a   Write the correct preposition from the box next to words 1–10.

about   for   in   on   to

1	worried *about*	6	refer _____
2	talk _____	7	lead _____
3	succeed _____	8	listen _____
4	interested _____	9	concentrate _____
5	believe _____	10	work _____

b   **12.5**))) Listen to ten sentences and check your answers.

9   **12.5**))) Listen to the sentences in exercise **8b** again. Work with a partner and decide how we pronounce the prepositions.

10a   **TASK**   Work with a partner. Complete questions 1–10 with a dependent preposition and your own ideas. Use the Vocabulary focus box to help you.

1   Are you good _____?
2   Are you interested _____?
3   Have you ever worked _____?
4   Are you afraid _____?
5   Do you find it hard to concentrate _____?
6   Do you ever get bored _____?
7   Do you believe _____?
8   Would you like to succeed _____?
9   Do you ever worry _____?
10   Do you find it difficult to talk _____?

b   Ask and answer the questions.

12.4 Speaking and writing

Listening & Speaking agreeing and disagreeing

1a Work with a partner. Add at least three more things to this list of things that can go in and out of fashion.

clothes restaurants cars diets
mobile phones   video games

b Discuss the questions with a partner.

1 Would you buy a new phone because yours felt old-fashioned? Why/Why not?

2 Do you notice if people's clothes are (un)fashionable? Does it affect your opinion of them?

2 **12.6**)))) Listen to three conversations about how fashionable things are. What three things in exercise **1** are the speakers talking about? Tick the words in exercise **1**.

3 **12.6**)))) Listen to the conversations again and decide if the sentences are true (T) or false (F).

Both speakers think that …

1 Andrew's new phone will be good for taking photos on holiday.

2 old-fashioned things sometimes look better than newer things.

3 the prices at the new restaurant are too high.

4 the restaurant is in a good position.

4a Use the phrases from the listening to complete the table.

You might be right.   I was just going to say that!   Don't you think …?   I'm not sure about that.   I couldn't agree more. That's just what I thought.   Absolutely!   I totally disagree.

Agreeing	Disagreeing	Asking if someone agrees

b Look at the phrases in the first two columns of the table in exercise **4a**. Write S if the phrase shows strong agreement or disagreement, and W if it shows weak agreement or disagreement.

c Check your answers in the Language for speaking box.

LANGUAGE FOR SPEAKING
agreeing and disagreeing

Asking if someone agrees

Don't you agree?	*Would you agree?*
Don't you think …?	*Wouldn't you say that …?*

Agreeing	**Disagreeing**
Agree strongly	Disagree strongly
I was just going to say that!	*I totally disagree.*
That's just what I thought.	*Rubbish!*
Absolutely!	
I couldn't agree more.	Disagree weakly
My thoughts exactly.	*I'm not sure about that.*
That's a good point.	*Yes but I can't help thinking …*
	I agree up to a point …
Agree weakly	
I suppose so.	
You might be right, but …	

d **12.7**)))) Listen and repeat the phrases for agreeing and disagreeing in the Language for speaking box.

5 Work with a partner and choose two topics. Use the prompts to have a conversation.

- There is no difference between expensive branded clothes and cheaper versions.
- We don't need books any longer.
- We have too many possessions nowadays.
- Everyone should speak at least two languages.
- People who follow fashion have no originality or ideas of their own.

A Give an opinion on topic 1. Ask if B agrees.
B Agree strongly. Add another reason.
A Agree or disagree not very strongly.

B Give an opinion on topic 2. Ask if A agrees.
A Agree strongly. Add another reason.
B Agree or disagree not very strongly.

6a Work with a partner. Read the statement and write down three reasons to agree with it and three reasons to disagree.

'We spend too much time, money and effort staying in fashion.'

b Join another pair. Decide which pair will agree with the statement and which pair will disagree and discuss.

c Do most people agree or disagree with the statement?

Writing advantages and disadvantages essay

7a Work with a partner. What do you think fast fashion is?

b Check your ideas in the first paragraph of the essay.

---

1 Broadly speaking, 'fast fashion' companies make and sell the latest fashions very quickly. The clothes are heavily influenced by the international fashion shows in London, Milan, etc., and can even appear on the high street within two weeks of the show. They introduce new clothes into the shops every two or three months, not twice a year, like traditional fashion houses. The main objectives of 'fast fashion' are to bring high-fashion clothes into the shops quickly and cheaply. However, this has both advantages and disadvantages.

2 One advantage ¹_____ customers can buy very up-to-date, fashionable clothes. ²_____ major ³_____ is that there is a greater variety of clothes in the shops. This means that a smaller number of each item of clothing is made, so you probably won't find other people wearing the same clothes as you.

3 ⁴_____ hand, there are also several ⁵_____ with 'fast fashion'. ⁶_____ disadvantage can be that the designs are not original; they are copied from the fashion shows of famous designers, which people should be discouraged from doing. Another ⁷_____ the clothes are usually made very cheaply, which can mean that the quality is poor and that the people who make the clothes are not well paid. This can give the companies a negative image.

4 Overall, we have seen that fast fashion can be a good or a bad thing. We need to realize that we are responsible for the choices we make when we are shopping, and the difference those choices make to other people in the world.

8a Work with a partner and write down two good things and two bad things about fast fashion.

b Read the rest of the essay and underline any ideas you thought of.

c Which paragraph talks about advantages? Which talks about disadvantages?

9a Read the information in the Language for writing box.

LANGUAGE FOR WRITING
advantages and disadvantages

Advantages
There are several benefits.
One advantage is that …
Another major positive is that …

Disadvantages
One disadvantage can be that …
Another drawback (of fast fashion) is that …
On the other hand …
… there are also problems with …

---

b Complete the essay in exercise **7b** with one to three words in each gap.

10 Find and underline two generalizations in the introduction and conclusion.

11a Look at the essay title.

What are the advantages and disadvantages of buying the latest technology?

Work in small groups and complete the table with your ideas.

Advantages	Disadvantages
•	•
•	•
•	•

b Work with a partner. Complete the essay plan with two ideas for each paragraph.
- Introduction (general points about buying technology)
- Advantages
- Disadvantages
- Conclusion (general points/need to consider both sides)

12a **TASK** Write an essay on the topic below.

The advantages and disadvantages of buying the latest technology.

Write 200–250 words.

b Swap your essay with another student. Read your partner's work and tell them two things you like about the essay and one thing they could improve (e.g. the ideas, the organization, spelling, use of tenses).

Starbucks

1 Work with a partner. Follow the instructions below.

> When you see the Starbucks logo, what do you think of?
> In one minute, list as many words and phrases as you can
> which you connect with this famous coffeehouse. Use the
> photos to help you.

2 Compare your list with another pair. Did you write any of
the same words or phrases?

3 ▶ Watch the video. Use the words below to give a brief
description of Starbucks to your partner.

> the criticism   a global brand   the logo   the philosophy
> a slogan

4 ▶ Watch again. Add events to the timeline below to show
the history of Starbucks through the decades.

1970   1980   1990   2000   2010   now

5a **TASK** Work in pairs. Student A, work with another Student
A and read the situation.

> You both own a busy family-run café in a medium-sized
> English town. Starbucks would like to open a new coffeehouse
> next door to your café. List 4–5 reasons why you are strongly
> against the idea.

Student B, work with another Student B and read the
situation.

> You both work for Starbucks in the business development
> department. You are planning to open a new coffeehouse in a
> medium-sized English town. List 4–5 reasons why you think a
> new coffeehouse in this town would be very successful, and
> why it would benefit the town.

b Pair A, work with Pair B. Present your ideas to each other.

c As a class, list the main points from both sides. Decide
which side has the winning argument.

Review

1a Read the text and underline six words related to advertising.

A new way of seeing the world

Recently Google announced plans for a new advertising system using Google Glass. It is a kind of wearable computer which looks a little like a pair of glasses which allows you to google information on the go. Currently companies pay Google every time someone clicks their advert to find out more about their product. But in the future, it seems that just looking may be enough. Imagine you are walking down the street and glance at a billboard by the side of the road, or a poster at a bus stop. Google Glass will be able to tell exactly what your eyes are looking at and for how long. And there's more. It will probably also be able to measure how you feel about the brand. If you find something surprising, funny or interesting, the pupils in the middle of your eye get bigger, and Google will be able to track that as well. So they will be able to tell how effective the slogan or image actually is.

b Work with a partner and discuss the questions.

1 Do you or would you use Google Glass? Why/Why not?
2 How do you feel about advertisers knowing which ads you are looking at, or how you feel about them?
3 In what other ways do you think advertising might change in the future?

2a **12.8**))) Listen to some different opinions about adverts and match them to an adjective with a similar meaning.

> amusing clever confusing memorable persuasive
> unpleasant

b **12.8**))) Work with a partner. Listen to the opinions again and report what each person said, using reported speech.

1 He said _____   4 _____
2 _____   5 _____
3 _____   6 _____

3a **12.9**))) Listen to six questions and write them down.

1 _____   4 _____
2 _____   5 _____
3 _____   6 _____

b Work with a partner. Ask and answer the questions in exercise **3a**.

c Now write a short report of the questions you asked and the answers you received, using reported speech.

4a Match the two halves to make six phrases.

1 bring people round   a objections
2 get   b people over
3 get people to   c your own way
4 overcome   d other person's point of view
5 understand the   e see things your way
6 win   f to your way of thinking

b Tell a partner about when and how you did one of these things.

5a Complete the phrases with the correct preposition.

1 I don't usually worry _____ ...
2 I find it hard to concentrate _____ work when ...
3 I'm pretty good _____ ...
4 I don't believe _____ ...
5 I often listen _____ ...
6 I'm very interested _____ ...

b Complete the sentences in exercise **5a** in ways that are true for you. Tell a partner about your sentences.

6a Complete the conversation.

A Apparently the government is going to ban advertising for junk food during children's TV programmes. What's your opinion on that?
B I'm not sure ¹_____ that. I can't ²_____ thinking the government shouldn't be trying to control things like that.
A Well, I agree up to a ³_____, but children are so easily influenced, aren't they?
C My thoughts ⁴_____. Adults can decide for themselves, but it's different for children.
B I suppose ⁵_____.

b Work with a partner or in a small group. What do you think about banning the advertising of junk food during children's TV programmes?

Communication

a   Work with a partner. Look at the following structure for telling an anecdote. Identify the different sections in the two stories in exercises **2** on page 16 and **7** on page 17.

1 Announcing a story is about to start	That reminds me of … I remember the time when … I'll never forget that day …
2 Giving background information	The sun was setting … I was driving home when …
3 Main events	I had just opened the door when she suddenly appeared. I recognized him straightaway.
4 Conclusion	He was never seen again.
5 Final comment	I've never forgotten what happened. I can laugh about it now, but it was really scary at the time.

b   What verb forms are typically used in each section?

c   Work with a partner.

1   Use the notes and the structure for telling a story to plan a 'lucky escape' story.

2   Tell the story to a partner, with lots of detail. Try to use the correct narrative forms and some of the verbs in exercises **5** and **6** on page 17.

Surfer in Australia attacked by shark

Heard big bang

Flew through air

Discovered big bite mark in surfboard

Surfer unharmed

Work with a partner or in small groups. Choose one of the stories about a famous hoax, either the Cottingley fairies or the Near miss.

1   Match the sentences to the right picture.

2   Put the story in the right order.

3   Rewrite the story together, using appropriate verb forms and time linkers.

The Cottingley fairies

Near miss

1
- If people jumped in the air at 9.47 a.m., they would float.
- On 1 April 1976, the well-known astronomer Patrick Moore announced on the BBC that at 9.47 a.m. something strange was going to happen.
- One woman claimed that she and her friends all floated around the room.
- He reported that Pluto was going to pass behind the planet Jupiter.
- This would affect gravity on Earth.
- When it was 9.47 a.m., hundreds of people rang the BBC to tell their stories.

2
- Two years later, Polly was at a meeting and mentioned the photos.
- Perhaps surprisingly, Sir Arthur Conan Doyle, author of the Sherlock Holmes books, became interested and supported the story.
- Elsie's father saw the photos and decided they were fake, but her mother, Polly, believed the girls.
- In 1981 the cousins were interviewed for a magazine and finally confessed to the hoax.
- For decades many people believed the photos were real.
- In 1917 two young cousins, Elsie and Francis, living in Bradford, England, claimed to have taken photos of fairies.

2.4 Student A
Exercise 6

a Use the following notes to prepare to tell the story of another coincidence.
- American novelist Anne Parrish/on holiday in Paris.
- Look/bookstores with her husband
- Find/favourite childhood book/Jack Frost and other stories
- Anne/show book to husband
- Husband/open book/see Anne's name and address.
- Book/used to belong to Anne.

b Tell your partner your story, using the phrases in the Language for speaking box on page 22 to engage your listener. When listening to your partner, use the phrases to make sure you sound interested.

3.2 Student A
Exercise 8

a Work with a partner. Read the paragraph about a *Faking It* episode. Use the notes and your own ideas to write a similar paragraph about a similar type of programme.

| Home | Categories | A-Z | Programmes |

Faking It ▶

Chess player to football manager

FIRST BROADCAST: 26 September
DURATION: 49:03

Former professional chess player trades his chessboard for the football pitch as he attempts to fake it as a football manager in a month.

Past – make decisions, have time to think, spend hours playing chess

Now – manage people, lead, work under pressure, take responsibility, learn about football

b Now tell your partner about the person you wrote about.

6.2 Student A — Exercise 9

a Read about Manoon, a rice farmer from Thailand. Answer the questions.

1 What problems did the weather cause him?

2 What was his solution?

When it didn't rain, rice farmer, Manoon, had trouble getting enough water for his crops. There was a well nearby, but he couldn't get the water from the well to his fields. This meant that his crops wouldn't grow properly, even if his whole family spent time carrying water from the well to the fields. So he decided to build a windmill pump to get water from the well. He made the sails from old advertising boards. Now he has enough water for his crops, even if the rain comes late.

b Work with a partner who has read the other story. Take it in turns to interview each other. Answer as Manoon. Try to use present perfect simple and continuous in your answers.

- What has been happening to the weather in your area?
- What effect has this had on your crops?
- How has this affected your life and your family?
- What have you done to improve the situation?

7.1 Student A — Exercise 8

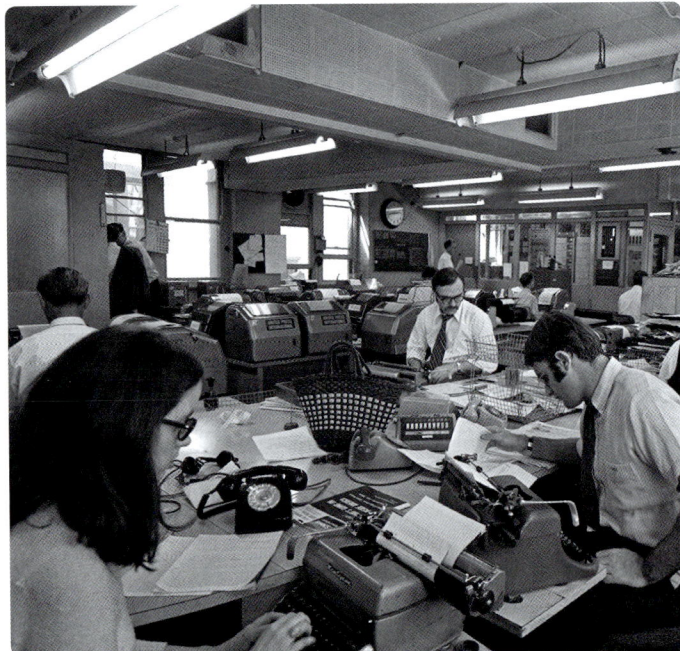

Prepare to talk for a minute about how offices have changed since the 1970s, using *used to* and *would*. Look at the photo and think about computers, paper, women at work, working hours and conditions, attitudes to work, etc.

7.2 Students A & B — Exercise 8

Choose one of the following activities.

a Decide on one of the people you chose in exercise **5** on page 69. Write 7–8 interesting interview questions you would like to ask them. You can make them direct or indirect. Then interview each other, taking the roles of the people you chose.

OR

b Write 7–8 interesting interview questions you would like to ask your partner. You can make them direct or indirect. Interview each other, then share some of the interesting things you found out with another pair, or with the whole class.

8.1 All students
Exercise 8

Work in groups of four. Imagine each student in each group is one of the government ministers.

1 Decide which government minister you are.
2 You have to decide together how much money to spend on healthcare, childcare, cultural activities and transport. Read your role card and prepare some good arguments. Use conditional sentences.

If we spend more money on a healthy eating campaign, more people will have a balanced diet and we will spend less on hospitals.

3 Discuss the budget together and decide what percentage of the budget should be spent on each area.
4 Explain your decisions to the class or another group. Give reasons.

Student A: Healthcare
You think a large percentage of the budget should be spent on healthcare. Think about people's need for physical activity, a balanced diet, access to good doctors and hospitals.

Student B: Childcare
You think a large percentage of the budget should be spent on childcare. Think about how childcare helps parents to work – which is good for individuals and the economy. Also think about how it can help children make a good start at school.

Student C: Cultural activities
You think a large percentage of the budget should be spent on cultural activities. Think about how it will improve people's social life and happiness, and how it will help them become better educated.

Student D: Transport
You think a large percentage of the budget should be spent on transport, including bicycles which are free for anyone to use. Think about how fewer private cars will reduce pollution, how cycling makes people healthier, and how cheaper public transport will help poverty.

8.2 All students
Exercise 6

a Work in small groups. Look at the three scenarios and discuss what you would do. Decide together on the best thing to do.

1 You have just bought a coffee on the way to work. You have left the café and you are in a hurry. You realize that the server has given you too much change.

2 In a car park, you accidently dent someone's car with your car door. Do you leave a note with your name and address?

3 You are working in a shop or café. A customer insists he has given you a £20 note, but you have only given him change for a £10 note.

b Write three similar scenarios for another group to discuss. Have some ideas about your own answers. Give these situations to a different group.

c Now discuss another group's three scenarios. Compare your ideas with those of the group that wrote the scenarios.

Work with a partner.

a   Look at the two pairs of sketches and describe the differences between them, using comparatives, superlatives and modifiers.

b   Can you tell which one was created from the woman's own description?

Work with a partner.

a   Take turns to describe your picture without showing it to your partner. Give as much detail as possible, using the vocabulary in exercise **2** on page 88, and making some deductions and speculations.

b   Listen to the description of a picture Student B gives, and try to imagine what you hear. Then look at the original picturc. How close was the description Student B gave?

9.4 Exercise 9
Students A & B

a Work with a partner. Choose a situation and a problem, then decide on …

1 background details of the story. What's the problem? Why does it cause you difficulties?

2 what you are going to say to the person you have a complaint about.

3 the result you want from your complaint.

> **work**
>
> A colleague arrives late for meetings all the time; he/she is usually very disorganized; your boss is getting angry when things don't happen as they should.

> **study**
>
> You are giving a presentation to your class; your partner didn't do much work for the project, but then says you did it together.

> **social**
>
> You are getting a bit fed up because when you and your friends go out, one of the group never pays for anything.

b Work with a different pair. Make your complaint to one of the pair. Use the phrases in the Language for speaking box on page 93 to make your complaint, explain the problem and try to agree on a solution.

c Go back to your original partner in exercise **9a**. Compare the results from your complaints. Who got the best result?

10.1 Exercise 10
Student A

a Read about the Kickstarter project called Everpurse and answer the following questions.

1 What was the service or product? What was special about it?

2 What evidence was there that the business is worth investing in?

3 What investment was needed? How many investors did Everpurse get?

b Join two or three students who have read the same text. Prepare a short presentation about your project, using the questions in exercise **5** on page 97 to guide you.

c Present your project to the rest of the class.

Discover   Start   Search   Sign up   Log in

Everpurse: easily charge your phone all day

Have you ever noticed that smartphones always run out of energy just when they're needed most? Smartphones are used for so many things nowadays – emailing, checking social media, finding out how to get somewhere – that most people get to the end of the day and need to charge their phones. With Everpurse, you can charge your phone while it's in your bag. It's the first bag with a built-in charger. Everpurse can be carried inside a bigger bag, or by itself. When you get home, you just drop it onto the white charging mat and leave it overnight. It's that simple.

Everpurse needed $100,000 to make Everpurses for as many people as possible. If you invested $99 or more, you were one of the first people to receive one. More than 1,400 investors pledged almost $240,000.

11.1 Student A Exercise 9

a Work with a partner. Read about another outlaw and answer the questions.

1 What crime(s) did the outlaw commit?

2 What were the reasons they became well known or popular?

MARIA BONITA

Maria Bonita (Beautiful Maria) was the girlfriend of the Brazilian outlaw leader, Virgulino Ferreira da Silva, known as Lampiao. Virgulino's father was killed by the police in 1919, which led Lampiao to fight back against the police, with a large group of other outlaws. Maria Bonita joined Lampiao in 1930, when she was in her early twenties. She and the other female outlaws in the group dressed like the men and were, apparently, just as tough. She took part in all the battles with the police, though people say that she sometimes stopped Lampiao from being cruel to his victims.

b Write three third conditional sentences about what happened to the outlaw.

c Tell your partner about what you found out and use the sentences you wrote.

d Decide together which outlaw you admire most/least. Explain why.

11.4 All students Exercise 4

1 A three-bedroomed apartment in the town centre. Near the children's school. No garden. Two bathrooms and a large kitchen/dining room. Expensive but just affordable.

2 A three-bedroomed house in the suburbs. A thirty-minute bus ride to school or fifteen-minute drive. Large garden. One bathroom. Reasonably priced.

3 A four-bedroomed house in a noisy and slightly dangerous area of town. Within walking distance to school. Two bathrooms and a small garden. Large kitchen/dining room.

2.1 Student B Exercise 9

a Work with a partner. Look at the following structure for telling a story. Identify the different sections in the two stories in exercise 2 on page 16 and exercise 7 on page 17.

1 Announcing a story is about to start	That reminds me of … I remember the time when … I'll never forget that day …
2 Giving background information	The sun was setting … I was driving home when …
3 Main events	I had just opened the door when she suddenly appeared. I recognized him straightaway.
4 Conclusion	He was never seen again.
5 Final comment	I've never forgotten what happened. I can laugh about it now, but it was really scary at the time.

b What verb forms are typically used in each section?

c Work with a partner.

a Use the notes and the structure for telling a story to plan a 'lucky escape' story.

b Tell the story to a partner, with lots of detail. Try to use the correct narrative forms and some of the verbs in exercises 5 and 6 on page 17.

Lorry driver escapes from crash unhurt

In Russia on motorway

Second truck crashed into him

Driver came through front windscreen

Walked away unhurt

2.4 Student B Exercise 6

a Use the following notes to prepare to tell the story of another coincidence.

- TV reporter Irv Kupcinet/in London on a work trip
- In hotel room/find items belonging to his friend/Harry Hannin.
- Meanwhile/Hannin in Paris.
- In his hotel room/find tie with Kupcinet's name on it.

b Tell your partner your story, using the phrases in the Language for speaking box on page 22 to engage your listener. When listening to your partner, use the phrases to make sure you sound interested.

3.2 Student B Exercise 8

a Work with a partner. Read the paragraph about a Faking It episode. Use the notes and your own ideas to write a similar paragraph about a similar type of programme.

| Home | Categories | A-Z | Programmes |

Faking It ▶

Newsagent to showbiz reporter

FIRST BROADCAST: 08 November
DURATION: 49:28

Twenty-nine-year-old working mum swaps bringing up children and working in the family newsagent's shop to become a TV showbusiness reporter.

Past – get up early, deal with customers, work hard, look after family

Now – be confident, work in a team, persuade people to talk to you, look good

b Tell your partner about the person you wrote about.

6.2 Student B Exercise 9

a Read about Thongsa, a rice farmer from Thailand. Answer the questions.

1 What problems did the weather cause her?
2 What was her solution?

Thongsa Juansang was a rice farmer. Growing rice needs a lot of water, and when the rain didn't come, her crop died. So she has introduced new crops, growing food that needs less water. Instead of growing rice, she's changed to growing fruit and vegetables, and she can now feed her family. She also has some food left over which she can sell at markets in order to buy rice.

b Work with a partner who has read the other story. Take it in turns to interview each other. Answer as Thonga. Try to use present perfect simple and continuous in your answers.

- What has been happening to the weather in your area?
- What effect has this had on your crops?
- How has this affected your life and your family?
- What have you done to improve the situation?

7.1 Student B
Exercise 10

Prepare to talk for a minute about homeworking using *used to* and *would*. Look at the photo and think about how people working from home can communicate with the office and customers nowadays, and how attitudes have changed over the past decades.

9.2 Student B
Exercise 10

Work with a partner.

a Listen to the description and try to imagine what you hear. Then look at the original picture. How close was the description Student A gave?

b Describe your picture without showing it to your partner. Give as much detail as possible, using the vocabulary, and making some deductions and speculations.

10.1 Student B
Exercise 10

a Read about the Kickstarter project called Good & Proper Tea and answer the questions.

1 What was the service or product? What was special about it?

2 What evidence was there that the business was worth investing in?

3 What investment was needed? How many investors did The Good & Proper Tea van get?

b Join two or three students who have read the same text. Prepare a short presentation about your project, using the questions in exercise 5 on page 97 to guide you.

c Present your project to the rest of the class. Try to get as many people to back you as possible.

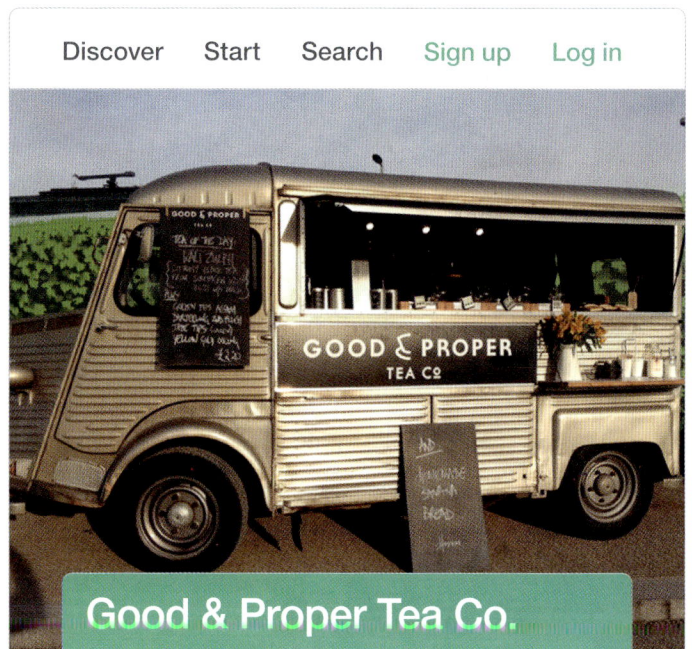

Discover   Start   Search   Sign up   Log in

Good & Proper Tea Co.

If you buy a cup of coffee these days, you can choose what style of coffee you want and even find out how the beans were roasted. But tea drinkers are rarely provided with the same kind of choice and quality. Instead, said Emilie Holmes, 'we are presented with a cup of not-quite-hot-enough water, with a teabag hidden somewhere in the depths'. She explained her idea in a video on Kickstarter, hoping to raise the £10,000 she needed to convert her van into a mobile tea stall. The money was raised in just one week. In fact, she raised £14,682 from 372 backers. It was a busy week. Every time some money was pledged, Emily received an email and she replied in person to every single investor. Her business is now well established, providing customers with an excellent cup of tea.

11.1 Student B Exercise 9

a Work with a partner. Read about another outlaw and answer the questions.

1 What crime(s) did the outlaw commit?
2 What were the reasons they became well known or popular?

TWM SION CATI

Twm Sion Cati was born in Wales in 1530 and became famous for his clever ways of stealing goods and money. For example, one story tells how a farmer came looking for Twm because he had stolen his cow. He arrived at Twm's house and asked a man nearby if this was Twm's house. The man said it was, and offered to hold the farmer's horse while the farmer went inside. As soon as the farmer went in, Twm (who was the man outside) jumped on the horse and went to the farmer's house. He then told the farmer's wife that her husband was in trouble and needed money straightaway. She believed him because he was riding the farmer's horse. Twm then escaped to London having stolen both the horse and the money.

b Write three third conditional sentences about what happened to the outlaw.

c Tell your partner about what you found out and use the sentences you wrote.

d Decide together which outlaw you admire most/least. Explain why.

12.2 Author's solution Exercise 4

Clearly option 1 is helpful, but you have little or no chance of making a sale.

Option 2 is a much better answer, but you're still guessing.

Option 3 is clearly the best. People like people who respect their opinions, and you have the best chance of matching his need to something you do have in the shop.

Grammar reference

1.1 Present simple, present continuous and present perfect simple

GR1.1a 🔊

1 Everyone **needs** friends. Real friends are important.
2 I **see** my old school friends every few months. We generally **have** dinner together.
3 He **doesn't like** all his Facebook friends.
4 **Do** you **talk** to all your friends regularly?

- We use the present simple to talk about:
  a things that are always or generally true.
  b things that happen regularly or repeatedly.

Remember the 's' for the third person singular (*like → like***s**).
Sometimes the spelling changes (*watch → watch***es**, *try → tri***es**).
We use *do/does* to form the present simple negative and questions.

GR1.1b 🔊

1 Please be quiet. I**'m watching** TV.
2 We**'re learning** about the history of music at school.
3 The Earth's temperature **is increasing**.

- We use the present continuous to talk about:
  a things that are happening at the time when we speak.
  b things that are happening around the time when we speak.
  c things that are changing.

We form the present continuous with *be* + *-ing* form.
Be careful with the spelling of *-ing* forms (*begin → begi***nn***ing*, *mak***e** → *making*).

GR1.1c 🔊

1 I**'ve lived** here all my life.
2 **Have** you ever **been** to Brazil?
3 **A** Is Marco here?   **B** No, he**'s** already **left**.

- We use the present perfect simple to talk about things up to now, our experience (our lives until now).
  things that have already or just happened.

We form the present perfect with *have* + past participle.
The past participle for regular verbs is the same as the past simple form (*live → lived*, *work → worked*), but some verbs are irregular (e.g. *know → knew → **known**, eat → ate → **eaten***).
See the Irregular verbs list on page 166.

---

1 Choose the correct options to complete the text about Facebook.

> There **1** *are* / *are being* over one billion Facebook users worldwide. And this number **2** *increases* / *is increasing* all the time. It is clear that Facebook **3** *changes* / *has changed* the way we **4** *look* / *have looked* at friendship. The word 'friend' **5** *becomes* / *has become* a verb, and 'friends' now **6** *include* / *have included* people we only **7** *know* / *are knowing* online and who we **8** *are never meeting* / *have never met*. One positive side to Facebook is that friends who **9** *lose* / *have lost* contact, often many years ago, **10** *are now able* / *have now been able* to get in touch again. 'More and more people **11** *connect* / *are connecting* with old friends via Facebook,' says a spokesperson for the website. 'And Facebook also **12** *means* / *has meant* that friends never **13** *need* / *have needed* to lose touch; people can stay friends for life.'

2 Complete the conversations with the present simple, present continuous or present perfect form of the verbs in brackets.

1 **A** Where _do you work_ ?
   B Well, normally I _____ in Berlin, but I _____ in Stuttgart at the moment. (work)
2 **A** _____ you _____ Jake?
   B Yes, we _____ each other for a few years. (know)
3 **A** _____ you _____ in London?
   B Yes, I do. Actually, I _____ there all my life. (live)
4 **A** Jameela's busy at the moment. She _____ a piano lesson.
   B Oh yes, of course. She _____ one every Wednesday. (have)
5 **A** _____ you _____ Andy yet?
   B I _____ him right now, actually. (email)
6 **A** How many Facebook friends _____ you _____?
   B Not many. I think I _____ about fifty or sixty. (have got)
7 **A** I _____ for my phone.
   B _____ you _____ in the kitchen? I think I saw it in there a few minutes ago. (look)
8 **A** You _____ Karen quite often, don't you?
   B Usually, yes. But I _____ her for a few weeks now. (see/not see)
9 **A** I _____ a great book at the moment – *Tribal Life* by Bruce James. _____ you _____ it?
   B No, but I _____ another one of his books. (read)

1.2 State verbs

> **GR1.2)))**
>
> 1 I **think** it's a great idea.
> 2 Do you **want** some coffee?
> 3 Who **does** this bag **belong to**?
> 4 The soup **tastes** delicious.

Most verbs express actions, and we can use them in simple tenses (e.g. *I use the internet all the time*) and continuous tenses (e.g. *I'm using the internet at the moment*).

Some verbs usually express states, such as thoughts, feelings, possession and things we experience. We most often use these verbs in simple tenses, even if we mean 'just now'.

Common state verbs include verbs for:

- how we think
  think, know, believe, agree, prefer, understand, mean, imagine, realize, remember, forget, recognize
  *Do you **believe** me?   I don't **agree**.*

- what we feel ·
  like, dislike, hate, love, want, feel (have an opinion), seem, appear, look, sound, need
  *How **do** you **feel** about the news?*

- what we possess
  have (got), belong, own, include
  *Do you **have** any money on you?*

- what we experience
  be, see, hear, look, smell, taste, seem
  *The flowers **smell** really nice.*

> Note that we can sometimes use some state verbs, particularly verbs that express how we feel, in continuous tenses when we want to emphasize that the feeling or attitude is temporary.
> *I'm **feeling** tired.*
>
> They can also be used in informal speech as a modern idiom.
> *I'm **loving** this pizza.*
>
> Some verbs are also used in the present simple and present continuous with different meaning.
> *I **have** a headache.* (illness)
> *I'm **having** lunch.* (action)
> *I **think** it's a great idea.* (opinion)
> *I'm **thinking of** getting a new phone.* (consider)
> *I **wasn't thinking about** what I was doing.*

1 Choose the correct options.

1 A Shall we take a break from bargain hunting and have a coffee?
  B That (sounds) / is sounding like a good idea.

2 A *Do you have / Are you having* a few minutes to help me?
  B Yeah, sure.

3 A I *don't understand / 'm not understanding*. What *do you mean / are you meaning* by 'trending'?
  B Oh, don't worry. I'll explain later.

4 A I *try / 'm trying* to download some photos. Can you help me?
  B Sure. Do you know why it *isn't working / doesn't work*?
  A I *think / 'm thinking* the file's too big. It *looks / is looking* like that's what *causes / 's causing* the problem.

2 Complete 1–11 using the correct form of the verbs in brackets.

1 This is Carlos. He _comes_ (come) from Spain.
2 Peter is on his way. He _____ (come) by bus.
3 I _____ (see) your point, but I _____ (not/agree) with you.
4 You're quiet? What _____ (you/think) about?
5 What _____ (you/think) of the new James Bond film?
6 I _____ (imagine) you're very tired after your journey.
7 Jamal isn't here. He _____ (have) his lunch.
8 _____ (anybody/have) any questions?
9 The umbrella's not mine. I think it _____ (belong) to Annette.
10 Yuck! This soup _____ (taste) horrible. And it _____ (look) disgusting, too.
11 I _____ (look) for my keys. _____ (you/know) where they are?

3 Complete the article about online shopping with the correct form of the verbs in the box.

> agree   be (x2)   include   increase   know   make   prefer   ~~seem~~

> Online shopping [1] _seems_ to become more popular every year. According to a recent report, over half of US consumers with internet access now [2] _____ shopping online, and just 1% say they have never shopped online. Experts [3] _____ that consumers spend on average around $100 per online order. The most common types of goods bought online [4] _____ electronics, books, clothing and household goods.
>
> There are a number of reasons why online shopping [5] _____. Cheaper prices and a large variety of products [6] _____ the main reasons, according to the survey. The ability to compare products and read reviews [7] _____ another reason. Most online shoppers say that they often [8] _____ a decision to buy a product when five or more reviewers [9] _____ that the product is good value for money.

2.1 Narrative forms

GR2.1)))

1 I **arrived** at midnight.

2 He **didn't realize** how dangerous it was.

3 **Did** they **arrive** in time to save him?

4 We **were walking** along the beach, when we saw someone waving at us.

5 We **had been** on the train for about an hour, when it suddenly stopped.

A narrative is a description of a past event. We generally use three main verb forms in a narrative.

• We use the past simple for the main events in a story.

Most past simple verbs are formed by adding *-ed* to the infinitive (*want → wanted*). However, many common verbs are irregular (*make → made*).
*We **wanted** to leave early the next morning so we went to bed at 10 p.m.*
*Something **made** a loud noise.*

Negatives and questions are formed with *did* and the infinitive without *to*.
*We **didn't recognize** the stranger who was standing outside the house.*
*What **did** he **want** with us?*

• We use the past continuous for background events. We also use it for longer actions interrupted by a shorter event.
*She **was sitting** in the corner of the room.*
*They **were having** dinner when the phone rang.*

We form the past continuous with *was/were* and the *-ing* form.
*I **was feeling** nervous.*

• We use the past perfect for events that happened *before* one of the main events or that happened before the time of the story.
*I'**d stayed** in the same hotel twice before.*

We form the past perfect with *had* and the past participle.
I'd taken the train to London an hour before.

---

1 Put the underlined events in the order they happened or started.

1 (a) Jenny and I started our website in order to market (b) the clothes we had designed while (c) we were studying together at university.

[c] [ ] [ ]

2 (a) I decided that I wanted to become a pilot while (b) I was sitting in the garden one day and (c) saw several aeroplanes crossing the sky.

[ ] [ ] [ ]

3 (a) I first noticed the man while (b) I was travelling by train from Paris to Milan. (c) He was reading a book by my favourite author. (d) I'd been watching him for about an hour when (e) he spoke to me.

[ ] [ ] [ ] [ ] [ ]

2 Choose the correct options to complete narrative extracts 1–8.

1 We *were walking* / *'d walked* about two kilometres before we *realized* / *were realizing* that we *left* / *'d left* the map behind.

2 We *went* / *'d gone* for a walk when we *were finishing* / *'d finish*ed the meal.

3 The sun *was shining* / *had shone*. People *sat* / *were sitting* on the grass in the park.

4 I *was* / *'d been* exhausted after a long day at work, so I *went* / *was going* to bed early.

5 Sam *didn't recognize* / *wasn't recognizing* me, even though we *were meeting* / *'d met* a few weeks before.

6 I *locked* / *was locking* the office door after I*'d checked* / *was checking* that everyone *went* / *had gone* home.

7 My parents first *met* / *had met* when they *were* / *had been* at university together. They *were both studying* / *had both studied* history.

3 Complete the text with the correct form of the verbs in brackets.

I'll always remember the time we were struck by lightning when we ¹ *were flying* (fly) back from Singapore. We ² _____ (be) in the air for about an hour, and the plane ³ _____ (move) up and down quite a lot. Outside you ⁴ _____ (can) see flashes of lightning across the sky and dark clouds. Suddenly there ⁵ _____ (be) a loud bang. At first a few people ⁶ _____ (start) screaming. But then the whole plane ⁷ _____ (become) strangely quiet. The pilot ⁸ _____ (speak) to tell us we were about to land, which was a great relief to everyone. But just as we ⁹ _____ (land), the whole plane ¹⁰ _____ (start) shaking violently again. In the end we ¹¹ _____ (land) safely. When we ¹² _____ (get off) the plane, we ¹³ _____ (see) that there ¹⁴ _____ (be) an enormous hole in the tail fin.

2.2 Time linkers

GR2.2))

1 They realized the story was false **as soon as** they found the boy.

2 I saw Paul **while** I was walking to work.

3 They were working for the same newspaper **when** they met each other.

4 We were waiting for Julia outside the cinema. **Meanwhile**, she was waiting for us at the bus station.

5 **By the time** I realized, it was too late.

6 There were many scientific discoveries **during** the 18th century.

7 We lived in Warsaw **until** I was twelve.

We use time linkers to show how the timing of events in a story relate to one another. Some of the more common time linkers include:

as soon as/while

• **as soon as** (one thing happens immediately after another)
*I called her **as soon as** I saw the story on TV.*

• **while** (something happens while something else is in progress, or two things are in progress at the same time)
*I met Ursula **while** we were skiing.*
*Could you wait here **while** I find the manager?*

We can often use *when* in a similar way to *while*.
*They lost their passports **when** they were waiting in the airport.*

We use *when* (not *while*) to introduce an action that 'interrupts' an action already in progress.
*I was cycling to the shops **when** I fell of my bike.*

meanwhile/by the time (that)

• **meanwhile** (two things happen at the same time, but in two different sentences)
*Tom and I drove to the city centre. **Meanwhile**, Anna drove to our house. As a result, we missed each other.*

• **by the time (that)** (something is completed before the main event happens)
By the time we got there, Mark had left.

during/until

• **during** (something happens at a point within a certain period of time)
*I fell asleep **during** the film.*

• **until** (something happens up to a particular point in time)
*I was awake **until** about four in the morning.*

---

1 Choose the correct options.

1 I found some old newspapers (while)/ meanwhile / during I was tidying up the attic recently. They all had stories about famous hoaxes in them.

2 I almost fell asleep *during / while / meanwhile* the meeting this afternoon. It was so boring.

3 The US belonged to the UK *by the time / until / while* 1776, when it gained independence.

4 I was looking for my phone. *By the time / Meanwhile / As soon as*, my wife had found it and was looking for me.

5 We called the police *by the time / meanwhile / as soon as* we discovered the house had been robbed.

6 We spent ages looking for the shop and *as soon as / while / by the time* we found it, it was closed.

7 There were many important discoveries *during / while / by the time* the 1800s.

8 Luke and I met *during / meanwhile / while* we were working together in a café.

2 Complete the text with the time linkers in the box.

| as soon as   by the time   during (x2)   meanwhile   while |

Although it's very popular nowadays, ¹*during* the 1950s pasta was an unusual meal in the UK. Not many British people had been to Italy, and very few people knew how pasta was made. So, for April Fool's Day in 1957, the BBC news programme *Panorama* decided to make a story about spaghetti growing on trees. ²_____ the programme, viewers were told that the harvest that year was particularly good because of the weather. And ³_____ the presenter explained how spaghetti was grown, there was a film of workers in the background cutting the spaghetti from the trees. ⁴_____ the programme had been broadcast, the BBC started receiving phone calls from people who wanted to grow their own spaghetti. ⁵_____, the BBC continued the joke by instructing anyone who wanted to grow a spaghetti tree to 'place a piece of spaghetti in a tin of tomato sauce.' ⁶_____ the story was revealed to be an April Fool's Day joke, hundreds of people had contacted the BBC.

3 Complete the sentences with the correct time linker.

1 I woke up three times *during* the night.

2 Sorry I didn't speak to you earlier, but I phoned you _____ I could.

3 We were very late and the party had finished _____ we got there.

4 We walked all day _____ it got dark, and then we went home.

5 We just couldn't find the plane tickets. We looked everywhere. _____, the taxi to the airport was waiting for us outside.

3.1 Ability

GR3.1))

1 The researchers discovered that some children **are able to wait** for fifteen minutes to eat the marshmallow.

2 I **could ride** a bike by the age of six.

3 She **was able to speak** French in the restaurant because she'd studied it for years at school.

4 We **weren't able to get** tickets for the concert. They'd sold out.

5 **Will** you **be able to finish** the report on time?

6 They **didn't succeed in winning** the prize.

7 I'm sure you**'ll manage to** resist the temptation.

Can, could and be able to

We generally express ability using *can, could* and *be able to.*

Present

- We use *can/can't* + infinitive or *am/are/is(n't) able to* + infinitive to express general ability.
  *I **can wait** for things I want.   I **can't resist** chocolate.
  Some people **are able to resist** most temptations.*

Past

- We use *could/couldn't* + infinitive or *was(n't)/were(n't) able to* + infinitive to express general ability in the past.
  *I **could run** 100 metres in twelve seconds when I was younger.
  I **was able to swim** when I was about four.*

- We use *was(n't)/were(n't) able to* to talk about ability on a specific past occasion.
  *We **were able to ski** even though there wasn't much snow.
  Alex **wasn't able to help** me.*

Future

- We can use *will/won't be able to* + infinitive to express general ability and ability on a particular future occasion.
  *I**'ll be able to help** you in a few minutes.
  I **won't be able to give** you a lift tomorrow, I'm afraid.*

Manage to and succeed in

- We can use *manage to* + infinitive or *succeed in* + *-ing* when there is some difficulty in achieving the task.

Present

*She usually **manages to achieve** her ambitions.
She usually **succeeds in getting** what she wants.*

Past

*I didn't **manage to speak** to the boss.
He **succeeded in getting** a place at university.*

Future

*I'm sure you**'ll manage to get** a ticket.
I'm sure she**'ll succeed in persuading** you.*

---

1 Choose the correct options.

1 My parents say I *can* / *could* walk when I was about nine months old.

2 The DVD player wasn't working, but in the end we *could* / *managed to* fix it.

3 Do you think you'll *manage to* / *succeed in* finish your assignment by the weekend?

4 How many languages *do you manage* / *can* you speak?

5 I *couldn't* / *won't be able to* meet you tomorrow, I'm afraid.

6 Some people *can* / *succeed in* learn languages easily.

7 Did they *manage to* / *succeed in* reaching the top of the mountain?

8 Anyone *is able* / *can* to learn a musical instrument if they try.

2 Complete the sentences with the verbs in the box.

can   can't   could   couldn't   manage (x2)

1 A Are you able to resist temptation?
  B No, I never *manage* to stick to a diet!

2 When I was a child, I _____ never resist eating all the biscuits as soon as we got them.

3 A We _____ decide where to go on holiday. Can you recommend anywhere?
  B Yes, I _____. I went to Rome last year, it was beautiful.

4 A I usually _____ to resist temptation. Apart from video games, that is. Last night I just _____ stop playing a game. I stayed awake until well after midnight trying to finish it!

3 Complete the text with the words and phrases in the box.

is able   was able   can   could   managed to   ~~succeeded in~~

Daniel Tammet has an amazing ability for mathematical calculations, memorizing facts and language learning. He holds the European record for memorizing pi (π). In 2004, he [1] *succeeded in* writing the numbers in pi up to 22,514 in just over five hours, without error. He has entered the World Memory Championships twice, but he has never [2] _____ win. Tammet [3] _____ also speak eleven languages. Because of his incredible memory, he [4] _____ to learn new languages very quickly. To prove this for a television documentary, he was challenged to learn Icelandic in one week. Seven days later he appeared on television in Iceland and he [5] _____ to have a conversation in Icelandic. Tammet's abilities first became clear as a child. He [6] _____ read and do complex mathematics at a very early age and he says he has always loved counting.

3.2 Obligation, permission and possibility

must, have to, need to

GR3.2a))

1 Raúl is unhappy because he **has to work** very long hours.
2 **Must** you **leave** so soon?
3 I **don't have to work** on Saturdays or Sundays.
4 In my last job we **had to ask** permission if we wanted to work at home.
5 Before I became the team leader, I didn't **need to set** other people's goals.

Present

- We use *must* and *have to* to say that something is necessary or an obligation. We often use *must* to talk about the feelings and wishes of the speaker and *have to* to talk about obligations that come from someone or somewhere else.
  *You **must work** hard to be successful in life.*
  *In my job, I **have to manage** a team of twenty people.*
  *Do you **have to wear** a suit and tie at work?*

- We use *mustn't* to say it is necessary or an obligation NOT to do something.
  *You **mustn't be** late for work.*

- We use *don't have to* and *don't need to* to say something isn't necessary or an obligation.
  *We **don't have to wear** a suit and tie at work.*
  *We **don't need to be** at work until nine o'clock.*

Past

- We use *had to* to say something was necessary or an obligation in the past.
  *We **had to wear** a uniform when I was at school.*

- We use *didn't have to* and *didn't need to* to say something wasn't necessary or an obligation in the past.
  *We **didn't have to wear** a uniform when I was at school.*

can, could

GR3.2b))

1 In my present job I **can set** my own goals.
2 Employees **can't make** personal calls while at work.
3 At school we **could choose** which foreign languages we studied. I chose German and Spanish.
4 Women **couldn't study** to become doctors in the UK until 1876.

Present

- We use *can* to say something is allowed or is OK and *can't* to say something isn't allowed or isn't OK.

Past

- We use *could* to say something was allowed or was OK in the past and *couldn't* to say something wasn't allowed or wasn't OK.

1 Complete the sentences with the words in brackets.

1 I _can_ usually choose my own hours at work, but I _have to_ work at least forty hours a week. (have to, can)
2 You _____ use your mobile. It _____ be switched off. (must, can't)
3 You _____ pay in pounds. You _____ also pay in euros or dollars if you prefer. (can, don't have to)
4 The main requirements in my job are that you _____ be good at making decisions and you _____ be a good leader. (must, have to)
5 Sorry I'm late home. I _____ stay at work and finish a report. I _____ leave until I'd sent it to my boss. (couldn't, had to)
6 You _____ have a university degree to work here, but you _____ have a lot of relevant experience. (don't need to, must)
7 We _____ study at least one foreign language at school, but we _____ study English. We _____ choose from English, Russian, German and Chinese. (could, didn't have to, had to)

2 Choose the correct options to complete in the job description.

A PA (personal assistant) gives support to managers or directors. To be a PA, you **1** *mustn't /* (*don't have to*) have any specific qualifications, but you **2** *can / must* have the right skills and personal qualities. PAs **3** *must / can* have good knowledge of the organization in which they work, and they **4** *can / have to* know who the important people in the company are. Managers often communicate with customers and collegues through their PA, so they **5** *must / can* be good communicators. In the past, PAs **6** *must / had to* have good typing skills, but today this isn't as important.

3 Rewrite the sentences using the verbs in the box. Begin with the words given.

can   could   have to   don't have to   had to   must
mustn't

1 It's the law to wear a seatbelt in a car in the UK.
   You have to wear a seatbelt in a car in the UK.
2 It's not necessary to book a ticket for the concert.
   You _____.
3 In all jobs, being reliable is extremely important.
   In all jobs, you _____.
4 I missed the bus, so my only option was to get a taxi.
   I missed the bus, so _____.
5 It's not OK to take photos in the museum.
   You _____.
6 Sorry I'm late. I wasn't allowed to leave work early.
   Sorry I'm late. I _____.

4.1 will/be going to for predictions and decisions

Predictions

> **GR4.1a** 🔊
> 1 Climate change **will cause** huge problems.
> 2 Soon there **won't be** space in cities for all the people who want to live in them.
> 3 Look at the traffic! It**'s going to take** a long time to get there.

We can use both *will* + infinitive without *to* and *be going to* to talk about predictions for the future.

• We generally use *will/won't* when we want to say what we believe or think about the future. This is often when the prediction is based on personal feeling or opinion.
*You***'ll have** *a great time on holiday.*
You **won't pass** *the test. You haven't studied enough.*

> We often say *I don't think … will* for a negative prediction NOT ~~I think … won't~~.
> *I* **don't think** *people* **will** *live in floating cities in the future.*

• We generally use *be going to* when there is some evidence in the present to support the prediction or an action is starting or clearly on the way.
*There isn't a cloud in sight. It***'s going to be** *a lovely day.*
*I***'m not going to finish** *this report today. I haven't got enough time.*

Decisions

> **GR4.1b** 🔊
> 1 What a lovely day! I**'ll have** a swim later.
> 2 We**'re going to have** a few days in Paris next month.

We can use both *will* and *be going to* to talk about decisions.

• We generally use *will* when we make a decision at the moment of speaking.
*I'm exhausted. I think I***'ll go** *to bed*
I'm full. I **won't have** *dessert.*

> We often use *will* in cafés and restaurants when we are ordering drinks and meals.
> *I***'ll have** *a pizza and a green salad, please.*

• We generally use *be going to* when we have already made a decision. This is often when we are talking about plans and intentions.
*My brother***'s going to visit** *us in the summer.*
*I***'m not going to take** *my driving test until next year.*

---

1 Complete the conversation with *will* or *be going to* and the verbs in brackets.

1 **A** Do you know any good travel websites?
  B Just a minute. I'*ll show* (show) you some.
2 **A** You're going to the US this summer, aren't you?
  B Yes. We _____ (hire) a car and drive round California.
  A Lucky you! You _____ (have) a great time.
3 **A** Look at those clouds! I think it _____ (rain).
  B Yes. I think you're right. I _____ (get) my umbrella.
4 **A** Are you free on Wednesday?
  B Sorry. I'm _____ (see) my grandparents in London. How about the week after?
  A OK, I _____ (call) you early next week.
5 **A** Here's the book I was talking about. I think you _____ (enjoy) it.
  B Thanks. I _____ (give) it back to you next week, if that's OK.
6 **A** I think you've missed the last bus.
  B I _____ (get) a taxi, then. How much do you think it _____ (cost)?
  A I'm really not sure, but I guess it _____ (not be) more than ten euros.
7 **A** Where are you going?
  B To the shops. I _____ (get) something to eat.
  A While you're there, we need some milk.
  B OK, I _____ (get) some milk as well.
8 **A** Oh no! The plane's delayed by four hours. It _____ (be) a long day!
  B Oh well. In that case, I _____ (do) some work while we're waiting.

2 Complete the text with *will* or *be going to* and the verbs in the box. In some cases, both forms are possible.

be   do (x2)   go   have   not have   help   ~~rent~~

> Hi Jules,
>
> You asked about our summer holiday plans. Well, we [1]'*re going to rent* a boat in Turkey and spend two weeks sailing along the coast. I've never sailed before, so I think I [2]_____ a couple of lessons before we go. They have courses near here at the sailing club in Portsmouth, so I [3]_____ there. But the other people we are going with are all experienced sailors, so I'm pretty sure we [4]_____ any problems. I guess they [5]_____ most of the sailing and I [6]_____ a little when needed. Anyway, I'm really looking forward to it – I think it [7]_____ fun. What about your holidays? [8]_____ you _____ anything this summer?
>
> See you soon,
> Denise

4.2 *will/may/might* to talk about probability

GR4.2))

1 People **will continue** to move from the countryside to the city, so in the next fifty years there **may be** many cities with populations of more than ten million.

2 Owning their own home **might become** impossible for most people.

3 Temperatures **are likely to rise** over the next century, and this **may possibly have** an impact on weather.

Modal verbs

- We can use the modal verbs *will*, *might* and *may* to talk about how sure we are about something. *Will* generally expresses more certainty. *Might* and *may* have very similar meanings.

  *The population **will continue** to rise, and it **may reach** ten billion by the end of the century.*
  *Walking in the countryside **might have** a number of health benefits.*

Adverbs and adjectives

- We can use the adverbs *probably*, *possibly* and *definitely* with *will/might/may* to give more information about how sure we are. However, this is most common with *will*. The adverb generally goes after *will* and before *won't/will not*.

  *They **probably won't arrive** before midnight.*
  *We'**ll possibly go** for a walk later this afternoon.*
  *I'**ll definitely see** you sometime next week.*
  *Deforestation **may possibly continue** for another 100 years.*

- We can also use the adjectives *likely* and *unlikely*. We use the infinitive with *to* after *(un)likely*.

  *Urban living **is likely to continue** increasing.*
  *They'**re unlikely to arrive** before midnight.*

Here is a summary of degree of certainty:

Certain	Possible	Unlikely	Impossible
will (definitely)	*will probably* *will possibly* *may* *is likely to* *might*	*is unlikely to* *probably won't*	*(definitely)* *won't* .

---

1 Put the words in the right order to make sentences.

1 likely / is / global warming / for several hundred years / continue / to .
   Global warming is likely to continue for several hundred years.

2 might / with animals / in the future / communicate / be able to / humans .
   In the future, _____.

3 will / the planet Mars / one day / humans / colonize / possibly .
   One day, _____.

4 spend / computer screens / will / we / probably / in front of / more and more time .
   We _____.

5 to / are / with aliens / unlikely / we / ever make contact .
   We _____.

6 will / in the future / inside buildings / humans / most of their time / spend .
   In the future, _____.

7 to be / ever live / won't / humans / two hundred years old /probably .
   Humans _____.

3 Rewrite the sentences using the words in brackets.

1 I don't think they will arrive in time. (unlikely)
   They are unlikely to arrive in time.

2 Cities of the future are likely to have more green spaces. (probably)
   _____

3 It's probable that unemployment will continue rising. (likely)
   _____

4 The ice caps are unlikely to melt completely. (probably)
   _____

5 It will possibly rain later. (may)
   _____

6 I don't think I'll finish my report before Friday. (unlikely)
   _____

7 If United Nations forecasts are correct, by 2050 the global population might be between nine and ten billion. (likely)
   _____

5.1 *-ing* form and infinitive with *to*

GR5.1))
1 They **finished filming** in January.
2 I **don't feel like going** out tonight.
3 I **ran** five kilometres **without stopping**.
4 We **agreed to meet** at 6.30.
5 Carole **chose not to go** to the party as she had a job interview the next day.

When a verb which isn't a modal verb is followed by another verb, the second verb is either in the *-ing* form (e.g. *I like **watching** TV*) or the infinitive with *to* (e.g. *I want **to watch** TV*).

-ing form

- We use the *-ing* form after the following verbs: *admit, avoid, consider, deny, finish, help, imagine, miss, practise, recommend, suggest.*
  David **recommended** see**ing** the latest Bond film.

- We also use the *-ing* form after verbs expressing likes and dislikes, such as: *can't stand, enjoy, feel like, hate, like, love, (don't) mind, prefer.*
  I really **enjoy** go**ing** to the cinema.

- We also use the *-ing* form after prepositions such as: *about, after, at, before, by, in, of, on, to, without.*
  Justyna insisted **on** pay**ing** for the meal.
  We're thinking **of** go**ing** to the cinema tonight.

Infinitive with *to*

- We use the *infinitive with to* after the following verbs: *afford, agree, aim, appear, arrange, attempt, choose, decide, demand, expect, fail, forget, hope, intend, manage, need, offer, plan, start, seem, tend, want, would like.*
  Amir **offered to give** us a lift to the conference.
  I **promise** not **to tell** anyone.

> Note that to form the negative, we put *not* between the two verbs.
> I decided **not** to say anything.

-ing form or infinitive with *to*

- The following verbs can be followed by both the *-ing* form and the infinitive with *to*, with little or no change in meaning: *attempt, begin, can't stand, continue, hate, like, love, prefer, start, stop.*
  We **continued** work**ing**.   We **continued to work**.
- We don't usually use two *-ing* forms next to each other.
  I'm starting to feel better.   NOT ~~I'm starting feeling better.~~

Spelling rules

Note that we sometimes make changes to the spelling of a word when we add *-ing*. For example, we may drop the final *-e*, change *-ie* to *-y* and sometimes we double the final letter.
make → making   lie → lying   begin → beginning

---

1 Make sentences using the prompts.

1 I / want / see / the new James Bond film .
   I want to see the new James Bond film.
2 my friend / insisted on / pay / for the cinema tickets / last night .

   _____
3 Adam / hopes / get / to London / at about two-thirty .

   _____
4 I / didn't expect / enjoy / the film / so much .

   _____
5 let's / watch / a film at home tonight / instead of / go / to the cinema .

   _____
6 we / have / great memories of / live / in Austria .

   _____
7 did you / manage / finish / write / your report ?

   _____

2 Complete the conversations with the verbs in the box. Use the *-ing* form or infinitive with *to*.

| act   become   come   do (x2)   go (x3)   take |

1 A We're thinking of *going* to see a film. Would you like _____ with us?
   B Great, thanks. I'd do anything to avoid _____ this work!
2 A I'm thinking of _____ acting lessons.
   B You're going to start _____! I never knew you were interested in _____ an actor.
3 A Are you interested in _____ to that film exhibition? I'm going with Francesca tomorrow.
   B I'd really like to, but I've promised _____ out for the day with my mum. I think she's planning _____ all sorts of things. I can't let her down.

3 Rewrite the sentences to make one sentence with similar meaning. Use the words in brackets.

1 He was late. He didn't apologize. (for)
   He didn't apologize for being late.
2 Francesco left. He didn't say goodbye. (without)

   _____
3 Carmen plays the guitar. She's very good. (at)

   _____
4 Ingrid wants a new a car. She can't afford it. (buy)

   _____
5 I take my driving test tomorrow. I'm nervous. (about)

   _____
6 I didn't book the tickets. I didn't remember. (forgot)

   _____

5.2 Time expressions with present perfect and past simple

GR5.2)))

1 Marco**'s eaten** three bars of chocolate **so far today**. He'll be sick.

2 **A** When **did** you **arrive**?
   B We**'ve been** here **since** Tuesday.

3 **A** **Have** you **ever been** to Egypt?
   B Yes, I **went** about four years ago. It was fantastic.

We can think of time periods as being unfinished (e.g. *this week, recently*) or finished (e.g. *yesterday, in 2014*).

Unfinished time periods

We generally use the present perfect for unfinished time periods.
*I***'ve sent** lots of emails **today**.
Have you **seen** Okito **recently**?
*We***'ve been** here **since nine o'clock**.

Expressions of unfinished time that we often use with the present perfect include:
recently, already, just, never, ever, yet, so far, for (ten minutes, three weeks, etc.), since (2013, ten o'clock, etc.), over the past (two days, six months, etc.), since

Finished time periods

We generally use the past simple for finished time periods.
I **got** my first games system **when I was ten**.
I finally **went** to bed **at midnight**.
Did you **see** Jamal **last week**?

Expressions of finished time that we often use with the past simple include:
yesterday, last (night, weekend, year, etc.), in (January, 2012, the summer, etc.), on (Wednesday, my birthday, etc.), (a few days, three years, etc.) ago, when (I was at university, etc.), recently

Unfinished or finished time periods

Note that some time expressions can refer to both unfinished or finished time, depending on the context.
Have you **seen** Luciana **this morning**?
(it is still this morning)

Did you **see** Luciana **this morning**?
(the morning is finished)

*I***'ve bought** a few new video games **recently**.
(focus on time until now)

I **bought** a new phone **recently**.
(focus on the time of buying the phone)

---

1 Choose the correct options to complete the conversations.

1 **A** When *did you move*/ *have you moved* to Frankfurt?
   B *Six months ago / Since six months.*

2 **A** I've been very busy *yesterday / recently*.
   B Me too. I started a new project at work *since last week / last week*.

3 **A** I haven't had lunch *yet / already*. I'm starving.
   B Oh, I *went / 've been* to that new café for lunch. It *was / has been* really good. You should go there.
   A Yes, I went there *a few days ago / already*. I agree – it's good.

4 **A** I *didn't see / haven't seen* Junko's new apartment yet. *Did / Have* you?
   B Yes, I *saw / 've seen* it a few days ago.

5 **A** We *lived / 've lived* in Venice for seven years. From 2005 to 2012.
   B I *never went / 've never been* to Venice. I hear it's beautiful.

6 **A** Have you finished your exams *on Friday / yet*?
   B No, I've done two of them *last week / so far*.

2 Complete the text with the correct form of the verbs in brackets. Use the past simple or present perfect.

Video games [1] *have existed* (exist) for over sixty years. The first video games [2]_____ (appear) in the 1940s, when academics [3]_____ (begin) designing simple games, simulations, and artificial intelligence programs as part of their computer science research. However, video gaming [4]_____ (not/reach) mainstream popularity until the 1970s and 1980s, when arcade games, gaming consoles and home video games [5]_____ (become) available to the general public. Before the development of realistic computer graphics that [6]_____ (occur) recently, the games that [7]_____ (drive) the industry in the 1970s [8]_____ (be) basic games like *Ping Pong* and, a little later, *Space Invaders*. Since then, video gaming [9]_____ (become) a popular form of entertainment and a part of modern culture in most parts of the world, and today almost everyone under the age of fifty [10]_____ (play) a video game at least once.

6.1 Defining and non-defining relative clauses

There are two types of relative clause: **defining** and **non-defining**. In both types, the relative clause gives information about a person or thing. The relative clause comes after this person or thing has been mentioned and starts with a relative pronoun (*who*, *which*, *that* or *whose*).

Defining relative clauses

GR6.1a))

1 I want to meet the person **who** found my handbag. I'd like to thank them.
2 What's it called? It's the gadget **that** is used for opening cans.
3 Look, isn't that the woman **whose** handbag you found?
4 The man I met yesterday told me how to get to the concert hall.

- We use defining relative clauses to identify who or what we are talking about. We can use:
  a **who** – for people
  b **which** or **that** – for things
  c **whose** – for possessions and family relationships
- We can leave out the relative pronoun if it is the object of the verb. *The first car **(that) I had** was a ten-year-old Volkswagen.*

Non-defining relative clauses

GR6.1b))

1 Nicolaus Otto, **who** died in 1891, was the inventor of the petrol engine.
2 The Bugatti Veyron, **which** is one of the most expensive cars ever, was first produced in 2005.
3 It was invented by Richard Beeston, **whose** father and grandfather were also inventors.

- We use non-defining relative clauses to give extra information. Non-defining relative clauses do not identify who or what we are talking about. It is usually already clear who or what we are talking about. We can use:
  a **who** – for people
  b **which** – for things
  c **whose** – for possessions and family relationships
- We do not usually use *that* in a non-defining relative clause. ~~The Bugatti Veron, that is one of the most expensive cars ever, was first produced in 2005.~~

Note that we use commas around a non-defining relative clause. Or before the relative clause if the clause is at the end of the sentence.

We can also use the relative adverbs *when* and *where* in relative clauses.
*Is this the hotel **where** we stayed last year?*
*Rush hour is the time of day **when** people drive to or from work.*

---

1 Complete the text with appropriate relative pronouns.

An automobile, or motor car, is defined as a vehicle with wheels **1** *that* has its own engine or motor and **2**_____ is used mainly for transporting passengers. The invention of the automobile goes back to 1886, when the German inventor Karl Benz, **3**_____ is generally regarded as the inventor of the first modern automobile, introduced the Motorwagen to the public. Motorized vehicles soon started to replace animal-powered carriages, **4**_____ had for centuries been the main form of long-distance transport. The first affordable automobile **5**_____ sold in large numbers was the Model T, **6**_____ was introduced in the USA in 1908 and **7**_____ was produced by Henry Ford, **8**_____ Ford Motor Company had been founded in 1903. Many other automobile manufacturers soon began producing vehicles in the same way as Ford, and by the 1930s there were hundreds of different automobile companies around the world.

2 Which of the relative clauses in the text in exercise **1** are defining and which are non-defining?

Defining: [1] [ ] [ ]
Non-defining: [ ] [ ] [ ] [ ] [ ]

3 Rewrite the two sentences as one sentence using a relative clause.
1 I've just read a book. I think you'll like it.
   I've just read a book which/that I think you'll like.
2 They're building a new factory. It will have no humans and only use robots.
   _____
3 What's the name of the scientist? The one who discovered the X-ray?
   _____
4 You can book an $80,000 balloon flight. It goes into space.
   _____
5 I've got a new mobile phone. It's got a 128GB memory.
   _____
6 I met someone yesterday. He knows you.
   _____
7 Is that the girl? We went to her party last weekend.
   _____
8 The program isn't working properly. You loaded it yesterday.
   _____

4 In which sentences in exercise **3** do we not need to use a relative pronoun?

[ ] [ ]

6.2 Present perfect simple and continuous

GR6.2 〉〉

1 The bus **hasn't come**. I**'ve been waiting** here for ages.
2 Stefan **hasn't been working** for this company for very long.
3 How long has Caroline **been teaching** at that school?
4 **Have** you **had** breakfast yet?

- We use the present perfect continuous (*have/has + been + -ing*) for unfinished actions which started in the past and continue up to now. It often answers the question *How long …?*
  It**'s been raining** all afternoon.
  Scientists **have been investigating** climate change.
  How long **have** you **been working** here?

- We use the present perfect simple (*have/has + past participle*) for completed actions which happened at some point before now and still have an influence on the present. We don't know or aren't focusing on exactly when the action happened.
  It**'s stopped** raining.
  Have you **seen** the weather forecast?

- There is sometimes little difference between the present perfect simple and continuous. The choice is often about how we see the action.
  The weather**'s been improving**. (We see this as something in process.)
  The weather**'s improved**. (We see this as a finished state.)

We generally don't use the present perfect continuous with state verbs such as *be, have,* and *know.*
~~We've been knowing about global warming for over 100 years.~~

1 Choose the correct options to complete the sentences.

1 It*'s rained* / *'s been raining* since I got up.
2 Have they *finished* / *been finishing* the experiment yet?
3 Have you ever *seen* / *been seeing* a tropical storm?
4 We*'ve tried* / *'ve been trying* to find a solution to the problem for weeks.
5 Good news! Sam's *found* / *been finding* a solution to the problem!
6 Sorry I'm late. How long have you *waited* / *been waiting*?
7 Scientists have *tried* / *been trying* to find a solution to climate change for decades.
8 It hasn't *snowed* / *been snowing* for ages.

2 Complete the sentences with the verbs in the box. In each pair, use the present perfect simple in one sentence and the present perfect continuous in the other.

fix   increase   investigate   snow   speak

1 The average global temperature *has been increasing* for at least 100 years.
  The average global temperature _____ every year for at least the last hundred years.
2 It _____ a couple of times so far this year.
  It _____ since this morning.
3 Researchers _____ the phenomenon for a number of years.
  Researchers _____ the phenomenon on several different occasions.
4 He _____ the washing machine all morning.
  _____ he _____ the washing machine yet?
5 I _____ _____ French for ages — not since I left school.
  We _____ French for the past hour or so.

3 Complete the text about Arctic sea ice with the verbs in brackets in the most probable tense: present perfect simple or continuous.

Scientists ¹ *have been studying* (study) changes in Arctic sea ice for around 100 years. As measuring devices and satellite analysis ² _____ (become) more accurate, it ³ _____ (become) clear that the amount of Arctic sea ice ⁴ _____ (decrease) steadily for several decades. In fact, the Arctic ⁵ _____ (lose) 75% of its summer sea ice volume over the past three decades. This is mainly due to global warming. However, the amount of ice lost each year ⁶ _____ (depend) not only on global warming, but on a number of other things such as local weather patterns. In some years these things ⁷ _____ (cause) more or less sea ice to melt. However, even though in one year there may ⁸ _____ (be) more sea ice than in the previous year, the trend is that Arctic summer sea ice ⁹ _____ (disappear) at a rate of around 2.5% per year.

7.1 *Used to* and *would* for past habits and states

We can use both *used to* and *would* to talk about situations that existed in the past but do not exist now.

GR7.1 》

1 I **used to like** listening to my grandmother reading me stories when I was a child.

2 **Did** people ever **use to think** the Earth was flat?

3 Leo **didn't use to like** cooking, but now he's really into it.

4 In the past children **would learn** everything by heart, but nowadays people rarely do that.

5 My grandfather **would tell** me the names of all the trees and flowers when we went for walks in the countryside.

Used to

We use *used to* + infinitive for both past habits and past states: things that were true but are not now.
We **used to live** in Madrid. (but now we don't)
There **used to be** an office block here. (but now there isn't)
I **used to drive** to work. (but now I don't)
I **didn't use to like** my job. (but now I do)

Note that there is no final '*d*' in negatives and questions.
I didn't **use** to drink tea.   Did you **use** to work for the UN?
NOT I *didn't used to drink tea.*   Did you used to work for the UN?

Remember that *used to* is only for past habits. For present habits we use the present simple.
Oliver **cycles** to work.

Would

We can also use *would* + infinitive to talk about past habits and typical past behaviour.
I **would** usually **drive** to work.
I **would** usually **get** to work at about 7.30 and I generally **wouldn't leave** until after six o'clock.

However, we do not use *would* to talk about past states, only actions and typical behaviour.
We would live in London.
There would be an office block here.

---

1 If possible, rewrite these sentences with *would*. If this is not possible, put a cross.

1 I used to hate job interviews, but now I like them. ✗

2 My grandfather used to wear a suit and tie every day.
   My grandfather would wear a suit and tie every day.

3 The boss used to arrange a party every year.
   _____

4 I used to like visiting my mum's office.
   _____

5 Anna used to sit at her desk and write all day.
   _____

6 In the past, a lot of people used to do the same job all their life.
   _____

7 People used to be more formal at work.
   _____

8 I used to see the park from my window, but now I'm in a different office.
   _____

2 Complete the text using *would* or *used to* and the verbs in brackets. Use *would* where possible; only *used to* if *would* is not possible.

Office life – it's so much better now

It's a good time be an office worker.

Technology has made the biggest change. Communication is easier and work is more interesting. In the past, people [1] *would spend* (spend) ages at work doing boring jobs; these days computers can do these same jobs quickly and easily. Attitudes to men and women at work have changed a lot over the last fifty years, too. 'In the 1960s, my boss was a woman who was the same age as me,' says David Harper. 'When we went to meetings together, people [2] _____ (be) surprised that she was the boss, not me. I [3] _____ (tell) people how good she was.'

Offices have become more pleasant places to work in. Companies [4] _____ (have) strict rules about clothes and behaviour in the office, but these days things are more easy-going. Relationships are more equal now. People [5] _____ (speak) to their manager very formally, but now conversations can be more relaxed; and offices themselves are nicer places to work in. 'The office where I worked was small and it [6] _____ (smell) really bad,' one of my friends told me. 'Every morning I [7] _____ (open) the window as wide as I could, but it never helped!'

Perhaps not everything is better, though. These days, people often stay at work late and take their work home with them. It wasn't always like that. 'When I worked in an office, we [8] _____ (start) work at 9.00 and we [9] _____ (go) home at 5.30,' said my uncle. 'The manager would [10] _____ (tell) us all to go home at 5.30 and we didn't think about work until the next day!'

7.2 Questions

GR7.2)))

1 What **does she** think of your new car?

2 Where **did he** use to work?

3 Who **opened** the box of chocolates?

4 Can you tell me **where the railway station is**?

5 Would you mind telling me **if the hotel dining room is open** after 10 p.m.?

Object and subject questions

There are two basic types of question: object questions and subject questions.

- In object questions, the question word is the object. We normally put an auxiliary verb before the subject. For the present and past simple tenses, we use the auxiliary *do/does/did*.

  Who **do you** most admire? – I most admire my parents.
  What **did she** buy? – She bought some books.

- In subject questions, the question word is the subject. We don't use *do/does/did*.

  Who **inspired** you to become an athlete? – My sports teacher inspired me to become an athlete.
  Who **invented** the computer? – Several people helped invent it.
  NOT ~~Who did invent the computer?~~

Indirect questions

We use indirect questions to make questions softer or more polite.

- Indirect questions begin with a question phrase (e.g. *Could you tell me…; I'd like to know …; Would you mind telling me …*).

- After the question phrase, the word order is like a statement rather than a question: we do not invert the auxiliary verb and the subject and we do not use *do/does/did*.
  Could you tell me **who you most** admire?
  NOT ~~Could you tell me who do you most admire?~~
  I'd like to know **why you decided** to leave university.

- We use *if* (in place of a question word) for indirect questions where the answer is *yes* or *no*.
  I'd like to know **if** you have any further ambitions.

1 Read the text and then write the questions. There are both object and subject questions.

> William James Sidis was a child genius, born in the US in 1898. After his death, his sister claimed he was the most intelligent person who ever lived, with an IQ between 250 and 300. He could read at eighteen months. He had written four books and was fluent in eight languages before he was ten. Harvard University accepted him as a student when he was just twelve. After he graduated at sixteen, he joined Rice University as a maths professor. However, the students at Rice didn't take him seriously because of his age and he left after only eight months. He went back to Harvard to study law. While he was studying law he became concerned with social issues, and in 1919 he was arrested while he was taking part in a political parade that turned violent. He spent eighteen months in jail. After his release from prison, he hid away and started writing books on subjects such as the universe, American history and psychology. William James Sidis died in 1944.

1 *When was James Sidis born?* In 1898.
2 _____? His sister.
3 _____? Between 250 and 300.
4 _____? Harvard University.
5 _____? He was arrested.
6 _____? Eighteen months.
7 _____? In 1944.

2 Urban free-climber Claudette Dubois has climbed up the outside of some of the tallest structures in the world, including the Eiffel Tower, Sydney Opera House and the Petronas Twin Towers. Rewrite the direct questions in this interview with Claudette as indirect questions. Begin with the words given.

1 How do you feel before you do a big climb?
   Could you *tell me how you feel before you do a big climb?*

2 When were you last truly scared?
   Would you _____

3 What did you want to be when you were growing up?
   I'd like _____

4 Is there anyone famous you'd like to meet?
   Could _____

5 How would you like to be remembered?
   I'd like _____

3 Match the questions in exercise **2** to answers a–e.

a Just before my last climb. I always get scared.

b I feel very nervous, but quite calm at the same time.

c As a funny and disciplined person who liked to challenge herself.

d Yes, Phillipe Petit. I've always admired him.

e A Hollywood stuntwoman.

8.1 Sentences with *if* – real conditionals

GR8.1 》

1 If people **enjoy** their job, they **are** happier in general.
2 If you **eat** a balanced diet, you**'ll feel** healthier.
3 If we **have** a positive attitude, we **won't feel** down when things don't work the way we want them to.
4 If people **don't have** any friends, they **can** become very lonely.
5 They'll arrive at 7 p.m. **unless** the plane is delayed.
6 My brother is quite shy; he won't speak in public **unless** he has to.

In sentences with *if*, we usually talk about situations and events which are uncertain. *If*-sentences usually have two clauses: the *if*-clause and the result clause. They are also called conditional sentences.

- When things can possibly happen, so *can* be real, we use the same tenses with if as with other conjunctions. So, we can use the present tense to refer to the present.

  If + present simple, → present simple
  *If people **enjoy** their job, they **are** happier in general.*
  *If people **work** a thirty-seven hour week, they **have** quite a lot of leisure time.*

- When we talk about specific situations in the future and their possible results, we normally use a present tense in the if-clause to talk about the future.

  If + present simple, → will
  *If you **eat** a balanced diet, you**'ll feel** healthier.*
  *You**'ll be** happier as a country if you **pay** higher taxes.*

The conditional clause and the result clause can usually go in either order. When the conditional clause is first, it is followed by a comma. When the result clause comes first, there is no comma.
If I see Jim, I'll give him your message.
I'll give Jim your message if I see him.

- We can use modal verbs, particularly *can*, *may* and *might* in either clause.

  *If a country **has** quite high taxes, it **can provide** free healthcare to everyone.*
  *If you **can cycle** for thirty minutes a day, it **may add** one to two years to your life.*
  *If Aydin **can't get** a job, he **might do** some voluntary work.*

- *Unless* usually means *if … not* or *except if*.

  *We'll go for a walk later **unless** it **rains**.* = *We'll go for a walk later **if** it **doesn't rain**.*
  *Money doesn't make you happy **unless** everyone **has** enough.* = *Money doesn't make you happy **except if** everyone **has** enough.*

1 Complete the conversations with the best form of the words in brackets.

1 A What do you think is the secret to happiness?
   B Well, lots of things. But I believe that if people _have_ (have) a positive attitude towards everything, they generally _____ (feel) much happier.
   A And what's the secret to a long life?
   B As well as a positive attitude, if you _____ (exercise) regularly and _____ (be) careful about what you eat, you _____ (probably/live) longer.
2 A I think I need to improve my diet.
   B Well, for a start, if you _____ (eat) at least five portions of fruit and vegetables each day, you _____ (start) to feel much healthier. And if you _____ (drink) lots of water all the time and less coffee and tea, you _____ (have) more energy.
3 A If you _____ (not/hurry), we _____ (not/get) to the cinema in time.
   B OK, I'm getting ready as fast as I can. What _____ (happen) if we _____ (get) there after the film starts? Can we still get in?
   A Well, yes. But what _____ (be) the point of going in if we _____ (miss) the beginning of the film?

2 Match 1–5 to a–e to make sentences about happiness.

1 Happiness is like a cloud. If you stare at it long enough,
   _b_
2 If you spend your life waiting for the perfect moment,
   ___
3 You will never be happy ___
4 Unless you love what you are doing, ___

a you probably won't be successful.
b it goes away.
c it may never arrive.
d if you spend all your time thinking about what happiness means.

3 Complete the second sentences so they mean the same as the first sentences.

1 You won't succeed if you don't make an effort.
   You won't succeed unless _you make an effort_.
2 We'll get the bus unless we see a taxi first.
   _____ if _____.
3 If you spend it wisely, money can buy happiness.
   Unless _____.
4 We should arrive at about 3.30 unless we get delayed.
   If _____.
5 You're not allowed in the club except if you're dressed smartly.
   _____ unless _____.

8.2 Sentences with *if* – unreal conditionals

GR8.2))

1 If I **had** more time, I**'d take up** marathon running.
2 They **wouldn't drive** to work if there **was** a good bus or train service.
3 If we **lived** in London, we **could go** to the theatre more often.
4 If he **were** Prime Minister, he **would change** the law.

If sentences usually have two clauses: the conditional clause (often using *if*) and the result clause.

Unreal conditionals express something that is imaginary or hypothetical.

• To talk about an unreal situation and its result in the present or future, we use *If* + past tense + *would* (or *'d*) + infinitive without *to*. The *if* clause talks about an unreal situation and the *would* clause talks about the hypothetical or imaginary result. This is sometimes called a second conditional.

If + **past tense,**   **would** (**'d**) + infinitive without *to*
*If someone **needed** my help, I**'d do** my best to help them.*
*If we **were** all less selfish, the world **would be** a better place.*
*I**'d be** much happier if the weather **wasn't** so bad.*

The conditional clause and the result clause can usually go in either order. When the conditional clause is first, it is followed by a comma. When the result clause comes first, there is no comma.
If I were you, I'd be more careful.
I'd be more careful if I were you.

• When we are not sure about the result, we can use the modal verbs *might* and *could* instead of *would*.
*If I were braver, I **might do** a bungee jump for charity.*
*If you didn't know what you were doing, you **could hurt** yourself.*

• We also use *could* to mean *would be able to*.
*If it wasn't raining, we **could go** for a walk.*

• In the conditional clause, with *I/he/she/it*, we often use *were* instead of *was*. This is considered a more formal style.
Formal: *If I **were** younger, I'd take up snowboarding.*
Informal: *If Katia **was** here, she'd be able to help us.*

We also use *were* in certain fixed phrases:
If I were you, I'd do more exercise.

1 Complete the dilemma questions with the correct form of the words in brackets.
1 If you *found* (find) a wallet in the street, what *would you do* (you/do)?
2 If you _____ (see) someone being attacked in the street, _____ (you/try) to help them?
3 If you _____ (do) something heroic, _____ (you/want) to be in the newspaper or on the TV news?
4 If you _____ (see) someone stealing from a shop, _____ (you/tell) a shop assistant?
5 What _____ (you/do) if you _____ (know) a new work colleague had lied on his or her CV?
6 If you _____ (find) a winning lottery ticket, _____ (you/claim) the money?
7 Where _____ (you/live) if you _____ (can/live) anywhere in the world?
8 If you _____ (can/have) any job, what _____ (it/be)?

2 James wants some things in his life to be different. Write conditional sentences using the prompts.
1 be richer → buy a bigger house
   If I were richer, I'd buy a bigger house.
2 be younger → play more sports
   _____
3 have more time → read a lot more
   _____
4 not rain so much → be much happier
   _____
5 my job be not so boring → enjoy life more
   _____
6 not eat so much junk food → be much healthier
   _____

3 Rewrite sentences 1–6 in the conditional.
1 I can't buy a new mobile because I haven't got enough money.
   If I had more money, I could buy a new mobile.
2 I can't go out tonight because I have to write a report.
   _____
3 Julia isn't here so we can't ask her to help.
   _____
4 We can't go skiing because there isn't enough snow.
   _____
5 I can't help you because I'm so busy.
   _____
6 I work such long hours and I'm always tired.
   _____

9.1 Comparatives and superlatives

GR9.1 》)

1 George is a banker. He's **richer** than most of his friends.
2 Living in London is **more expensive** than living in Birmingham.
3 Some people think that watching golf is **less exciting** than watching football.
4 It's **the best** meal I've ever had.
5 The Pyramids in Egypt are some of **the oldest** buildings in the world.

Comparatives

We use the comparative form of adjectives to compare people and things with each other.

*I'm **taller** than my sisters.*   *Paris is **more beautiful** than London.*

• For one-syllable adjectives, we add -er (or -r for adjectives that end in -e). For multi-syllable adjectives, we use *more*.
  short → shorter   ancient → more ancient
• For some two-syllable adjectives, we can either add -er or use *more*. However, for two-syllable adjectives ending in -y, we generally change the -y to i and add -er
  gentle → gentler/more gentle   happy → happier
• To make a negative comparison, we use *less* + adjective
  *Beards are **less popular** than they used to be.*
• We use *than* when we make a direct comparison between two things.
  *Pedro's hair is darker **than** Lucca's.*
• To say something is the same, we use *as … as*. To say something is not the same, we use *not as/so … as*.
  *I'm **as tall as** my dad.   Paola's hair is **not as long as** before.*

We use modifiers when we want to give more detail about the degree of difference between two things.
*I'm **a bit taller** than my brother.*
*Anna is **much older** than Andre.*

• To make the difference between the things being compared stronger:
  a lot   far   much   so much   very much
• To make the difference between the things being compared smaller:
  a bit   a little   slightly
• To say there is no difference between the things being compared:
  not any   no

Superlatives

We use superlatives to compare people and things with everything in their group.
*Alex is **the tallest** person I know.*
*She's **the most intelligent** person I've ever met.*

For one-syllable and most two-syllable adjectives we use *the* and add -est. For multi-syllable adjectives, we use *the most*.
short → the shortest   beautiful → the most beautiful

---

1 Complete the sentences with the correct comparative form of the adjectives in brackets.

1 Helen is *much shorter* (short) than her younger brother, David.
2 People who live in _____ (warm and dry) climates are often _____ (healthy) than people who live in _____ (cold and damp) climates.
3 It is _____ (easy) and slightly _____ (quick) to cycle to work than to go by bus.
4 The doctor told Steve he was _____ (likely) to get ill because he didn't do much exercise.
5 The cities here are _____ (much/big) than in my country, where the population is _____ (small).
6 You should wear _____ (good) sunglasses than those. Your eyes should be _____ (well/protected) from the sun.

2 Complete the text with the comparative or superlative form of the adjectives in brackets and any other necessary words.

Physical changes in human appearance have occurred ever since we first appeared. However, ¹*more recent* (recent) changes have not been ² _____ (dramatic) they were in the ³ _____ (distant) past. This is because we have become ⁴ _____ (much/good) at adapting the environment to suit us rather than evolving to fit in with the environment.

Some changes have been ⁵ _____ (global) whereas others have been ⁶ _____ (regional) and localized. The ⁷ _____ (important) change affecting us is that the human body has become ⁸ _____ (slightly/small). Humans are not ⁹ _____ (tall or heavy) they used to be.

The ¹⁰ _____ (tall) humans lived around 40,000 years ago, with an average height of 183 cm. This is ¹¹ _____ (much/tall) today's average height of 175 cm.

Perhaps surprisingly, the human brain is also not ¹² _____ (big) as it used to be. In fact, the human brain is now the ¹³ _____ (small) it has been at any time in the past 100,000 years, and is about ¹⁴ _____ (10%/small) when humans first appeared.

9.2 Modals of deduction and speculation

GR9.2 》)

1 The lights are on. Someone **must be** at home.

2 He **can't be** English. Listen to his accent – I think he's South African.

3 It's very cold. It **might snow** soon.

4 Don't you think she looks a bit like Andrea? She **could be** his sister.

When we are making a deduction or speculating (= making a guess, usually based on evidence), we use the modal verbs *must*, *can't*, *might* and *could* to express how sure we are about something.

Must and *can't*

- We use *must* when we are very sure something is true.
  *You've been driving all day. You **must be** tired.*
  *My keys **must be** here somewhere!*

- We use *can't* when we are very sure something is not true.
  *This photo **can't have been taken** in the UK. They're driving on the right.*
  *This **can't be** Satiana's coat. It's too big.*

- We do not use *mustn't* in this way.
  ~~This mustn't be Satiana's coat. It's too big.~~

Might and *could*

- We use *might* or *could* when we are not sure, but we think something is possible. *Might* and *could* have the same meaning.
  *This photo **might/could** be in the UK. They're driving on the left.*
  *This **might/could** be Alex's phone. He's got one like this.*

- We can use *might not*, but we do not use *could not*.
  *This **might not be** Jenny's house. I think hers has a green door.*
  ~~This could not be Jenny's house. I think hers has a green door.~~

We use **look** + adjective – when something **appears to be** …
It **looks** cold.

1 Complete the second sentence using *must*, *can't* or *might/could* so the meaning is the same as the first sentence.

1 Perhaps my keys are in the kitchen.
My keys *might be in the kitchen* .

2 I guess Erika likes black. She always wears black.
Erika _____. She always wears it.

3 Perhaps that apartment over there is Frank's.
That apartment _____.

4 It's possible that this painting is by Rembrandt. It's his style.
This painting _____.

5 It's impossible that this is Ute's house. She said hers has a bright red door.
This _____. Hers has a bright red door.

6 Ten euros for a coffee! Surely there's a mistake.
Ten euros for a coffee! There _____.

7 Ten euros for a coffee! I'm sure that's not right.
Ten euros for a coffee! That _____.

2 As part of a competition, two people are trying to match some photos with the countries: the UK, Australia, the USA and South Africa. Complete the conversations using *must*, *can't* or *might/could*.

A What about this photo? Where do you think this is?

B Well, it ¹_____ be the UK – the weather's too nice, and there are no beaches like that in the UK. But it looks a bit like the UK. It ²_____ be Australia, maybe. Ah, look – I think that's the Australian flag in the background. It ³_____ be Australia.

A OK, and what about this one?

B Well, I'd say this one ⁴_____ be the UK, but I'm not sure.

A Yes, I agree. Look at that cloudy sky. I think you're right. And the number plate looks British. Yes, this one ⁵_____ be of the UK.

B OK, so this next one ⁶_____ be the UK or Australia – we've already got those. So, it ⁷_____ be either the US or South Africa. Which do you think?

A Well, it's difficult to say. It ⁸_____ be either, I suppose. There's nothing obvious. Oh, hang on. I'm not sure, but I think this one ⁹_____ be South Africa.

B What makes you think that?

A Look at the roads in the distance – the cars are driving on the left. I think they drive on the left in South Africa, don't they?

B Yes, I think they do. So it ¹⁰_____ be the US – they drive on the right there.

A OK, so this one ¹¹_____ be South Africa. And that means the last one ¹²_____ be the US.

10.1 Active and passive forms

- We form the passive with the verb *be* + past participle.
  *Thousands of new websites **are set up** every day.*
  *The business **was started** by James Davis in 1997.*
  *Over a million units **have been sold**.*
  *When **was the** business **started**?*
  *Most things **can be bought** online these days.*
  *Smoking is **not allowed** in the restaurant.*

  Note that we form the negative of simple tenses by putting *not* between the auxiliary *be* and the past participle (e.g. *I was **not** asked*). For other tenses, *not* goes between the two auxiliary verbs (e.g. *The office has **not** been cleaned*).

- We use active verbs to describe what someone or something does.
  *Perry Chen, Yancey Strickler and Charles Adler **started** Kickstarter.*

- We use passive verbs to describe what happens to someone or something.

  Often the person or thing that does the action is not known, or is obvious or unimportant.

  *Over two million dollars **was invested** in the business.*
  *The product **is manufactured** in over twenty countries.*

- We use *by* if we want to say who or what does the action.
  *Kickstarter **was started by** Perry Chen, Yancey Strickler and Charles Adler.*

- We often use the passive to continue talking about the same thing or person.
  *Kickstarter is a crowd funding platform. **It was started** in 2009.*

1 Complete the sentences with the passive form of the verbs in the box.

> develop eat make order send ~~start~~ use

1 The first online retail site *was started* in 1994.
2 The internet _____ in the 1960s by the US military.
3 Today, the internet _____ regularly by over a billion people.
4 Billions of internet searches _____ every day.
5 The first mobile phone text message _____ in the late 1990s.
6 About three billion pizzas _____ in America every year, most of these _____ online.

2 Complete the text about online shopping using the correct passive or active form of the verbs in brackets.

> The first version of online shopping [1] *was invented* (invent) in 1979 by UK businessman Michael Aldrich. His system, which [2] _____ (call) VideoTex, [3] _____ (connect) a modified TV to a computer using a phone line. In 1980, he [4] _____ (set up) a system which [5] _____ (allow) customers and suppliers to be connected so that business could [6] _____ (complete) electronically. During the 1980s, he [7] _____ (create) a number of online shopping systems, using Videotex technology. These [8] _____ (use) mainly by large corporations.
>
> Online shopping [9] _____ (not/become) popular until the introduction of the World Wide Web in the early 1990s. In 1994, Pizza Hut was the first business to offer online ordering. Many other commercial websites soon [10] _____ (follow). Amazon and eBay [11] _____ (launch) in 1995. Today millions of items [12] _____ (sell) online every day.

3 Rewrite the sentences using the passive.
1 They started the business in 2012.
   The business was started in 2012.
2 People invested over ten million dollars in the business.
   _____
3 They don't use the euro in Switzerland.
   _____
4 When did someone send the first text message?
   _____
5 The Chinese invented paper about 4,000 years ago.
   _____
6 People buy and sell millions of items online every day.
   _____

10.2 *a/an, the* and no article

GR10.2))

1 What would you like, **an** apple or **a** banana?
2 **The** Shard is one of **the** newest buildings in London.
3 I can see **a** car in the distance. I think **the** car's red.
4 Football is probably **the** most popular sport in the world.
5 I became interested in astronomy when I was at school.

We use *a/an*:

- when something is one of many
  *Have you ever been to **a** football match?*
  *Did you have **a** good seat in the stadium?*

- when we mention something for the first time
  *My town has got **an** indoor and **an** outdoor swimming pool. The outdoor pool is open only in the summer.*

We use *the*:

- when it's the only one of something, or the only one in a place
  *I love **the** Olympics.*
  *Can you close **the** door, please?*

- when we have talked about the thing(s) before:
  *Did you have a good seat in **the** stadium?*
  *My town has got an indoor and an outdoor swimming pool. **The** outdoor pool is only open in the summer.*

We use – (no article)

- when we talk about plural and uncountable nouns in general
  Some schools have banned (–) competitive sports.
  I love watching (–) swimming on TV.

- in some common expressions after a preposition (e.g. *at school, at university, in hospital, in bed, to bed, on TV*)
  *I was in the athletics team **at** (–) **university**.*
  *I'm tired. I'm going **to** (–) **bed**.*

With *school, university, college, hospital, church, prison* and *bed* you sometimes use *the* and you sometimes use – (no article).

- You use *the* when you are talking about the 'physical' place.
  ***The** station is very old.*
  *The football stadium is near **the** university.*

- You use – (no article) when you are talking about the 'activity' associated with a place.
  I go to church every Sunday. (= I go to a religious ceremony every Sunday.)
  What did you study at university? (= What did you do as a student?)

1 Choose the correct options to complete the conversations.

1 **A** Did you play any sports when you were at *the* / (–) school?
   B Yes, I was in – / *the* school football team. I was *a* / *the* captain, actually.

2 **A** I think *the* / – competition is good for *a* / – child's development.
   B I agree. But it can also have *a* / *the* negative effect if someone is always on *the* / – losing side.

3 **A** I think it's totally wrong that *the* / – celebrities get paid so much money.
   B Well, they do give *the* / – entertainment to millions of *the* / – people. And also, they can have *a* / *the* short career, so they need to earn *a* / *the* lot of money in *a* / *the* short period of time.

4 **A** Is *a* / *the* game on *the* / – TV this evening?
   B Yes, it is. I think *the* / – start is at 7.45. Are you going to watch it at *the* / – home or shall we go to *a* / – bar to watch it?

5 **A** Have you got *a* / *the* favourite sport?
   B Not really, I'm not *a* / *the* big sports fan. But I generally like winter sports like – / *the* skiing and – / *the* ice skating. I always love *the* / – Winter Olympics.

2 Complete the text about the origin of the Olympic Games with *a/an, the* or – (zero article)

¹ *The* Olympic Games originated long ago in ancient Greece. One story about ²_____ origin of ³_____ Games concerns ⁴_____ god Zeus. It is said that Zeus once fought his father, Kronos, for ⁵_____ control of ⁶_____ world. They fought at ⁷_____ top of ⁸_____ mountain that overlooked ⁹_____ valley in south-western Greece. After Zeus defeated his father, ¹⁰_____ temple and ¹¹_____ enormous statue of Zeus were built in ¹²_____ valley below ¹³_____ mountain. ¹⁴_____ valley was called Olympia, and soon ¹⁵_____ religious festivals were held there as ¹⁶_____ people came to worship Zeus and celebrate his physical strength. It is believed that these religious festivals eventually led to ¹⁷_____ Olympic Games.

Although we do not know exactly when ¹⁸_____ Games first took place, ¹⁹_____ earliest recorded Olympic competition occurred in 776 BC. It had only one event, ²⁰_____ running race, which was won by ²¹_____ cook named Coroebus. Over time, ²²_____ new sports involving running, jumping, throwing and fighting were added to ²³_____ Games. ²⁴_____ winner of each event received ²⁵_____ wreath of ²⁶_____ olive leaves and was considered ²⁷_____ hero. Only ²⁸_____ men were allowed to compete, and ²⁹_____ women were not even allowed to watch ³⁰_____ Games.

11.1 Sentences with *if* – unreal past conditional

GR11.1 》)

1 If the bank robber **had escaped**, he **wouldn't have gone** to prison.

2 The burglar **might have escaped** if the alarm **hadn't gone off**.

We use the unreal past conditional to talk about unreal situations in the past. We use it to talk about situations or events that are contrary to, or the opposite of, what actually happened.

• *If* + **past perfect**   ***would have*** + **past participle**
  *If you **had locked** the car, no one **would have stolen** it.*
  (You didn't lock the car, so it was stolen.)
  *If he'**d been caught**, he **wouldn't have been able to** commit any more crimes.* (He wasn't caught, so he was able to commit more crimes.)
  *If the police **had arrived** five minutes earlier, they **would have caught** the burglar.*

The *if*-clause and the result clause can usually go in either order. When the *if*-clause is first, it is followed by a comma. When the result clause comes first, there is no comma.
If I'd seen you, I would have said hello.
I would have said hello if I'd seen you.

• We can also use the modal verbs *could* and *might* instead of *would*.
  *If the police had arrived five minutes earlier, they **might** have caught the burglar.*
  *If we'd left earlier, we **could** have stopped off on the way.*

In informal spoken English and in informal writing (e.g. *social media*), we usually contract *had* and *would* to *'d*, especially after pronouns. We sometimes also contract *have* to *'ve*.
*If I'**d** seen anything, I would'**ve** told you.*

---

1 Complete the unreal past conditional sentences in the conversations with the correct form of the verbs in brackets.

1 A Sorry we're late. We got stuck in traffic.
   B Well, if you *'d set off* (set off) earlier, you *would've missed* (miss) the heavy traffic. I did warn you.

2 A Was the thief who burgled you arrested?
   B No. There wasn't enough evidence. They _____ (arrest) him if they _____ (find) the things he'd stolen.

3 A Did you get the job?
   B No, I didn't bother applying.
   A Oh, I'm sure you _____ (get) the job if you _____ (apply) for it.

4 A I see you didn't manage to clean the kitchen.
   B Well, if you _____ (ask) me earlier, I _____ (can/clean) it. But I was too busy, sorry.

5 A I thought you and Johann had met a few years ago.
   B No, I don't think so. I'm sure I _____ (remember) if I _____ (met) him before. I didn't recognize him at all.

2 Rewrite the summary with conditional sentences to show how things might have been different.

Johnny didn't work hard at school. → He failed all his exams. → He didn't get a job. → He had no money. → He went back to school. → He went to university. → He got a good job.

1 If *Johnny had worked hard at school, he wouldn't have failed all his exams.*

2 If he hadn't failed his exams, _____

3 If _____

4 If _____

5 If _____

6 If _____

3 Write an unreal past conditional sentence for each story about how things might have been different.

1 A nineteen-year-old man stole $200 from a shop. A few days later he saw a security camera photo in a local newspaper and showed it to his mother. She contacted the police and he was arrested.
   If he hadn't shown the picture to his mother, she wouldn't have contacted the police.

2 A man was robbing a shop in Madrid in Spain and he pulled a bag out of his pocket to put the money in. He pulled out his ID card at the same time by mistake. It fell on the floor. An hour later he was arrested.

   _____

3 A man robbed a shop and jumped onto a bus to escape. He didn't have the correct money to pay for a ticket, so he got back off the bus and was arrested by a policeman who was passing by.

   _____

11.2 *should/shouldn't have*

GR11.2 𝅘

1 You really **should have contacted** me sooner about the problem.

2 They **shouldn't have spent** so much money on a holiday.

3 Who **should we have told** about the change of arrangements for the meeting?

4 They **shouldn't have taken** the money.

We use *should have* or *shouldn't have* + past participle to criticize things we or other people did or didn't do in the past and to say what was the correct or better thing to have done.
*I **should have waited** before I sent the email.*
*She **should never have posted** the letter.*
*You **shouldn't have said** anything to him. He's really upset now.*
*I didn't know what to do. In your opinion, what **should I have done**?*

In spoken English, we usually contract *have* to *'ve*.
*We should**'ve** waited a little longer.*
*You shouldn't**'ve** said anything.*

---

1 Read the situations and write what was the correct or better thing to have done in each situation, using *shouldn't have*. Begin with the words given.

1 In 2000, millions of people received an email with the subject line 'I love you'. Opening the email was a mistake as it activated one of the worst computer viruses, the 'Love Bug' virus, which infected over fifty million computers around the world.
People *shouldn't have opened the email.*

2 A few years ago, an employee of an insurance company started a rumour via email that another company had serious financial problems. The other company saw the email and took the company that had started the rumour to court. They received £450,000.
The employee _____

3 A CEO of an international company criticized 400 of his employees by email. The email became public and the value of the company fell by almost 30%.
The CEO _____

4 In 2010, a fourteen-year-old girl posted on Facebook that she was having a party. 21,000 people clicked that they were going to attend. Her parents cancelled the party.
The girl _____

5 In 2009, the University of California emailed 46,000 applicants and told them they were accepted as students of the university. The university had accidentally sent the email to all the applicants rather than just to the successful applicants.
The university _____

2 Look at the things Dmitry did and didn't do when he went for a job interview. Write what was the correct or better thing to have done, using *should have* or *shouldn't have*.

He didn't have a shave. He wore jeans and a T-shirt. He didn't arrive on time. He kept looking at his phone. He didn't ask any questions. He didn't say goodbye.

1 *He should have had a shave.*
2 _____
3 _____
4 _____
5 _____
6 _____

12.1 Reported speech

We use reported speech to talk about what someone said. We often use the reporting verbs *say* and *tell* most commonly (the past forms *said* and *told*).

GR12.1a))

Direct speech	Reported speech
1 'It**'s** a great idea.'	He said that it **was** a great idea.
2 'I really **like** the new ad.'	She said that she really **liked** the new ad.
3 'It **was** a long journey.'	He told us that it **had been** a long journey.
4 'I**'ve** never **been** there.'	She told us she**'d** never **been** there.
5 'We**'re hoping** sales will increase.'	He said they **were hoping** sales would increase.
6 'It**'ll get** easier with practice.'	He told them it **would get** easier with practice.

- *Tell* must have a personal object (e.g. *He told **me**, I told **them***). *Say* does not have a personal object (NOT ~~He said me~~).
- We can generally use reported speech with or without *that* (e.g. *He said ...* or *He said that ...*).

Tense changes

When we use reported speech, tenses usually move one tense back (*do → did, is → was, did* or *have done → had done, will → would* etc.). This helps to show that the words were spoken in the past. The pronoun can also change (e.g. from *I* to *he*).

> However, we sometimes do not change the tense. This is usually when something is still true or important.
> *She said they**'ll be** ten minutes late.*

'Here and now' words

Words which talk about time and place may also sometimes change when the reporter's 'here and now' is not the same as the original speaker's.

GR12.1b))

Direct speech	Reported speech
1 'The film was released **last summer**.'	He said (that) the film had been released **the previous summer**.'
2 'The filming is **tomorrow**.'	She said (that) the filming was **the next day**.
3 'I saw him here **yesterday**.'	He said (that) he'd seen him there **the day before**.
4 'It's on TV **this Monday**.'	She told me (that) it was on TV **that Monday**.

---

1 Complete the sentences with *said* or *told*.

1 David _said_ he was an actor.
2 He _____ he'd been in several TV ads that year.
3 Anna _____ me she wanted to be a model.
4 Kate _____ she had designed the brochure.
5 Andy _____ us he was from Canada.

2 Rewrite the statements as reported speech.

1 'I'll watch the film with you.'
  Tom said _(that) he'd watch the film with us._
2 'We don't understand what the advert is selling.'
  They said _____
3 'Marek watched TV all day.'
  Joanna told us _____
4 'I think we're going to the cinema at the weekend.'
  Sharon said _____
5 'We don't like action movies.'
  Andrea and Pawel said _____
6 'I've seen this documentary before.'
  Andy told me _____

3 Alexia is talking about her acting experience and her hopes for the future. Report what she says.

> '**1** I really want to be an actor. **2** I think I have a natural talent for acting. **3** I've been in a few plays. **4** I was once in a TV advert. **5** I played a woman queuing in a bank. **6** It was a great experience and I really enjoyed it. **7** I hope I'll get another chance to be on TV again. **8** I'm determined to become a professional actor.'

1 _She said/told me (that) she really wanted to be an actor._
2 _____
3 _____
4 _____
5 _____
6 _____
7 _____
8 _____

4 The time and place references in these statements have now changed. Report the statements, changing the 'here and now' words.

1 'I saw this film last week.'
  He said _(that) he'd seen the film the week before/the previous week._
2 'We're having a meeting tomorrow.'
  She told me _____
3 'I'm going to London this Monday.'
  He said _____
4 'The award ceremony will be held here in the hotel.'
  They announced _____

12.2 Reported questions

GR12.2a))

Direct question	Reported question
1 'When **are they** going?'	She asked when **they were** going.
2 'Where **does he** live?'	He asked me where **she lived**.
3 'What **have you** done?'	She wanted to know what I'**d done**.

We use reported questions to say what someone asked. We usually use the reporting verb *asked*. We can use *asked* with an object (e.g. *He asked **me** what ...*) or without an object (e.g. *He asked what ...*). We can use *wanted to know* instead of *asked*.

When we report questions, as with reported speech, we usually move one tense back (*do → did, is → was, will → would*, etc.). This helps to show that the words were spoken in the past.

Because a reported question is no longer a direct question, we do not invert the subject and the auxiliary verb, and we do not use the auxiliary verb *do*.

GR12.2b))

Direct question	Reported question
1 'Did you understand?'	She asked us **if** we'd understood.
2 'Have you seen Hitoshi?'	He wanted to know **if** I'd seen Hitoshi.
3 'Do you read a lot?'	She asked **whether** I read a lot.

To report *yes/no* questions we use *if* or *whether*.

With questions with *be*, we sometimes put the verb at the end of the reported question. This is more usual when the question is short.
'What's your favourite film?'
He asked what my favourite film was.
NOT usually *He asked what was my favourite film.'*

1 Rewrite the questions as reported questions.
   1 'Where do you work?'
      He asked where I worked.
   2 'Do you live near Istanbul?'
      She _____
   3 'Have you lived there long?'
      He _____
   4 'Where did you go to university?'
      She _____
   5 'Can you give me some advice?'
      He _____
   6 'Will you help me later?'
      He _____
   7 'Have you ever read any Shakespeare?'
      She _____
   8 'What are you doing this evening?'
      She _____

2 Read this interview with businessman Peter Horspath and then report the questions.
   1 I   What makes a good leader?
      P   A good leader needs people to follow them.
   2 I   What is the highest compliment you have been paid?
      P   It's that I am always honest and fair.
   3 I   What is the worst thing anyone has said about you?
      P   Someone once said that my success was a result of luck.
   4 I   What do you look for in the people you do business with?
      P   I look for honesty and hard work.
   5 I   What is your worst fault?
      P   I sometimes don't give people a second chance.
   6 I   What is the best piece of career advice you can give?
      P   It's important to step outside your comfort zone on occasions.
   7 I   Do you have a favourite book?
      P   My favourite book is *How to Win Friends and Influence People* by Dale Carnegie.
   8 I   What do you do to relax?
      P   I go to the gym.

   1 The interviewer asked *what made a good leader.*
   2 She asked _____
   3 _____
   4 _____
   5 _____
   6 _____
   7 _____
   8 _____

Audioscripts

Unit 1 Trends

1.1 》
S So, how many friends would you say you had?
J Well, it all depends what you mean by friends, doesn't it? I mean, I get on well with a lot of people at work – that's maybe twenty people I'd say were friends …
S Do you socialize outside work?
J Oh, yes. Maybe not that often, but we meet up after work from time to time … Then there are the friends I play football with. I guess I don't have a lot in common with them apart from football, but I'd say they were friends all the same.
S But how many of those friends would you ask to help you out if you were in trouble?
J Ah, well, that's different. Friends you can really trust … there aren't so many of those. Maybe five or six?
S And what about online? Do you have a lot of Facebook friends?
J No, not really. I can't be bothered with it, really. I guess I've got about fifteen to twenty, but I don't use it much. What about you?
S Oh, I have a lot of friends on Facebook, about 150, I think.
J 150?! Do you keep in touch with all of them?
S Yes, well, kind of – you know, we send the occasional message to each other.
J And have you actually met all of them, face-to-face?
S No. Some of them are people I've met on holiday or something, and we wanted to keep in touch. Some of them are old friends from school. But there are quite a lot of friends who are people I've never actually met at all. I just made friends with them on Facebook.
J I don't see how you can be friends with someone you've never met.
S Of course you can. I probably chat to some of them more than you talk to your friends from football!
J Hmm. And what about in the real world? How many friends do you have in real life?
S Well, a lot of the friends I see often in real life are on Facebook, too, actually. I've got friends from work like you, and then there are the people in my evening class. I'm learning German …
J And what about really close friends?
S I've only got a couple of really close friends that I share everything with. Actually, if I'm honest, recently just one, because I've fallen out with one of my best friends. We're not speaking to each other at the moment.
J Did you have a big argument?
S Not exactly. It all started when …

1.2 》
get on well with someone
meet up with someone
have a lot in common with someone
fall out with someone
help someone out
trust someone
get in touch with someone
keep in touch with someone
make friends with someone
have an argument with someone

1.3 》
1 I often meet up with groups of friends in the evening.
2 You don't need to have a lot in common with someone to be friends. It's fine to have different interests.
3 I get on well with most people I know. There aren't many people I don't like.
4 A really good friend is someone you can call at midnight and ask them to help you out.
5 The friends you make at school are often friends for life.
6 I'm always pleased when someone I haven't heard from in ages gets in touch.
7 I'm quite easy-going. I rarely fall out with my friends.
8 I'm not speaking to my sister at the moment, we've had an argument. It seems a bit childish.
9 I can trust my closest friend with all my secrets.

1.4 》
P And now, in our regular look at what's trending on social media, and why: right now, it's something called *Black Friday*. This term has been used more than two million times on Twitter in the last 48 hours. *Black Friday* is the fourth Friday in November, when the shops have amazing special offers in the run up to Christmas. Many items are half price or two for the price of one, and it's now the busiest shopping day of the year in some countries. It started in the USA, but it's spreading round the world now, to the UK, Australia and more recently to shoppers in Brazil, Mexico and other Latin American countries. Many shops have been opening very early in the morning, and in some places people have been so keen to get a bargain that they have started queuing outside the shops the night before. Last year it is estimated that shoppers in the USA spent over eleven billion dollars on *Black Friday*.
However, while you may get a good discount on your purchases, you should be careful. Firstly, there's the real danger of spending more than you intended or can really afford, buying things on credit, and owing a lot of money. And secondly, it may be dangerous, with over fifty injuries in the past five years, caused by people fighting over things in the sales.

1.5 》
P Let's go over to a busy shopping centre and find out what shoppers there think.
I Today is one of the busiest shopping days of the year, and this shopping centre is full of people shopping. However, today something different is happening here. It's *Buy Nothing Day*, and some people are here to try to persuade the rest of us to do just that … to buy nothing. Lewis Castle is one of them. He's standing here in the main entrance of the shopping centre, holding a big sign saying 'Stop Shopping, Start Living.' Lewis, can you explain a little about what *Buy Nothing Day* means?
L Yes, of course. It's pretty simple, really. We're asking everyone to think about their spending habits and buy nothing at all for just one day.
I And what difference will that make?
L Well, the idea is to make people stop and think about what they're buying. When you really think about it, the idea of buying things as a way of spending your leisure time is crazy. We are all buying more things than we really need. We believe shopping makes us happy, but it doesn't. In fact, it can do the opposite if people end up owing a lot of money.
I Yes, I agree, that's a good point. People often buy things they don't really need or want.
L Exactly, it's amazing to realize that only 20% of the world's population is consuming over 80% of the Earth's natural resources. Does that seem fair to you? In countries like the UK, we all own far too much.
I Does it make any difference what you buy?
L Yes, that's part of it, too. We're trying to get people to think about the effect their buying choices have on the rest of the world. Something might seem a great bargain, but that could be because it's been made in a country where the workers aren't paid enough. In addition, most of the time we prefer people to buy locally because transporting goods by air has a harmful effect on the environment.
I But will it really make a difference if we stop shopping for just one day?
L Actually, most people don't understand how difficult it is to last 24 hours without spending any money. But you'll feel great if you achieve it.
I Are a lot of people taking part in *Buy Nothing Day* this year?
L Yes, and more and more do every year. I think it started in Canada more than twenty years ago, but now there are *Buy Nothing Day* movements in over 65 countries.

1.6 》
1 Can you explain a little about what *Buy Nothing Day* means?
2 When you really think about it, the idea of buying things as a way of spending your leisure time is crazy.
3 We believe shopping makes us happy, but it doesn't.
4 Yes, I agree, that's a good point.

5 We all own far too much.
6 Most of the time we prefer people to buy locally.
7 Most people don't understand how difficult it is …

1.8))
This is a fascinating book. We all know that the internet is changing the way we do things, but Carr believes that it is also changing the very way our brains work. With the printed book, he argues, our brains learnt to think deeply. In contrast, the internet encourages us to read small bits of information from lots of different places. We are becoming better and better at multitasking, but much worse at concentrating on one thing.

1.9))
1 Shopping and banking online is unsafe.
2 Looking at screens all day is bad for our eyes.
3 People will forget how to talk to each other.
4 People don't spend enough time outside.
5 Online information is not always reliable.
6 Hyperlinks in online texts are very distracting.
7 We are now using far more electricity to power all our screens.
8 Multitasking online makes us work less effectively.

1.10))
A So, this week we're going to be talking about *The Shallows*, a book by Nicholas Carr, in which he argues that using the internet is actually changing the way our brains work. How is that?
B Well, it's actually a very interesting book because, rather than just talk about all the ways people say the internet is bad for us … you know, that staring at a screen is affecting our eyesight or making our children fat because they don't go outside and play any more, Carr takes quite a scientific approach. He isn't exactly saying that the internet is bad for us, but he is saying that it is making our brains work differently, and that the changes may be permanent.
A In what way?
B Well, he starts off by talking about when people started writing and reading books. That was a huge change as well, and lots of people felt it was a bad idea. What would happen, they argued, if people didn't have to memorize everything because it was all written down in books? Sounds a bit like the arguments people make today about people looking facts up online – that they don't remember things any more. But Carr says that in fact books taught us to really focus on one thing at a time, whereas now we are constantly looking at lots of different things at the same time. Hyperlinking, where we are encouraged to click on an underlined word or phrase and we go off to a different website, is a particular problem.
A But isn't multitasking good for the brain?
B Well, according to Carr, no. The studies show that when we try to do two things at once, we do both of them less well. We are also less likely to remember what we've done or read. There are some obvious benefits to the internet, but all the same, it is changing our culture so that we are less able to concentrate or make deep connections in our brain, and that can't be a good thing, can it?

1.11))
P It seems like every day we find another reason to feel guilty about what we buy. Maybe it's food that we know isn't good for us, or clothes which are made by poorly paid workers, or products which are damaging the environment. Manufacturers know we feel this way, and the latest trend is for so-called 'guilt-free brands' – brands which claim to be better for us, for workers and for the planet – so that we can buy them and not feel guilty. Sounds great, but is it as good as it sounds? With us today we have Gosia Szlachta and Jem Norris, both members of the same environmental group but with very different views on the idea of guilt-free brands. So, Jem, what do you think about the idea?
J Well, as far as I'm concerned, anything which makes people think more about what they're buying is a good idea. Take the Fairphone, for example. Until that was produced, most people didn't even realize how bad conditions were for electronics workers in many parts of the world. Now there's a lot more awareness …
G There's a lot more awareness, but don't you think it would be better if people understood that there is no need at all to keep buying new phones? There seems to be an idea that you have to have a new phone every two years. I'm convinced that if people really understood how much damage this causes, to workers and to the planet, they wouldn't do this. I think people should feel guilty. Producing guilt-free brands just gives people an excuse not to think about these issues, and just keep buying more and more stuff …
J Well, according to the people who make Fairphone, their phones will last longer and be easier to repair. If you ask me, we have to give people the option of buying something which is better for the planet, not just say they shouldn't buy something at all.

1.12))
1 So, Jem, what do you think about the idea?
2 Well, as far as I'm concerned, anything which makes people think …
3 There's a lot more awareness, but don't you think it would be better if …
4 I'm convinced that if people really understood …
5 Well, according to the people who make Fairphone, …
6 If you ask me, we have to give people the option …

1.13))
1 How do you decide when you can trust someone?
2 Do you have a lot in common with your closest friend?
3 When was the last time you made friends with someone new?
4 How do you keep in touch with family or friends who live far away?
5 When was the last time you fell out with someone?
6 Who in your family do you get on with best?

Unit 2 What a story!

2.1))
That reminds me of another story I heard about a man who had a lucky escape. He had been at a barbecue restaurant on top of a mountain, and after the meal he decided not to take the cable car down with his friends but to walk down instead. While he was looking for the path, he fell into a stream and broke his leg. Unable to move, he tried to phone for help, but his mobile wasn't working because he'd dropped it in the stream. Knowing he was missing, teams of people were looking for him, but it was twenty-four days before they found him. Luckily he'd brought a bottle of barbecue sauce with him to the barbecue, and he survived by drinking water mixed with the barbecue sauce.

2.2))
1 That reminds me of another story I heard about a man who had a lucky escape.
2 He'd been at a barbecue restaurant.
3 While he was looking for the path …
4 Knowing he was missing, teams of people were looking for him.

2.3))
P So … to our next story. A national newspaper was embarrassed recently after publishing a story about a super-fruit, the blue melon, which, it turns out, was another internet hoax. Does the internet make hoaxing too easy? Laura, you work for a national newspaper; do you think there are more hoaxes these days?
L Well, there have always been hoaxes, but, yes, there are more of them now. It is easy to create a hoax now that everyone can change photos and videos digitally. And the internet makes it easier to spread the hoax around the world. Everything moves so fast nowadays, and online stories aren't checked before they're published.
P One recent hoax I remember was the so-called Balloon Boy hoax.
L Oh yes, that was a big story. A couple, Richard and Mayumi Heene, let a large gas balloon float off into the air and then, as soon as it was high in the sky, they said that their six-year-old son was inside the balloon. The police were informed and helicopters were sent up to track the balloon until they could find a safe way of getting him down. By the time the balloon landed an hour or so later about 80 kilometres away, the story was live on television. When the boy was not found inside, the media reported that he had fallen out during the flight, and a huge search started. Meanwhile, the boy was actually safe at home, hiding. The parents suddenly announced that they'd found him at home asleep.
P Did the parents really think he was in the balloon?
L Well, we can't say for sure, of course, because they never admitted it; but while reporters were interviewing the family on TV, the boy accidentally mentioned that they'd done it to be on TV. He was supposed to keep quiet about that, of course.

P That's incredible. Do you think most hoaxes are carried out to become famous?

L Yes, and that's not a new thing. Take the example of Piltdown Man. The scientists who claimed to discover that skull became very well known as a result. The publicity you get from a good hoax can also be useful in marketing a product. There have been quite a few advertising campaigns like that. But I don't think becoming famous or getting publicity is the only reason. Quite often, no one knows who started the hoax. Take the blue melon, for example. I imagine someone did that because they thought it was funny to make people believe it.

P But not all hoaxes are funny. For example, people in Britain have been calling the emergency number 999 because of a hoax saying that calling this number charges your phone battery.

L Really?

P Yes, it sounds stupid, but a lot of people believe this hoax, and it's caused real problems for the police and fire service. Some people seem to like creating hoaxes to cause as much trouble as possible.

2.4 》

1 A couple, Richard and Mayumi Heene, let a large gas balloon float off into the air and then, as soon as it was high in the sky, they claimed that their six-year-old son was inside the balloon.

2 The police were informed and helicopters were sent up to track the balloon until they could find a safe way of getting him down.

3 By the time the balloon landed an hour or so later about 80 kilometres away, the story was live on television.

4 When the boy was not found inside, the media reported that he had fallen out during the flight, and a huge search started. Meanwhile, the boy was actually safe at home, hiding. The parents suddenly announced that they'd found him at home asleep.

5 We can't say for sure because the couple never admitted it, but while reporters were interviewing the family on TV, the boy accidentally mentioned that they'd done it to be on TV. He was supposed to keep quiet about that.

2.5 》

During the early twentieth century, scientists were keen to find some evidence that would prove the link between early man and apes. In 1912 that evidence seemed to have been found while Dawson and Woodward were digging on a site in Piltdown, in the south of England. As soon as they saw the jawbone and the skull, they decided that this must be the evidence science needed. Woodward claimed that both bones belonged to a human being who had lived about half a million years ago, during what is known as the Lower Pleistocene period. Most scientists accepted this opinion until nearly forty years later, when it was discovered that the Piltdown Man was a fake. Meanwhile, Dawson, who most people consider responsible for making the fake, had died.

The Piltdown Man hoax truly damaged science because by the time the hoax was discovered, scientists had wasted nearly forty years believing a lie.

2.6 》

A I heard this incredible story from a friend about a woman who lost her wedding ring …

B What happened?

A Well, she'd lost her wedding ring years ago, in … 1995, I think, while she was baking in her kitchen; and although she looked everywhere, even taking up the kitchen floor, she couldn't find it anywhere.

B Oh no, that's awful.

A Yes, but then she found it again more than ten years later.

B How?

A You're not going to believe this, but she was in the garden digging up carrots and she suddenly noticed that one of the carrots was 'wearing' her ring!

B What, you mean the ring was on the carrot?! Really?

A Yes, it's true, the carrot had grown *through* the ring …

B No way! That's incredible!

A It is, isn't it? I'm sure she's keeping it safe now!

2.7 》

1 What happened?
2 Oh no, that's awful.
3 You're joking.
4 What, you mean the ring was on the carrot?!
5 Really?
6 No way! That's incredible!

2.8 》

1 Last Tuesday my computer broke while I was trying to finish an important piece of work.
2 So I called a friend who knows about computers, and he came over straightaway.
3 He had a look at it, but he couldn't fix it.
4 He took my keys so he could come back to fix it the next day while I was at work.
5 The next morning when I tried to leave for work, I discovered that he had locked my front door from the outside, and I couldn't get out of the flat.
6 My parents were travelling abroad, and no one else I know had a spare key.
7 I tried to call my friend, but he had left his phone in my flat. It rang right next to me.
8 I had to wait for him to arrive, and so I was very late for work.

2.9 》

1 to think or believe that something will come or happen
2 to not be able to remember something
3 to ask yourself questions about something
4 to know again someone or something that you have seen or heard before
5 to help someone remember something
6 to suddenly be seen
7 to know or understand that something is true, or that something has happened
8 to cry out loudly in a high voice

2.10 》

1 You're not going to believe this, but I've lost my job.
2 Someone told me there's going to be a bad storm tonight.
3 I heard that Jack has won the lottery.

4 Apparently, the office is closed this week.

Unit 3 Life skills

3.1 》

In the late 1960s, Walter Mischel, a professor at Stanford University in the United States, carried out an experiment which is known as the Marshmallow Test. He and his researchers took four-year-old children into a room, all by themselves, and put a marshmallow in front of them.

Then the researcher told the child: 'You can eat this now if you want. Or, if you can be patient and wait until I come back, and not eat the marshmallow, you can have two marshmallows as a reward.' Then they left the child alone with the marshmallow for fifteen minutes. Of course, they filmed what the children did.

3.2 》

Fifteen minutes is a long time if you're a child and you really like marshmallows!

So, what happened? How many children do you think ate the marshmallow? Well, nearly 70% ate it. Some ate it straightaway, some managed to wait a while before giving in. Only 30% of the children were able to resist temptation and wait the full fifteen minutes. OK, the researchers found out that most of the children preferred to have something immediately to having to wait for what they really wanted. Not that surprising, really.

But some years later, they discovered something much more interesting. When these children became adults, the researchers contacted them again. And what do you think they discovered? All the children who were able to wait were very successful. They had done well at school, had good relationships, and were healthy. They earned a lot more money, too. The children who couldn't resist temptation were generally less successful in all these ways.

In the original marshmallow test, the researchers noticed the children who managed not to eat the marshmallow were using some effective techniques. Those children who stared at the marshmallow, or picked it up, or smelt it, always ended up eating it. The successful children found a way to deal with the problem, by looking away from the marshmallow, or covering their eyes.

Watching the successful children made the researchers realize that the important thing was to avoid thinking about the marshmallow at all. Then the children didn't have to make an effort not to eat it. In a later experiment, Mischel proved that when he taught the children some simple techniques, such as imagining the marshmallow wasn't real, that it was just a picture of a marshmallow, nearly all the children succeeded in waiting the full fifteen minutes.

So, everyone can learn to wait if they want to. This is important because this experiment isn't just about waiting for a marshmallow. If you can wait for a marshmallow, then you'll be able to choose to study rather than watch TV, knowing it's better for your future. You'll succeed in saving up money for something you really want, rather than spending it without thinking. And, in this way, you will be able to make better decisions about your future, and eventually get a better, and higher-paid, job.

3.3 》

In the Marshmallow Test, researchers left four-year-old children alone in a room with a marshmallow. If the children managed to resist temptation and not eat the marshmallow, the researcher promised them a reward of two marshmallows. However most of the children found it difficult to be patient and gave in before the time was up. They preferred to have something immediately rather than wait for what they really wanted. The researchers found that, as adults, those children who could rise to the challenge were generally much more successful than the others.

The best technique was to avoid thinking about the marshmallow at all. The successful children dealt with the problem by looking away or covering their eyes. If they didn't think about the marshmallow, they didn't have to make an effort not to eat it.

When Mischel taught a different set of children this technique, nearly all the children succeeded in waiting the full time. Learning these techniques can help in adult life because being able to wait helps us to make the right choices.

3.4 》
achieve
avoid
manage
observe
prefer
resist
succeed

3.5 》

When he was working in the burger van, Ed had to be reliable and turn up for work on time. He also had to be polite to the customers. However, he didn't have to take much responsibility as his boss dealt with the money. He didn't need to get up early because the van opened at 11 a.m. When he wanted to, he could even take a day off work.

Now that he's training to be a chef, it's very different. He has to manage a team, even though he finds it difficult to tell people what to do. It's also a very high-pressure job, so he must work to tight deadlines. However, he doesn't have to work outside any more, and he can take home really nice food when the restaurant has closed.

3.6 》
1 easy-going
2 home-made
3 five-star
4 over-priced
5 five-hundred-page
6 second-hand
7 English-speaking
8 well-known

3.7 》
I So, today I'm going to show you how to do something amazing using only seven things – 1 a plastic bottle, 2 some water, 3 some bleach, 4 a piece of metal, 5 some glue, 6 sandpaper and 7 a metal roof. What are we going to make?
We're going to make a light that doesn't use electricity. The light goes in the roof and is strong enough to give light to a whole room.

So, let's get started … The first thing you do is cut a hole in the metal sheet.
A How do you do that?
I Like this. Look. You need to use special metal-cutters, and you need to measure carefully. And make sure you don't cut the hole too big. Got that?
A Yeah, thanks. OK, what next?
I Next, rub the plastic bottle with sandpaper. When you've done that, put the bottle in the hole in the metal and glue it in place. Like this. While the glue's drying, fill the bottle with water and add ten millilitres of bleach. Then put the top on the bottle. It should look like this one I made earlier.
A Can you say the part about the glue again?
I Yes, let me show you again.
Put the bottle in the normal way up, like this, and put the glue all around near the top. Make sure you use enough glue … OK?
A Yeah, thanks.
I After you've done that, it's time to go to the roof. So you need to cut a hole in the roof the same size as the bottle.
A Can you show us how to start cutting the hole?
I Yes, of course. Look. You do it like this. Then you continue cutting round. OK?
A That's great, thanks.
I Now, you put the bottle in the hole this way, and add more glue to make it secure. And there you have it! A light that needs no electricity, but with sunlight outside, it can light up the whole room.
A Wow, that's incredible!

3.8 》
1 The first thing you do is cut a hole in the metal.
2 When you've done that, put the bottle in the hole in the metal …
3 While the glue's drying, fill the bottle with water …
4 After you've done that, it's time to go to the roof.

3.9 》
Next, rub the bottle with sandpaper. When you've done that, put the bottle in the hole in the metal and glue the bottle in place.

3.10 》
1 If I come into work early, I can leave early.
2 In my last job I had to wear a uniform.
3 You can't use the phone for private calls.
4 You don't need to wear a tie.
5 You must remember to lock up before you go.

3.11 》
1 good-
2 English-
3 well-
4 hard-
5 easy-
6 second-

3.12 》
A The first thing you do is to put some flour in a bowl, with a little salt. Then you crack an egg into the bowl.
B I'm not very good at that. How do you crack the egg without getting bits of shell in the bowl?
A No problem, Let me show you. Look, you crack it on the edge of the bowl, like this. Then you mix it in and add the milk. Make

sure you mix it very thoroughly, so there aren't any lumps.
B What next?
A Then you have to wait for about 30 minutes. While you're doing that you can get ready whatever you want to put on the pancakes. Then you heat some oil or butter and put some mixture in the pan. When the first side is cooked, you flip it over. Look, you do it like this.
B Wow! That's clever.

Unit 4 Space

4.1 》
So, yesterday we took the train from La Paz, Bolivia, into Peru, stopping at Puno, and today we're going to visit the floating islands on Lake Titicaca. I can't wait. Ever since I first heard about these islands in a geography class many years ago, I've wanted to see them. Actually, I don't really enjoy boat trips, but I'm sure the water on the lake will be quite calm, as it's a clear sunny day. It's quite cold, though, so I'm going to take an extra sweater to keep warm.

I'm really interested in finding out more about how people live there. I believe that we'll be able to ask them questions through a guide. I'd love to know what people eat – a lot of fish, I suppose! I'd also like to know what they think the future holds for them and their families. Do they think their children will stay on the islands? What effect is technology going to have on their lives? I know they already have solar power and even black and white TVs.

Just thought! It would be great to have some photos for the blog, so I'll take my camera, too. Just hope I don't drop it in the water …

4.2 》
1 It was the end of September and a beautiful sunny day. Autumn is the most beautiful season here and the leaves on the trees were beginning to turn golden in places. As we climbed through the forest, we enjoyed the fresh air and the smell of the soil. Moving slowly up the steep, winding path, we came to the edge of the forest and suddenly we could see a gorgeous lake at the edge of a mountain range in the distance. The peaks and cliffs of the mountains were partly covered in snow, even at this time of the year. The scenery was just amazing.
2 We had been walking all day and it was slowly getting dark. We had seen gorgeous mountains with lovely greenery, refreshing waterfalls and clear pools amongst the rocks. We had enjoyed playing in the pools in the hot sunshine, but at the end of the day we had descended back into the valley. Walking down towards where we were staying for the night, the sunset was amazing, beautiful and red with the silhouettes of the palm trees in the distance. I don't think I've ever seen such a beautiful and unusual landscape.

4.3 》
P Good afternoon and welcome to *Science Matters*. Walking through the park yesterday, it was full of people enjoying the sunshine. Recent research, however,

suggests that people are spending less time outdoors. One study looked at trends in visits to national parks in the United States, Japan and Spain, and found that the number of visits had gone down by 18% since the late 1980s. A recent British study found that even during the summer, people spend just one to two hours outside per day. So, why is this happening, and what should we do about it? Our science reporter Julie Mayers has been researching into the benefits of being outdoors. So Julie, why do we stay indoors so much?

J Hello. Well, it may be that rather than enjoying the beauty of nature, we prefer to sit in front of a screen. Statistics show that people in the US now spend around eight and a half hours a day looking at a screen, and this trend will definitely spread around the world as smartphones become more common. Another explanation is that more people live in cities. In 1950, 79% of the UK population lived in cities, but that percentage is likely to rise to around 92% by 2030. And even traditionally less urbanized countries may end up in a similar situation. For example, Botswana in 1950 had less than 3% of its population living in cities; now it has about 61%, and this percentage will probably rise further over the next few years.

P But does it actually matter if we don't get outside much?

J Well, yes, obviously there are the physical benefits. We know that people who live near green spaces are more likely to be physically active. In fact, nearly 45% of Californian teens who live near a park take part in physical activities for at least one hour a day, at least five days a week, whereas only one third of teens who don't have access to a nearby park have the same level of physical activity.
But there's more than that. According to researchers at Heriot Watt University, in Edinburgh, people's brains actually change when they spend time in natural environments, reducing stress and improving mood. The Japanese have known this for some time. Shinrin-yoku, or forest bathing, is simply visiting a forest or other natural area and walking slowly, taking in everything you see, hear, smell, and even taste. Scientific research shows that walking in the forest for 30 minutes will reduce depression, and lower your blood pressure. They even think it might prevent you from becoming ill.

P Really? That seems very hard to believe. How's that?

J It seems that the trees give off chemicals which help to keep you healthy. One study showed a 50% increase in the white blood cells needed to fight illness after a two-hour walk. Research taking place at the moment will tell us more about how this works. The Japanese government has already built forty-eight official forest bathing trails, and say they will definitely build another fifty-two within the next ten years.

P Really? That's a lot. Do you think it could become as popular in other countries?

J Yes, it probably will. In fact, South Korea has already started building its own forest bathing centres, and other countries, like Finland, may soon follow.

4.4))
1 In the US people now spend 8.5 hours a day looking at a screen, and this trend will definitely spread around the world as smartphones become more common.
2 The percentage of British people living in cities is likely to rise to 92% by 2030.
3 Countries such as Botswana, where, in 1950, only 3% of people lived in a city, may end up in a similar situation.
4 Nowadays 61% of Botswana's population lives in cities and this percentage will probably rise further.
5 Walking in a forest for 30 minutes improves mood and might even stop you getting ill.
6 After a two-hour walk, some people showed a 50% increase in the white blood cells needed to help fight disease.
7 The Japanese government will build 52 more forest bathing trails within the next ten years, and other countries may follow.

4.5))
1 This trend will definitely spread around the world.
2 The number is likely to rise.
3 This percentage probably won't rise much further.
4 People who live near green spaces are more likely to be active.

4.6))
1 neat and tidy
2 in a bit of a mess

4.8))
1 What a mess!
2 in a while
3 take up too much space
4 peace and quiet
5 a nice drink
6 a big apartment

4.9))
1 What a mess this room is! We need to tidy it up.
2 I hope to finish the decorating in a while.
3 I wanted to put the bookshelf here, but it takes up too much space.
4 The best thing about this house is the peace and quiet.
5 Would you like a nice drink?
6 She lives in a big apartment in Berlin.

4.10))
I Can you tell me about your problem?
M Well, I'm a hoarder. I just can't throw things away. So my house is full of … stuff. I'm starting to run out of space.
I What kind of stuff do you keep?
M Everything – newspapers, old yoghurt pots, clothes, toys …
I Old yoghurt pots? Why do you keep those?
M Well, because they might come in useful one day. You know, I might decide to grow plants in them.
I But don't they take up a lot of space? Where do you keep them?
M In my shower cubicle.
I You're joking!

M No, seriously. I've got a load of newspapers, too, going back to 1995. They're in a shed in the garden.
I So your house must be pretty full, then?
M There's no room for anything. Our front garden is full of old machines like dishwashers and fridges.
I What a nightmare! And how does your wife feel about this?
M To be honest, she's not very happy. But what can I do about it?

4.11))
A So, how's it going? Enjoying your new flat?
R Yes, I love it.
A You've got a fantastic view from the windows.
R Yes, we're on the top floor. I spent the whole weekend going up and down the stairs with boxes.
A Yes, I can see!
R Look, make yourself at home. Have a seat.
A Er … where?
R Yes, I see what you mean. Well, why don't you sit on a box?
A No, don't worry, I can make room on this sofa, if I just … move this suitcase … How did you manage to move all your stuff over a weekend?
R Oh, I didn't do it all at the weekend. I took some time off from work last week.
A It'll look great once you've got everything unpacked. You've got a lot of room here …
R Yeah, it's so much bigger than my old place. Mind you, I've really got too much stuff. This old sofa and chairs take up so much space, and there's furniture in the flat already.
A Maybe you should get rid of your old furniture.
R Yes, perhaps. I think I really need to get everything unpacked first, and then I can see what I need and don't need. Are you going to give me a hand?
A Sure …

4.12))
W Hello, Bell's Bistro.
C Oh, hello. I had lunch at your restaurant today and I think I may have left my mobile phone there on one of the tables … I wonder if you could check for me?
W Certainly. Could I just take some details first?
C Yes, of course.
W Could you tell me the make of the phone?
C Yes, it was a …

4.13))
R Hello, how can I help you?
C Hello, I understand that the hotel has a gym?
R Yes, that's right. It's in the basement.
C Thank you. Could you tell me the opening hours, please?
R It's open from 7 a.m. until 9 p.m.
C Thank you, that's great.
R Can I help you with anything else?
C Yes, just one last question. Do I need to take a towel with me, or are they provided?

4.14))
R Hello, Grand Hotel. How can I help you?
G Hello, I think I may have left my briefcase at reception this morning. I wonder if you could check if it's been handed in?
R Certainly. Could I just take some details? What colour was it?

G It's black, and it has my initials on it, MHG, Miguel Hernandez Garcia.

R Thank you … one moment … Yes, we have it.

G That's great. I wonder if I could come and pick it up this evening?

R Yes, any time. Can I help you with anything else?

G No, that's all. Thank you for your help, though. I really appreciate it.

Unit 5 Entertainment

5.1)))

The first film we're looking at today is *The Secret Life of Walter Mitty*, starring Ben Stiller and Kristen Wiig. A remake of a classic comedy from 1947, based on James Thurber's book, which was written even earlier, in 1939, the film manages to bring the story up to date quite well. Walter Mitty is a quiet man who secretly dreams of being an action hero, rescuing people from burning buildings or travelling into space. Soon, however, his adventures start to become real, as he decides to set out on a journey to find a missing photographic negative. The special effects are pretty impressive, especially in the scenes set in Iceland and the Himalayas; but despite a cast with several excellent comic actors, the film just isn't very funny. Kristen Wiig, who plays the woman Mitty is secretly in love with, is just wasted, with no real humour in what she has to say. Stiller's performance is better, but overall the film's a bit disappointing.

The other film we're looking at today is *Rio 2096: A Story of Love and Fury*. I enjoy going to see animated films with my kids, but to be honest, I'm not usually a big fan of animated films for adults. So I didn't expect to enjoy this one. After about ten minutes, though, I realized I was wrong. It's fantastic.

The film is set in four different periods of Brazil's history. It starts in the future, in 2096, where a man and a woman, voiced by Brazilian stars Selton Mello and Camila Pitanga, stand at the top of a skyscraper in the middle of the night. 'To live without knowing the past is like walking in the dark,' says the man. Suddenly the film goes back in time almost 600 years, to 1566, when the Portuguese arrived in Brazil.

The man explains that in 1566 he was a Tupinamba Indian, attempting to save his tribe, who were all killed when Rio de Janeiro was first built. Having failed to save any of them, including his great love, Janaina, he magically turns into a bird. He will return as a man in the future, when he hopes to be with Janaina once more. We then see the couple living through slavery in 1825 and the military dictatorship in 1970 before returning to the future in 2096. It is a disturbing future where poor people can't afford to buy water, but he and Janaina continue to fight against evil, as they've done throughout the last 600 years.

The plot is a little complicated if you aren't familiar with Brazilian history, but the story is told with such passion that you can't help enjoying it. It really deserved to win the top prize at the 2013 Annecy International Animated Film Festival.

5.2)))

A beautiful film about the dreams of village school children in rural Indonesia, *Stepping on the Flying Grass* is both visually stunning and truly moving.

When their teacher asked them to write an essay about their dearest dreams and wishes, a group of village schoolchildren begin to think seriously about what they plan to do with their lives.

Puji enjoys being useful and just wants to help others. Mei fantasizes about becoming an actress. She spends hours practising in front of the mirror, but does she really love acting, or is it actually her mother's dream? Agus's family can't afford to eat any special food at home, but he really wants to eat at an authentic Padang restaurant in the city. When an opportunity arises to make some money, he decides to make his dream come true. As the film progresses he gradually realizes that for dreams to come true you need to work at them.

5.3)))

amusing
surprising
ordinary
violent
enjoyable
intelligent
original
predictable
disappointing
entertaining
unexciting

5.4)))

I've lived in New York for about three years now. It's an exciting place to live, but there are quite a few annoying things about it, too. For a start, it's incredibly expensive.

When I moved into my flat three years ago, the rent was already quite high, but it has gone up three times since then.

It can also be quite a violent place. I haven't been mugged yet, but my best friend has. Luckily, she wasn't actually hurt; they just took her bag.

And the traffic – it's dreadful. It took me more than an hour to get to work today, and nearly as long to get home.

However, I've never lived anywhere where there is so much to do. Over the past month I've been to the theatre three times as well as to a number of great art exhibitions. I've also just started salsa classes. You can find everything from everywhere here.

So, although living in New York has some bad points, on balance I don't think I want to live anywhere else in the world.

5.5)))

1 I'm absolutely exhausted.
2 She was absolutely amazed.
3 That smells absolutely delicious.
4 It's absolutely astonishing.
5 It's absolutely enormous.
6 It's absolutely freezing in here.

5.6)))

1 I can't walk any further. I'm absolutely exhausted. I'll have to sit down.
2 She was absolutely amazed when she saw her sister standing at the front door. They hadn't seen each other for ten years.
3 That smells absolutely delicious. I love the smell of garlic. What are you cooking?

4 It's absolutely astonishing. This is the first time you haven't been late this year.
5 I can't carry that. It's absolutely enormous. I'll need help to get it up the stairs.
6 Put the heater on. It's absolutely freezing in here.

5.7)))
Conversation 1

A Did you see that stuff on Facebook about how much music people listen to every day?

B Yes, but I'm not sure I believe it, though. The statistics look much higher than I'd expect. I mean, who listens to music when they're going to sleep?

A Me – and 32% of the people they asked!

Conversation 2

A What do you fancy watching on TV tonight?

B I thought we could watch the programme on climate change.

A Aw, no. That sounds really boring. I really don't want to watch *another* programme about the weather.

B Well, I thought it looked quite interesting; but if you're really sure you don't want to watch it, there's a sci-fi movie on the other channel.

A That sounds much more interesting.

Conversation 3

A Have you tried this new film site? Is it any good?

B Yes, it's great. I expected it to be really expensive, but it isn't. But you have to be careful.

A Oh, why?

B I stayed up till 4 a.m. this morning watching a whole series. I wouldn't recommend that if you have to go to work the next day! I'm exhausted!

5.8)))

1 I feel tired.
2 The film was good.
3 That meal was tasty.
4 It's cold today.
5 That piece of cake is large.
6 It looks bad.

5.9)))

1 It was nothing like as good as I expected it to be.
2 It's really not worth seeing.
3 I wouldn't recommend it.
4 I'm pretty sure you wouldn't like it.
5 It was much less interesting than I expected.

Unit 6 In control?

6.1)))

Your car is now in charge: driverless cars are already here.

Driving along the motorway in busy traffic, the driver presses a button on the steering wheel. The car is now driving itself.

This may sound like science fiction, but driverless cars are already on the roads in California. Many cars can already park themselves by the side of the road, brake automatically when the car needs to slow down, and warn the driver if they are slipping out of the correct lane, so going driverless is just the next step.

Driverless cars come with fast broadband, allowing them to overtake other cars safely, and even communicate with traffic lights as they approach junctions. Being stuck in traffic jams could become a thing of the past, as driverless cars will be able to drive at speed much closer to each other.

More than fifty million people die or are injured in road accidents every year, and 90% of these accidents are caused by human error. Google's driverless car sticks to the speed limit and doesn't get tired. So wouldn't it be much safer if all cars were driverless?

6.2))
Intelligent machines that can serve us in supermarkets, give us directions and even drive for us are becoming part of all our lives. Some of the things machines can do now would have seemed impossible just a few years ago. And there's more to come. Amazon promises robot drones which will deliver our packages, and Rolls-Royce says robo-ships, which won't need any crew, will soon be sailing our seas.

But what will this mean for our workers? Some think that only people whose skills are better than the machines' abilities will have work. Those who don't have high-level skills risk being unemployable, or will have to work for very low wages.

6.3))
climate change
crop damage
water shortages
global warming
strong winds
tropical storms

6.4))
P Welcome to *The World Today*.
   Today we're talking about extreme weather. Recently there seem to have been a lot of extreme weather events. While there have always been strong winds and tropical storms, many scientists now agree that climate change has been causing higher temperatures, and more storms, floods and droughts.
   It's a serious situation, and although governments have been trying to reduce pollution and stop the global temperature rising, we haven't been very successful so far. Could there be a different solution? With us in the studio today we have Neil Clough, our science correspondent, who has been researching ways in which scientists around the world have been trying to artificially control or change the weather. Neil, can anything be done to prevent these extreme weather events?
N Well, if these changes in weather patterns have been happening as a result of global warming, then we should try to prevent further warming, by reducing pollution, protecting trees and so on. However, scientists have been exploring another method. It seems possible that we might be able to actually do more to control the weather directly.

6.5))
P Tell us more about controlling the weather.
N Well, scientists have been working on techniques to create or prevent rain for quite some time now. The best-known

method is called cloud seeding. This involves putting chemicals into the air to encourage any water in the air to form clouds and hopefully rain.
P So, if we can make it rain when we want it to, why do we still have problems with droughts?
N Ah, well, unfortunately it isn't quite as a simple as that. If there is a drought, there probably won't be any clouds in the sky at all. The only thing you could do is to do cloud seeding when there are clouds and then save the water for when there is a drought.
P That could be helpful, I guess ... And can it help with storms and hurricanes as well?
N Yes. Hurricanes form in warm, tropical waters. That's why global warming is having an impact; as the seas get warmer, there are likely to be more hurricanes. But it seems possible that we could use cloud seeding to cool the seas down.
P That sounds incredible! But is it actually a good idea to try and change the weather? I mean, what about putting chemicals into the atmosphere? That can't be a good idea, can it?
N Well, this is one of the things we need to find out. There is some concern that creating rain in one area of the world might take it away from somewhere else. But in terms of the chemicals, it seems that one group of scientists have found a solution. Professor Jean-Pierre Wolf and Dr Jérôme Kasparian, at the University of Geneva, have been experimenting with using lasers to control the weather.
P Lasers?
N Their experiments have shown that pulses of light from a laser can be used to make rain clouds, without using any chemicals. They also think that lasers can be used to direct storms away from certain buildings, such as airports.
P Wow. That is quite amazing. I still feel that perhaps we shouldn't be playing with the weather like this.
N Yes, a lot of people would agree with you. But you've got to remember that we have been changing the weather for a long time anyway through global warming. This type of technology is nothing compared with that, and it could be helpful, rather than harmful.

6.6))
In recent years there has been a noticeable increase in extreme weather events. Many scientists now agree that climate change has caused this increase. The science correspondent in the programme has just finished researching ways in which scientists around the world have been trying to artificially control or change weather patterns. These scientists have been exploring various techniques, including cloud seeding, over the past few years. However, many people are worried about putting chemicals into the atmosphere. Recently one team of scientists in Geneva has discovered a way to use lasers to control the weather.

6.7))
It's important to get away from your everyday life at least once a year; and if you live here

in the UK, you need to find somewhere with guaranteed sunshine. What I mean is, somewhere where the weather is a bit more reliable. It's great to do something you'd never do at home. In fact, I'm sure the challenge keeps you healthy.

Anyway, we've just booked two weeks exploring the lakes and volcanoes of Nicaragua. I can't wait ...

6.8))
1 What I mean is, somewhere where the weather is a bit more reliable.
2 In fact, I'm sure the challenge keeps you healthy.
3 Anyway, we've just booked two weeks exploring the lakes and volcanoes of Nicaragua. I can't wait ...

6.10))
1 You know, as soon as I get behind the steering wheel, I feel great. I'm in control. I decide where I'm going and how fast. What I mean is, I'm in charge. I don't have to wait at the bus stop or get nervous about catching the train, or it not turning up. I find travelling by bus and train much more stressful.
2 I must have about twenty pairs, in all colours. I wear them so I can feel taller, and that makes me feel much more confident. My favourite ones are silver and very high. I only wear them to special events because, although they look great, they're rather uncomfortable. In fact, I usually wear flat ones to get to the event and then slip them on before I go in.
3 I suppose it's true. My whole life is on it – I just couldn't function without it. I mean, I've put everything on it, my friends' numbers, my Facebook, photos, music, games and loads of Apps. I'd be completely lost without it. I never write anything down; I just put it on here, let me show you ... Actually, where is it? I had it a moment ago ... wait ... it must be in here ...
4 I think it all began when I was a kid, and my grandma used to bring me a bar when she came round to babysit. Now I love it – in cakes, biscuits or just a big boxful. I have to have some every day – I feel a bit down if I don't. But as I was saying, I think the real reason I love it so much is because it reminds me of all the happy times I had with my lovely grandma.

6.11))
S Hi, Pedro – it's Sara.
P Oh, hi. I was just thinking about you, Sara. We're meeting for lunch with Estelle tomorrow, aren't we?
S Actually that's why I'm phoning. There's been a change of plan. I'm afraid I've got something else on tomorrow lunchtime – I've got a work meeting from 12 till 2 that I can't change – so how about getting together after work instead? Say 6 o'clock? We could go for an early dinner.
P Let me just have a look at my diary ... Hmm, I'm really sorry, but I can't make it then. I'm meeting someone in town at 6.30. Are you free on Thursday after work?
S Well, I'm supposed to be playing tennis with my sister, but we can probably change it to another day. I'll speak to her, then I'll

      why should we give it to you?

get back to you. OK? And will you see if Thursday is OK with Estelle?

P No problem. I'll speak to you later, then.
S Bye.

6.12
1 There's been a change of plan.
2 I've got something else on tomorrow lunchtime.
3 How about getting together after work instead?
4 I'm really sorry but I can't make it then.
5 I'm supposed to be playing tennis with my sister.
6 I'll speak to her, then I'll get back to you.

6.13
1 climate change
2 crop damage
3 global warming
4 heat waves
5 landslides
6 strong winds
7 tropical storms
8 water shortages

6.14
1 music
2 cloud
3 danger
4 luck
5 stress
6 success
7 fashion
8 comfort

6.15
J Hi, it's Joanne here.
M Hi, Joanne.
J You know we were supposed to be going to the cinema on Saturday? I'm really sorry, but there's been a change of plan. Can we go on Sunday instead?
M Oh dear. Sorry, but I'm not available then. How about next Saturday?
J Ah, I'm meant to be meeting my brother and his wife for dinner next Saturday. But I'll talk to them and get back to you.
M OK, that's fine.

Unit 7 Ambitions

7.1
1
I For many years people have moved to Europe in search of a brighter future and a higher standard of living. In recent years, however, the pattern seems to be changing, with thousands of young people moving from Europe to Africa, Asia and South America. We spoke to three people who have made the move to find out why they moved and how it has worked out for them. Dermot, you're from Ireland, aren't you, but you live and work in the Philippines.
D Yes, that's right. I came to the Philippines in 2005 for a job in property, selling office buildings. At that time, Ireland was doing really well economically, and a lot of people couldn't understand why I was going abroad. It was a fantastic opportunity for me, though, as I was quickly promoted to manager when I'd just been a sales person back in Ireland. The job also came with

rent-free accommodation in a beautiful apartment, and everyone was so friendly. And after two years I became a director. So my career prospects have definitely been improved by coming to Manila.
I didn't work such long hours in Ireland, it's true, but I didn't get the benefits I have now, like private medical care and great training. And the weather is a lot better!

2
I That certainly sounds like a very positive move. And Maria, what about you?
M Well, I'm a qualified architect, with a masters' degree, but when I was made redundant in Athens, I just couldn't find another job. I used to spend all day ringing people up and getting nowhere. I'd been unemployed for over a year when I decided to try Australia.
I still haven't been able to find work as an architect in Melbourne, but I have been able to retrain as a landscape designer, designing gardens instead of houses. It's great being outside so much, because the weather's nearly always good. I also have a lot of job satisfaction now.
Because I have relatives here, it wasn't too difficult to get a visa. In fact, Melbourne is the biggest Greek city in the world, outside of Greece!
I Do you think you'll stay as long as Dermot has?
M Probably. I really like it here.
3
I And what about you, Joaquim? You're currently working in Luanda, Angola, aren't you? Do you think you'll stay there?
J Well, the job is just temporary, for four months, but now I'm here I think I'll stay a lot longer. The working conditions are much better at the moment than in Lisbon, where I'm from. I get sick pay and holiday pay, and plenty of time off. My salary is a lot higher as well, although Luanda is a very expensive city these days. In fact, it's now supposed to be the most expensive city in the world! There's plenty of work, though, both skilled and unskilled. Angola has one of the fastest-growing economies in the world.

7.2
1 Which is more important – a good salary or job satisfaction?
2 At work, is it better to obey the rules, or to take risks?
3 Have you ever had a temporary job? What was it? Did you want it to become permanent?
4 Have you ever had a job where you had to supervise other employees? Did you like the responsibility?
5 Would you like a job where you had to come up with new ideas, or one where you simply followed the rules?
6 Do you find it easy to think creatively and come up with new ideas? How do you do it?

7.3
Li Yan
L I'm not sure I understand. Could you explain what you mean?
I Well, yes, of course … so, you've applied for this job and you want to get this job. But why should we give it to you?

L Oh, I see. OK, you should give me the job because I have a lot of experience that will help your company.
I Could you give some examples of that?
L Well, to give you a good example, I spent three years working in a similar situation in …
Parissa
A I'm not sure I understand. Do you mean what job will I have?
I Yes … in other words, what are your goals for the next few years? What do you want to do?
A Ah, I see. Well, I'm very ambitious. First, I'd like to get some good work experience with a company like yours and then, in a couple of years, I plan to start a part-time master's course in …
Sophie
S I'm sorry. Could you repeat that, please?
I Yes, of course. I asked when was the last time you had a difference of opinion with someone at work – a time you disagreed with someone?
S Ah, OK. Let me see … a time I had a different opinion. Well … actually, last month I was working in a project team, and I didn't agree with the team leader about the time we needed to complete the project.
I And how did you deal with that? What did you do?
S Well, I …
Marina
M Oh, that's a difficult question! Let me think … well, I suppose I would be something like an egg … yes, an egg!
I Why an egg?
M Well, because an egg is very … now, what's the word again? … Useful, yes, an egg is very useful – it goes in so many dishes, and it is one of those foods that is eaten all over the world … so, useful, international … and very healthy, of course!
Ken
K I'm sorry. Could you explain what you mean?
I Yes, of course. What I mean is, what makes you want to work, to do a good job … and the opposite of that – what stops you being interested or working well?
K Ah, OK, now I get it. Well, goals are very important to me. I work really well when I have clear goals – I know what I am doing, why I am doing it and when I need to do it by.
I Could you give some examples of that?
K Yeah, of course. One example was when …

7.4
1 Could you explain what you mean?
2 Well, to give you a good example, I spent three years working in a similar situation.
3 I'm not sure I understand. Do you mean what job will I have?
4 Yes, in other words, what are your goals for the next few years?
5 Could you repeat that, please?
6 Let me think.
7 What I mean is, what makes you want to work?
8 Could you give me some examples of that?

7.5
1 wanting to become rich or successful
2 not willing to let anything stop you from doing what you want to do
3 having special skills or knowledge

4 a lot of people have heard their name or know about them
5 putting in a lot of effort
6 very good at doing something

7.6 》
get
completely
take
positions
progress
risks
promoted
different
think
make
creatively
higher

Unit 8 Choices

8.1 》
According to a recent World Happiness Report, Denmark is the happiest country in the world. But just why is that, and what, if anything, can other countries learn from it?

The first point to make is that, clearly, Denmark, and most of the other countries in the top ten don't have much poverty. Money may not buy happiness, but a strong economy certainly helps. However, if you look a bit further down the list, you'll see that money isn't everything. Mexico, for example, comes higher up the list than the United States. Money doesn't make you happy unless everyone has enough. Big differences between rich and poor tend to make people unhappier.

Also, just because a country is rich, it doesn't mean that it looks after its people well. Many people in the United States, for example, don't have free healthcare. But if a country has quite high taxes, like Denmark, it can provide free healthcare to everyone. You may not believe that you'll be happier if you pay higher taxes, but as a country, you will.

And Danish people have a healthy lifestyle, too. They tend to eat a balanced diet and get plenty of physical exercise. In fact, 50% of trips to work and school in Copenhagen are made by bicycle rather than car or bus. As well as the positive impact on reducing pollution, doctors estimate that if you can cycle for thirty minutes a day, it may add one to two years to your life.

Denmark is also a very equal society. There aren't big differences between rich and poor, and men and women are treated equally, too. Both parents are allowed paid time off work after the birth of a baby, and they can decide how to share the time. It's a very family-friendly country, with free or very cheap childcare provided by the government.

The Danes only work thirty-seven hours a week on average. If people work a thirty-seven hour week, they have quite a lot of leisure time, and the Danes spend much of this time socializing and enjoying cultural activities. The winter may be cold and dark, but there is a special term, 'hygge', to describe a kind of cosy meeting with friends and family. People light candles, keep warm, and eat delicious food together.

And, finally more than 40% of Danes use their extra leisure time to do voluntary work, helping their neighbours.

I'm beginning to see just why it's such a great place to live.

8.2 》
1 If people spend more than an hour travelling to work, they are generally less content.
2 Unless you have some close friendships, you will find it hard to be happy.
3 If you do regular exercise outdoors, you'll be able to work more efficiently.
4 People tend to be happier if they are in a long-term relationship.
5 If people are active in work and free time, they'll probably be healthier.

8.3 》
1 If I were braver, I might be a firefighter.
2 We could volunteer more if we had more time.
3 What would you do if you saw someone being robbed?
4 If we won the lottery we could give some money to charity.
5 I wouldn't do a job if it were risky or dangerous.
6 He'd be so embarrassed if he knew people were talking about his heroism.

8.5 》
1 red pram
2 could be
3 white coffee
4 mild coffee
5 should go
6 cold metal
7 hot pepper
8 hot milk

8.6 》
If you could pick anywhere in the world to live, where would you go? Iceland might not be the most obvious choice, but I don't regret moving here. I came to study earth science at the University of Iceland. Iceland has volcanoes, glaciers and earthquakes. What can't you see here? I came to study the natural world, but I stayed in Iceland because I love the way of life.

8.7 》
There was a bit of culture shock at first. I was surprised at just how much time people spend outdoors. People are close to nature in a way that many other countries have forgotten, and even when the temperatures are freezing, people love getting out into the fresh air. Look outside any café and you're likely to see lots of babies sleeping outside in prams. Icelanders believe that the cold fresh air could be good for their health and helps them sleep better. And no one worries about their safety. Crime rates are very low indeed.

I also found it hard to get used to the way that time seems to have no meaning here. If friends arrange to meet between half seven and eight, you'd better not be surprised if they don't turn up until about half past nine. At first this used to drive me mad. I thought people were being really rude. Gradually, though, I realized that it wasn't rudeness – people just don't worry about punctuality the way we do at home.

The education system is much more relaxed, too. There isn't the same emphasis on tests and exams. In primary school children spend a lot of time playing outside and learning practical skills, such as knitting. But they are still very highly educated in the end, and, apparently, one in ten Icelanders is a published author.

The food took a bit of getting used to as well. There are some dishes I had to be persuaded to try, like sheep's head or shark. But my husband, Gustav, is such a good cook that he can make most things taste nice.

8.8 》
Hello, everyone. My name is Stuart French and I'm here to talk to you about something we all have to do about seventy times every day … make a decision. Obviously some are more straightforward than others. Most people don't have too much trouble deciding what to have for breakfast, for example, but some decisions can be a lot trickier.

So, in today's talk I'm going to look at how understanding the decision-making process can help us to make better decisions when we really need to. First, I want to tell you about some factors that affect our decision-making. Then I'll talk about methods people use to make decisions. And finally, I'll give you some tips about decision-making.

8.9 》
So, what factors affect our decision-making? The first thing I'd like to mention is the number of decisions we make. Recent research seems to show that making conscious decisions actually makes the brain feel tired. As we make more and more decisions, we become less effective. So, if you have an important decision to make, it's probably best to do it early in the day before you've had to make too many other less important decisions.

Another major factor that affects our decision-making is how much information we have to consider. It's obviously a good idea to have some information before we make a decision. However, studies show that if we have too much information to deal with, we're more likely to make the wrong decision. It seems that it's just too much for our brains.

The third and last factor I want to mention today is stress. Researchers have found that people making decisions under stress are more likely to think about the possible positive results of a decision and less likely to think about the negatives. So if you're under stress at work and trying to decide whether to leave, you're more likely to think about how great it will feel to leave and less about how you'll actually get a new job.

8.10 》
Now, let's move on now to look at how to make a decision. One common method is to gather the necessary information (but not too much, remember!), list the possible solutions and set a time limit. This helps you to be more decisive.

Another useful thing to do is to make two lists on a piece of paper – the advantages and the disadvantages – and then see if you have more advantages than disadvantages and how important each one is. In fact, Charles Darwin, the great evolutionary scientist is said to have used this method to decide whether to ask his girlfriend to marry him. Not a great romantic, though …

Many people believe that it's sometimes a good idea to be guided by our heart – our gut feeling – so remember that overthinking things can sometimes make your decision-making ability worse.

So, we've looked at some of the things that affect our ability to make decisions and some ways to make decisions; now I'd like to finish with a tip. Decision-making can be a difficult and complicated process. Don't expect everyone to agree with your decisions, and be prepared to accept that sometimes you will make the wrong choices.

Are there any questions?

8.11 》
1   If you spend it on the right things, money can buy happiness.
2   Most people will be happier if you spend time with them rather than spend money on them.
3   If you're going on holiday, you will be happier if you pay for it straightaway.
4   People should buy experiences rather than things, especially if they are older.
5   People don't enjoy things as much unless they have to work hard for them.

8.12 》
1   If I were president of my country, …
2   I would move to another country if …
3   If I spoke fluent English, …
4   I could earn more money if …
5   If I had more money, …
6   I'd be happier if …

Unit 9 Appearances

9.1 》
1   He's got dark hair and a bit of stubble on his chin. He looks quite middle-aged and he's got a bit of a double chin. He's quite well-built, possibly a bit overweight. Oh, and he's going bald. But he's got kind eyes!
2   I'd say he's in good shape. He's probably in his late twenties. He's got quite a square jaw and a big nose, but it looks good! He's got a bit of a beard and a moustache. His hair is shoulder-length and dark brown.
3   I think she's quite slim. She's got short blonde hair, with a bit of a fringe. Her hair might be dyed, actually. I'd say she was in her late thirties or early forties.

9.2 》
1   The descriptions were more positive.
2   The descriptions were much more positive.
3   The descriptions were far more positive.
4   The descriptions were a bit more positive.
5   Their descriptions weren't as positives as their friends'.

9.3 》
1   I love this painting because it's so detailed, and it really tells a story. The colours are quite soft, mainly white, brown and a kind of bluey-green. It's a landscape, and it must

be either an old painting or a painting of a historical scene. In the bottom left-hand corner there are some men with dogs. I think they might be going out to hunt. Ah, no, they can't be going out to hunt because I can see they've caught something. Just to their left, there's a group of women doing something with a big fire. I'm not sure exactly what they're doing! They could be cooking something. It all looks very cold. There's lots of snow on the ground and on the mountains in the distance. The river must be frozen over, because people are skating on it in the valley towards the right-hand side of the picture.
2   I think this painting is really beautiful. It's a portrait of a woman. She's wearing an old-fashioned long dress in a lovely bright shade of red, with a purple scarf round it. There's the same red on her lips, and on the side of the book she's got in front of her. She's drinking from a blue glass bowl. I have no idea why; it's really mysterious. It might be a picture of an old story or something. The woman is in the foreground of the picture, but the background is also really detailed. Behind her there's a curved window … no, actually, it can't be a window. I think it must be a mirror. It's reflecting the sea and two old-fashioned sailing ships. I'd love to know what this picture is actually about!

9.4 》
1   In the top right-hand corner there are some sharp, snowy mountain peaks.
2   In the foreground there are four or five tall black trees, with no leaves.
3   On the left there are some houses.
4   In the bottom right-hand corner someone is walking over a snowy bridge.
5   The people in the background look very small.

9.5 》
Speaker 1
1   The river must be frozen over, because they're skating on it in the valley.
2   It can't be summer, it looks too cold.
3   The hunters must be coming back from the hunt because one has something on his back.
4   The painting could be a few hundred years old, I suppose.
Speaker 2
5   It might be a picture of an old story or something.
6   It can't be a modern painting; it looks too old-fashioned.
7   It must be a mirror; I can see the reflection of her face.
Speaker 3
8   The abstract painting must be very modern. I don't think it was painted a long time ago.
9   It could be older than you think. People started painting abstracts more than one hundred years ago.
10 It can't be a painting of a mandrill. I can't see a mandrill in the painting at all!

9.6 》
1   The search for the missing climbers went on all night.
2   But in the end they had to give up.

3   Jon took up bird-watching in his teens, and he's never got tired of it.
4   Dan takes after his father in looks, but his mother in character.
5   I'm really looking forward to the concert tomorrow. I haven't seen any live music for years!
6   Jill and I get on really well, even though we only see each other every five years.
7   Why don't you come round later and we'll watch a DVD?
8   We had to put off the meeting because the projector broke down.

9.7 》
Conversation 1
J   Look, I'm sorry to have to say this, but I need to talk to you about something.
L   Oh, what's that? What's wrong?
J   Well, I'm afraid there's a problem with noise.
L   Noise?
J   Yes. There are a lot of us in this office trying to work, and, well, it's a bit noisy at times.
L   Yeah, actually you're right. It is noisy sometimes, isn't it?
J   No, what I mean is you're a bit noisy at times. On the phone.
L   Well, I did have one long call today – sorry about that.
J   To be honest, the problem's been going on for a while now. You keep making personal calls in our shared workspace.

Conversation 2
A   Dan, can I have a word?
D   Oh, hi, Andy. Yeah, sure. What's up?
A   Well, sorry to bother you, but …
D   Is everything OK?
A   Well, actually, no, not really. Look, it's a bit awkward, but I'm afraid there's something I'm not happy about …
D   Oh … what's that?
A   It's the office kitchen – well, you don't ever seem to wash up your stuff; you just leave your coffee cups for someone else to do, and you leave food out on the counter. Look, Dan, to be honest, we're all getting a bit fed up with it.

9.8 》
Conversation 1 continued
J   Do you think you could take your personal calls outside the office?
L   Yes, of course … I'll make sure I get up and go out in future, so people can't hear me.
J   Well, actually, would you mind taking the calls in your own time rather than when we're working? Maybe in your lunchtime? Sometimes you're too busy on the phone when one of us needs to speak to you.
L   Yes, of course I can do that. And listen, I'd really like to apologize for being so annoying. I didn't realize it was that bad.
Conversation 2 continued
D   Oh, Andy, I'm sorry about that. I just didn't think.
A   It's OK … it's just that it's a bit annoying at times, especially when everyone else manages to do it. Look, I know it might not seem such a big deal, but it would really help if you could just clear up your stuff –

you know, wash your mugs, put things away in the fridge.

D Yeah, of course. I'm sorry. I'll make sure I do that next time … I mean every time!

9.9))
1 I'm sorry to have to say this, but I need to talk to you about something.
2 Look, it's a bit awkward, but I'm afraid there's something I'm not happy about.
3 I'd like to apologize for being so annoying.
4 It would really help if you could just clear up your stuff.
5 Would you mind taking the calls in your own time?

9.10))
1 Her hair isn't straight at all.
2 He has been trying to grow a beard for a month.
3 She runs marathons every weekend.
4 He doesn't like beards or moustaches.
5 He has lots of hair.

9.11))
I think I'm more like my father than my mother. He's the kind of person who always looks forward to the future, and so am I. My mother always thinks about what might go wrong. Recently my father took up cycling and wanted to teach her how to ride, but she kept making excuses and putting it off. In the end he gave up trying to persuade her.

9.12))
C Sorry to bother you, but I've got a bit of a problem with this tablet.
A Oh, I'm sorry to hear that. What seems to be the problem?
C I only bought it a few weeks ago, but it keeps turning itself off.
A Do you have the receipt?
C Er, no I don't, actually.
A Well, I'm afraid I can't help you, then.
C Do you think you could get the manager? He might remember selling it to me.

Unit 10 Compete and cooperate

10.1))
1 Ali Ganjavian noticed that people who travel a lot often get very tired.
2 The Ostrich Pillow was invented to help long-distance travellers.
3 It's a kind of hat that is pulled over the head in order to take a nap.
4 So far over $195,000 has been pledged by its backers.
5 In the first three months of production, Ganjavian's company shipped five thousand pillows to fifty-two countries.

10.2))
1 Ali Ganjavian noticed that people who travel a lot often get very tired.
2 The Ostrich Pillow was invented to help long-distance travellers.
3 It's a kind of hat that is pulled over the head in order to take a nap.
4 So far over $195,000 has been pledged by its backers.

5 In the first three months of production, Ganjavian's company shipped five thousand pillows to fifty-two countries.

10.3))
As figures show that more and more children are overweight, the government has announced that highly competitive sports days and tournaments are to be re-introduced at schools. Under the new plans, schools will play against each other in an Olympics-style event, with sports such as football, athletics, rugby, swimming, tennis and cycling. Winning teams will compete in sixty county competitions before going on to a national final.

For too long, schools have been avoiding competitive sports, introducing activities such as yoga, trampolining, cheerleading and dancing instead. They seem to believe that losing a race will make people feel bad about themselves. We have to realize that taking part in competitive sport is not bad for people's self-esteem. Whether you win or lose, competitive sport teaches people to work together in a team and to try hard to be the best that they can be. These are skills which are just as important in the workplace as they are in school.

It is also hoped that the new plans will help Britain to break more records in future Olympic Games.

10.4))
1 It's just unrealistic for children to be told that everyone can win; life is competitive. If you lose a race, then you should just try harder. That's what I learnt when I was at school.
2 I don't think more competition is the answer. Sport at school isn't about teaching children how to be competitive; it's about encouraging them to exercise.
3 There are plenty of children who don't do well academically, who are brilliant at sports. Why shouldn't they be allowed to play against each other and prove how well they can do? No one says that trying to get a good mark in an exam is too competitive.
4 I went to a school that insisted on competitive sports. The school used to hold sports days in a public park, so everyone in the park could watch. I was small for my age and always came last in all the races. It was awful.
5 Competition is healthy, but taking part is more important than winning. Everyone should feel good about having done their best, whether they win or lose.
6 If everyone knows at the start of a race who the winner is going to be, then it can be boring and demotivating. Why can't children be encouraged to compete against themselves, to break their own personal records instead?

10.5))
1 It's just unrealistic for children to be told that everyone can win; life is competitive.
2 If you lose a race, then you should just try harder.
3 That's what I learnt when I was at school.
4 I don't think more competition is the answer.

5 The school used to hold sports days in a public park, so everyone in the park could watch.

10.6))
Sound of a crowd cheering at a baseball or football match.

10.7))
P There's nothing quite like the atmosphere of the crowd at a big game, is there? Well, actually a South Korean baseball team, the Hanwha Eagles, think they can create something like the atmosphere of the crowd by using robots instead of real live fans. The robots can cheer on their team, and human fans who aren't able to attend the game in person will be able to upload their faces onto the robot, and make the robots clap and wave. They can also send text messages which the robots will display to the players.

10.8))
1 The robots can cheer on their team.

10.9))
1 The robots can cheer on their team.
2 Then the robots can also cheer on their own team.

10.11))
1 The atmosphere at the match was amazing.
2 We couldn't have had a better result.
3 I was able to sit right at the front.
4 I rang my friend at the end of the first half of the game.
5 She couldn't come, but she was happy to hear the score.

10.12))
Convenient it might be, but attending a game virtually couldn't possibly be as exciting as being at a real game, surely? And what about the effect on the players? Don't the fans have a responsibility to turn up and encourage their team? Sporting teams always prefer to play in their home stadium, where 70–80% of the crowd will be made up of their own fans, and there is plenty of evidence to show that the home team really does have an advantage. On average, teams playing in their home stadium win about 53% of the time, and there are certain football stadiums, such as the Turkish team Galatasaray's Ali Sami Yen Stadium, which seem to be designed to take advantage of the noise fans make, using the shape of the stadium to make the noise as loud as possible. This then makes it very difficult for the visiting team to do well.

Some teams now train using recordings of the other team's fans, so that they can learn to take no notice of whatever their opponents might be shouting. However, there is some evidence to suggest that the biggest impact of the crowd is not on the players, but on the referees, or match officials, who have to take decisions about whether to allow goals and so on. It seems that shouting from the crowd can affect their decisions, and make them more likely to favour the home team.

But is the noise of their supporters always a positive thing for players or athletes? Not necessarily. In general, crowds seem to improve performance for team sports and sports that involve strength or the ability to keep going, such as running or cycling. However, sports which require a lot of concentration don't benefit from the excitement caused by the screaming crowd. These kinds of athletes need calm and quiet to do well, and noise from the crowd might cause them to take unnecessary risks and make a mistake.

10.13))
1 Don't the fans have a responsibility to turn up and encourage their team?
2 ... the home team really does have an advantage.
3 ... there are certain football stadiums ... which seem to be designed to take advantage of the noise fans make.
4 ... they can learn to take no notice of whatever the other team's fans might be shouting.
5 ... referees, or match officials, who have to take decisions about whether to allow goals and so on.
6 ... noise from the crowd might cause them to take unnecessary risks and make a mistake.

10.14))
Helsinki, Lisbon, Istanbul, Bologna, Liverpool, Riga, Santiago de Compostela ... what do they all have in common? They're all in Europe, of course, but they're also all past winners of the title of European Capital of Culture. Since 1985, when Athens was first given the title, a different city has been chosen each year to organize a series of cultural events. As well as the honour of being chosen, the winning cities have often been able to attract more visitors and improve their image, so competition is fierce.

10.15))
1
A So how long are you going to be in Spain?
B Six months. My company is opening an office in Seville, and I'm involved in setting it up.
A I loved living in Spain. You are so lucky to be going there.
B Yes, but I hope I don't get lonely being so far from home.
A Well, there's one thing you could do to meet people – you could try learning flamenco. I tried it and I loved it – I made loads of friends.
B But I'm not much of a dancer.
A That doesn't matter. There are fantastic schools – they can teach anyone to dance.
B OK, I'll give it a go!
2
I've just got back from Santiago in Chile. It's such a fabulous city, mountains in one direction, the beach in the other. If you like skiing, I'd strongly recommend Portillo or Valle Nevado, both world-class ski resorts. In the city itself, one of the most interesting things to do is to go to La Chascona, one of the houses of the famous Chilean poet, Pablo Neruda. It's fascinating.
3
A Didn't you use to live in Prague?
B Yes, why? Are you thinking of going there?
A We've just booked a weekend there. Is there anything we shouldn't miss while we're there?

B Well, you just have to go to the Charles Bridge and up to the castle – especially at night. It's very romantic. The area near the castle has lots of restaurants and bars where you eat traditional Czech food, and, of course, drink some of our famous beer.
4
A OK, I arrive in Kyoto on the Thursday. Where would you recommend I stay?
B Well, have you thought of trying a traditional Japanese inn? It's called a ryokan. I stayed in one last year and it was a great experience. They're the last word in luxury and relaxation – you can enjoy traditional Japanese foods and baths – just everything you could ever want.
A That sounds fabulous. I'll definitely try it.

10.16))
1 You could try learning flamenco.
2 OK, I'll give it a go.
3 If you like skiing, I'd strongly recommend Portillo or Valle Nevado, both world-class ski resorts.
4 Is there anything we shouldn't miss?
5 Where would you recommend I stay?
6 Well, have you thought of trying a traditional Japanese inn?
7 They're the last word in luxury and relaxation.
8 That sounds fabulous. I'll definitely try it.

10.17))
1 get money to start a business
2 put money into someone else's business
3 discover that you don't have very much money
4 promise that something will be done or will happen
5 think of something new
6 make money from a business

10.18))
A I'd really like to get a bit fitter. What sport or activity would you recommend?
B I strongly recommend running; you'll get fit very fast.
A That's a good idea, but I have some problems with my knees. Could you recommend something a bit gentler?
B Have you thought of swimming? It's really good for you.
A Thank you, that's a good idea. I'll give it a go.

Unit 11 Consequences

11.1))
P And now let's move on to a new film which has just been announced, about the life and crimes of Colton Harris-Moore, known as the 'barefoot bandit'. Apparently the money Colton makes from the film will be going straight to his victims, but can it be right to make films which celebrate someone's crimes in this way? Susie, will you be going to see the film?
S Yes, definitely. I think it's a fascinating story.
P Why do you think people are so interested in his story? Didn't he get a lot of fans on Facebook as well?
S Yes, he did. I think the biggest thing with Colton is that the story was just so entertaining. Everyone wanted to know what would happen next. And lots of people

just loved the idea of him teaching himself to fly – who wouldn't want to do that?!
P Er, me for one! But seriously, he wasn't really someone to be admired, was he? I mean, if he had crashed the plane in a town, he would probably have killed someone. But there are examples of criminals who actually did some good. I can understand those more. Take Ned Kelly, for instance.
S I've heard of him, but I'm not sure what he did.
P He was an outlaw in Australia in the 1800s. His trouble started when a police officer was shot in Ned's house. Ned was arrested for murder, but he claimed he hadn't done it and escaped with his brother and two friends. The four of them then went around robbing banks, but they were kind to the people who actually worked in the banks, and shared the money with other people. Ned claimed that he was being unfairly treated because his family was Irish. When he was finally arrested, thousands of people protested outside the prison.
S That reminds me of someone else I heard about – a Hungarian called Atilla Ambrus. He robbed banks as well, back in the early 1990s. No one was ever hurt, and he treated the people working at the bank very politely. He even gave the women working there flowers! He became popular because many people felt that the banks deserved it! Though I don't think he ever gave any of the money away. When he was arrested, he escaped from prison by tying his bed sheets together! It's a great story, and there's been a film made about him since.
P Really? People do seem to love this kind of story, don't they?

11.2))
1 I accidentally posted a video of myself and some friends at a party and my boss saw it. I didn't mean to post it. I was uploading a different video and accidentally clicked on this video, too. It was really embarrassing, and now my boss thinks I'm really unprofessional.
2 I had just had a job interview and one of the interviewers was very rude to me. So I tweeted about it. As soon as I pressed Send, I knew it was a mistake, but it was too late. Later I found out that I would have been offered the job, but someone saw my tweet and they changed their minds and gave the job to someone else.

11.3))
1 She should have been more careful when she posted the video.
2 She shouldn't have accepted her boss as a 'friend' online.
3 She shouldn't have behaved badly at the party.
4 She shouldn't have posted any videos online.
5 He should have thought before pressing Send.
6 He shouldn't have said anything negative about the interviewer online.
7 He should have waited until he was offered the job.
8 They should have given him the job anyway, if he was the best candidate.

11.4 》

She should have been more careful.

She shouldn't have behaved badly.

11.5 》

1 I really wanted to go to a big football game, but I was supposed to be working. So I told my boss I was ill. The game was brilliant, but unfortunately I got so excited I started tweeting about it and my boss saw the tweets, so she knew I wasn't at home sick. I ended up losing my job.

2 It really wasn't my fault. I was looking after my parents' house while they were away, and I decided to have a party. It was only going to be a few friends, but one of my friends decided to write about it on Facebook. He didn't realize it, but that meant that 500 people knew about the party and about 150 people turned up. It was a great party, but the house was a terrible mess afterwards.

11.6 》

Conversation 1

M Something horrible has happened at work.

W Oh no! What?

M I had to finish a report for Tuesday morning, and by Monday afternoon, I hadn't even started it. I decided to borrow a laptop from the office so I could write it at home, and bring it in on Tuesday morning.

W OK. So …?

M The thing is, it's against the rules. Our manager says we must get permission before we do that.

W Right …

M So I took the laptop home, and was writing the report at home. But then during the night I got really sick …

W You were probably feeling guilty …

M Hmmm. Maybe. Anyway, I couldn't go into work on the Tuesday after all, because I was sick. And they discovered the laptop was missing.

W And they realized it was you!

M No, worse than that, actually! They called in the police!

W Why don't you just phone in and tell them it was you?

M Because then they'll realize I was going to be late with the report …

Conversation 2

M Where were you last night?

W I had to help Professor Dudley with his new research project.

M Again? That's all you do at the moment.

W I know! I wish I'd never offered to help him.

M So why did you?

W I thought it would get me a better grade in my exams. But …

M But …?

W I have to work day and night for him – for free! And I don't think he even knows my name. I'm just a slave.

M Ha! Serves you right.

11.8 》

I Over the last three programmes, we've looked at the results of actions – both our personal actions and the actions of big business and government. Today we have Dr Michelle Hall with us. She's been researching into an area known as 'unintended consequences'. Good morning, Dr Hall. Just to start off with, can you tell us what you mean exactly by 'unintended consequences'?

H Good morning, Peter. Well, yes, the easiest way to explain is through an example: let's imagine that we pass a law which says that all young people must wear helmets when they are cycling. This looks like a very sensible law. Obviously our intention is that if a young cyclist were to have an accident, their head would be protected.

I Yes, it sounds like a very good idea!

H But the problem is that wearing helmets is very 'uncool', or unfashionable, so young people might say, 'I don't want to wear a helmet'.

I And so …?

H So they'll stop cycling, and go everywhere by car. This means they may take less exercise. And then they could put on weight, and later in life that might bring health problems. And that all means that the unintended result is as bad as the original problem.

11.9 》

A OK, so when do we have to move?

B By the end of the month; I think the last day's the 28th.

C I've been checking all the estate agent's sites on the internet, and there seem to be quite a few apartments that would suit us.

A Great. Let's see. It would be a good idea for us to decide what we have to have.

C Well, to start off, a bedroom each, and a nice living room …

B I'd like the apartment to have a balcony.

C Let's leave extras like that for now and concentrate on the essentials.

B Don't you think a balcony is essential? What will we do in the summer when it's hot?

A Well, another option would be to go for a ground-floor apartment, or a building with a shared garden.

C OK, we can see what's available. Could we move on to thinking about where we want to live?

A Near the centre – that would be good for you at the university and for our office.

B OK, now for the difficult question: how much rent can we afford to pay?

C Could we all go up by 100 euros a month? We'd get somewhere really nice for that.

A I suppose so.

C So, we're looking for a three-bedroomed apartment, near the city centre …

B With a balcony or garden …

11.10 》

1 Let's leave extras like that for now …

2 Don't you think a balcony is essential?

3 Another option would be to go for a ground-floor apartment …

4 So, we're looking for a three-bedroomed apartment …

11.11 》

1 In the square I saw …

2 The light was …

3 The match was rubbish – it …

4 Please can you give me the key – I need it to …

5 We need change – it's important because …

6 I'll meet you at the bank – bring some …

11.12 》

1 We're running out of time.

2 Are there any other suggestions?

3 That's settled, then.

4 Let's leave that for now.

5 You must admit that's true.

6 That would be another option.

7 I'm convinced that …

8 So what we're saying is …

Unit 12 Influence

12.1 》

1 The best ad I've seen had a serious point, but it was actually really amusing. There were three guys sitting outside somewhere in Australia. There was a house behind them, and the light was on. One of them asked another one to go and turn the light off because it was Earth Hour. You know, every year it's one hour when everyone around the world is supposed to turn off their lights to save energy and make people think about using less electricity. Anyway, the man couldn't be bothered to turn the light off – he said it was just one light and it wouldn't make any difference. Then, suddenly, he saw a HUGE cloud of moths coming towards them. Maybe every moth in Australia was heading for their light because all the others had been switched off! I really think that the most effective adverts are those that make people laugh.

2 I saw an amazing ad to raise our awareness of the problems homeless people have. It said that the weather was one of the biggest problems homeless people have, and that during the previous winter many of them had died. However, because they were homeless, no one really noticed them. So, in Germany, Switzerland, Russia and a few other countries they asked homeless people to present the weather forecast on TV. This helped people watching to see them as real people, just like them, and lots of them were offered help and jobs. They are now hoping more countries will do it next year.

3 I really liked a public service ad called 'The impossible texting and driving test'. It was really clever. It was made in Belgium, and the point was to persuade people not to send texts on their mobile phones while driving. Of course, no one likes being told not to do something – well, I don't anyway – so they decided the best way to convince people that it's a stupid idea was to show what happens when you actually force people to text and drive! So the ad shows real people learning to drive at a driving school in Brussels. The instructor told them that a new law had been passed and that they now had to prove they could use a mobile phone while driving. Of course, no one could do it, and there were lots of silly little accidents.

12.2))

1 The best ad I've seen had a serious point.
2 Earth Hour is about saving energy.
3 I saw an amazing ad …
4 Lots of them were offered help.
5 The instructor told them that a new law had been passed.
6 There were lots of silly little accidents.

12.3))

P So, Tania, you've been reading our book of the week, *How to Persuade and Influence People.* Did you enjoy it?
T Yes, actually. I thought it might be useful, but I didn't really expect to enjoy reading it. But it was really quite entertaining. There are a lot of personal stories by the author, and some of them are quite funny.
P Can you give an example?
T Er, well, the author probably tells the stories better, but there's one where a bird attacked the audience at a presentation …
P Really?!
T Yes, the author had thought it would be a good idea to have a real owl in his presentation, but it escaped! Amazingly, he still got the job.
P So, what did you actually learn from reading the book?
T Well, there were some very useful tips for remembering people's names. He says that's important in getting people to trust you, so that you can then influence them.
P Oh, I'm not very good at remembering names. What were the tips?
T Erm, to believe that you could do it, to listen carefully when the person first says their name, to use their name in the conversation, to look at their face and associate it with the name, and to write down their name and everything you can remember about them afterwards.
P That sounds sensible. Have you got better at remembering names since you read the book?
T Actually, I think I have … a bit, at least. It probably takes practice.
P And what does the book say about persuading people?
T Well, there's a lot of information – you'll have to read it, really. But probably the most important thing is to really listen to people and to ask questions to find out what's really important to them, what matters to them. When they see that you understand them, you'll be better able to influence or persuade them.
P I guess that makes sense, too … So, most important question: are you better at persuading people now?
T I'm not sure. Ask me again in a few months …
P I certainly will …

12.4))

1 Well, the interesting thing is that soft power is now all about business. Countries no longer depend on force or politics to increase their influence abroad. I mean, when the distinguished American political scientist Joseph Nye used the words 'soft power', he was referring to foreign policy, but now soft power is used in business, too. The idea is that to succeed in business, you need to influence people – so nothing new there – but the best way to do that is through communication and soft skills. You need to respond to your employees and show that you believe in them. Then they will work hard for you and make your business successful.
2 One thing that's really changed in business is the way we persuade people through communication skills and not force. We're not afraid of being more open in the workplace any more. Of course, we have women to thank for a lot of these changes. Women are starting more businesses than ever, so female influence is increasing. Poor leadership and communication lead to employees becoming dissatisfied with their boss and maybe even leaving. That's a disaster because we depend on our employees to make our business a success.
3 The thing we're all concentrating on now is working together and finding work that we find satisfying. We want to work in a group and deal with problems effectively, not spend our time blaming other people for the problems, or feeling jealous of other people's success. I think a lot of young people have stopped worrying about how they are going to get a promotion. They just want to be good at something and to feel they're working for a company that values them as a person.

12.5))

1 We're not worried about showing our emotions in public.
2 What we're talking about is a country's influence in business and culture.
3 The idea is that to succeed in business, you need to influence people.
4 We're becoming more interested in how other people see us.
5 You need to respond to your employees and show that you believe in them.
6 Joseph Nye was referring to foreign policy.
7 Poor communication can lead to employees becoming dissatisfied.
8 Managers need to listen to their staff.
9 The thing we're all concentrating on now is working together.
10 They just want to feel they're working for a company that values them as a person.

12.6))

1 Emily and Andrew
E Ooh? Is that new? Very fancy!
A Yes, well I decided to treat myself – my old one wasn't working properly. It has a really good camera – 12 megapixels. That'll be really useful for my holiday.
E I was just going to say that! You won't need to take your camera with you now.
A And the internet is really good on it as well, so I don't think I'll need my computer as much as before.
E I'm not sure about that. Don't you think the screen's a bit too small to read?
A Mm, you might be right. Maybe I'll still use the computer for work. It really does look good, though, doesn't it? Hey, maybe I can persuade you to get one as well!

2 Lena and Matt
L So how did you get home from the party last night?
M In the end I got a lift with Andre. Have you seen that thing he drives? It looks absolutely terrible. So old-fashioned.
L Oh no, I totally disagree … I think it's really cool to go around in something like that. It's so different.
M Yes, but I can't help thinking that 'different' doesn't mean good-looking!
L Well, I think some of the old styles look better than the modern ones. And anyway, we shouldn't be under pressure to buy new stuff.
M I couldn't agree more. But this model never was stylish! It's just awful!

3 Isabella and Marina
I Have you been to that new place in town yet – you know, at the top of the hill?
M Yes, I went last week, actually. What was your impression?
I Well, the food is fantastic, but so expensive. And they encourage you to order so much! Don't you agree?
M Yeah, that's just what I thought. I must say, we enjoyed it, but I didn't enjoy paying the bill. I think it's in a great spot, though, looking out over the city.
I Absolutely! It's a great view. It's even better if someone else is paying!

12.7))

Agree strongly
I was just going to say that!
That's just what I thought.
Absolutely!
I couldn't agree more.
My thoughts exactly.
That's a good point.

Agree weakly
I suppose so.
You might be right, but …

Disagree strongly
I totally disagree.
Rubbish!

Disagree weakly
I'm not sure about that.
Yes, but I can't help thinking …
I agree up to a point …

12.8))

1 It really makes me want to try the product.
2 I'll never forget that advert.
3 I didn't really understand what it was trying to say.
4 It was really funny.
5 I've never seen anything so horrible. Yuck!
6 It is really imaginative and different.

12.9))

1 Do you usually watch adverts on TV?
2 What kinds of adverts do you notice?
3 Have you ever bought a product because of advertising?
4 What slogans can you remember?
5 Was advertising better when you were a child?
6 What do you think about advertising to children?

Irregular verbs

Infinitive	Past simple	Past participle
be	was/were	been
beat	beat	beaten
become	became	become
begin	began	begun
bite	bit	bitten
blow	blew	blown
break	broke	broken
bring	brought	brought
build	built	built
buy	bought	bought
can	could	been able to
catch	caught	caught
choose	chose	chosen
come	came	come
cost	cost	cost
cut	cut	cut
dig	dug	dug
do	did	done
draw	drew	drawn
dream	dreamt/dreamed	dreamt/dreamed
drink	drank	drunk
drive	drove	driven
eat	ate	eaten
fall	fell	fallen
feed	fed	fed
feel	felt	felt
fight	fought	fought
find	found	found
fly	flew	flown
forget	forgot	forgotten
forgive	forgave	forgiven
freeze	froze	frozen
get	got	got
give	gave	given
go	went	gone/been
grow	grew	grown
have	had	had
hear	heard	heard
hide	hid	hidden
hit	hit	hit
hold	held	held
hurt	hurt	hurt
keep	kept	kept
know	knew	known
lay	laid	laid
lead	led	led
learn	learnt/learned	learnt/learned
leave	left	left

Infinitive	Past simple	Past participle
lend	lent	lent
let	let	let
lie	lay	lain
light	lit	lit
lose	lost	lost
make	made	made
mean	meant	meant
meet	met	met
must	had to	had to
pay	paid	paid
put	put	put
read	read	read
ride	rode	ridden
ring	rang	rung
rise	rose	risen
run	ran	run
say	said	said
see	saw	seen
sell	sold	sold
send	sent	sent
set	set	set
shake	shook	shaken
shine	shone	shone
shoot	shot	shot
show	showed	shown/showed
shut	shut	shut
sing	sang	sung
sit	sat	sat
sleep	slept	slept
speak	spoke	spoken
spend	spent	spent
spoil	spoilt/spoiled	spoilt/spoiled
stand	stood	stood
steal	stole	stolen
stick	stuck	stuck
swim	swam	swum
take	took	taken
teach	taught	taught
tear	tore	torn
tell	told	told
think	thought	thought
throw	threw	thrown
understand	understood	understood
wake	woke	woken
wear	wore	worn
win	won	won
write	wrote	written

Phonemic symbols

Single vowel sounds

/iː/	tree /triː/	/ə/	computer /kəmˈpjuːtə/
/ɪ/	his /hɪz/	/ɜː/	learn /lɜːn/
/i/	happy /ˈhæpi/	/ɔː/	four /fɔː/
/ʊ/	good /gʊd/	/æ/	hat /hæt/
/u/	usual /ˈjuːʒuəl/	/ʌ/	sunny /ˈsʌni/
/uː/	school /skuːl/	/ɑː/	car /kɑː/
/e/	ten /ten/	/ɒ/	clock /klɒk/

Diphthongs (double vowel sounds)

/ɪə/	near /nɪə/	/ɔɪ/	boy /bɔɪ/
/ʊə/	tour /tʊə/	/aɪ/	try /traɪ/
/eə/	wear /weə/	/əʊ/	so /səʊ/
/eɪ/	train /treɪn/	/aʊ/	out /aʊt/

Consonant sounds

/p/	pen /pen/	/s/	see /siː/
/b/	big /bɪg/	/z/	lazy /ˈleɪzi/
/t/	tea /tiː/	/ʃ/	shower /ˈʃaʊə/
/d/	do /duː/	/ʒ/	television /ˈtelɪvɪʒn/
/tʃ/	children /ˈtʃɪldrən/	/m/	man /mæn/
/dʒ/	journey /ˈdʒɜːni/	/n/	never /ˈnevə/
/k/	cat /kæt/	/ŋ/	sing /sɪŋ/
/g/	go /gəʊ/	/h/	hot /hɒt/
/f/	fly /flaɪ/	/l/	like /laɪk/
/v/	very /ˈveri/	/r/	river /ˈrɪvə/
/θ/	thing /θɪŋ/	/w/	water /ˈwɔːtə/
/ð/	this /ðɪs/	/j/	yes /jes/

OXFORD
UNIVERSITY PRESS

Great Clarendon Street, Oxford, OX2 6DP,
United Kingdom

Oxford University Press is a department of the
University of Oxford. It furthers the University's
objective of excellence in research, scholarship,
and education by publishing worldwide. Oxford
is a registered trade mark of Oxford University
Press in the UK and in certain other countries

© Oxford University Press 2015

ISBN: 978 0 19 456563 9

Printed in China

This book is printed on paper from certified
and well-managed sources.

ACKNOWLEDGEMENTS

Cover Image: Getty Images (light trails/teekid), Oxford
University Press (Laptop and tablet)

Alamy Images pp.14 (website/Jeff Morgan 02), 23 (taxi/i car),
28 (making burgers/ZUMA Press, Inc), 29 (footballer holding
ball/Cultura Creative), 33 (older man using laptop/Cultura
Creative), 34 (Emmeline Pankhurst statue/Justin Kase
zsixz), 38 (Savanna at dawn, Emas National Park, Brazil/
Frans Lanting Studio), 38 (Morskie Oko lake, Tatra
Mountains, Poland/Jan Wlodarczyk), 50 (woman watching
TV and using tablet/Graham Hughes), 52 (The Shawshank
Redemption poster/AF archive), 53 (One Day film still/AF
archive), 74 (Oxford skyline/James Osmond), 76 (family
dinner/Aurora Photos), 80 (natural geothermal spa, Iceland/
Greg Balfour Evans), 80 (knitting class/ZUMA Press, Inc),
80 (baby prams outside building/Arctic Images), 94 (statue/
imageBROKER), 94 ("John Adams" by Gilbert Stuart, 1821 –
Smithsonian National Gallery of Art, Washington, DC USA/
Washington Stock Photo), 98 (high school cheerleaders/H.
Mark Weidman Photography), 100 (Galatasaray Stadium,
Istanbul/dpa picture alliance archive), 101 (Turkish football
club scarves/Jochen Tack), 102 (Liverpool docks/CW
Images), 104 (Gareth Bale/ZUMA Press, Inc.), 105 (flip flops
on sale/Jenny Matthews), 106 (fingerprint/SDM IMAGES),
106 (crime scene tape/Michael Burrell), 108 (app icons/Lucie
Lang), 114 (Sophos headquarters/VIEW Pictures Ltd),
114 (businessman/Tetra Images), 116 (Sky TV billboard
advert/Clynt Garnham Business), 116 (teen girl taking
driving lesson/MBI), 122 (iPhone packaging/Andrew
Paterson), 123 (Uniqlo store/Iain Masterton), 123 (H&M
store/Per Andersen), 124 (Starbucks sign/Matthew
Horwood), 124 (Starbucks coffee shop/British Retail
Photography), 125 (Google Glasses/dpa picture alliance),
134 (silk screen printing/Hero Images Inc.); Atlantic Books
p.10 (The Shallows book cover/Courtesy of Nick Ritchie);
Bridgeman Images pp.88 (Hunters in the Snow – January,
1565, Bruegel, Pieter the Elder (c.1525–69)/
Kunsthistorisches Museum, Vienna, Austria), 88 (Destiny,
1900 (oil on canvas), Waterhouse, John William (1849–
1917)/© Towneley Hall Art Gallery and Museum, Burnley,
Lancashire), 88 (Mandrill, 1913 (oil on cardboard), Marc,
Franz (1880–1916)/Private Collection), 130 (Emperor Ch'in
Wang Ti (221–206 BC) travelling in a palanquin, from a
history of Chinese emperors (colour on silk), Chinese
School, (17th century)/Bibliotheque Nationale, Paris,

France/Archives Charmet), 134 (Portrait of Jeanne
Hebuterne in a large hat, c.1918–19 (oil on canvas),
Modigliani, Amedeo (1884–1920)/Private Collection/
Giraudon); City of Vancouver Archives p.115 (Port p.572/Bill
Miner); Corbis pp.14 (train tv/Bobby Yip/Reuters), 15 (model
using telephone in satin nightgown/Condé Nast Archive),
18 (first cast of Piltdown Man forgery/Bettmann), 36 (Lake
Titicaca, the floating islands of the Uros people/Atlantide
Phototravel), 36 (tropical beach), 37 (woman using solar
panel/Hugh Sitton), 41 (couple packing moving boxes in
living room/Hero Images Inc.), 42 (Rooftops Of Lucca/Chris
Caldicott/Design Pics), 56 (aerial view of road intersection/
David Jay Zimmerman), 58 (Hurricane Jimena/Jim Edds),
64 (Peruvians without Water/Mariana Bazo/Reuters),
64 (Abel Cruz/Mariana Bazo/Reuters), 66 (Luanda
undergoing major reconstruction, Angola/sergioafonso/
Demotix), 66 (Pink House, Buenos Aires/Michael Runkel/
Robert Harding World Imagery), 68 (Jane Goodall holding
chimpanzee/Kennan Ward), 68 (Rebecca Adlington/Philip
Brown), 68 (Daniel Barenboim conducting/Alonso
Gonzalez/Reuters), 92 (young man reading/Todd Warnock),
98 (group in lotus position in yoga class), 107 (Hungarian
bankrobber Attila "The Whiskey Robber" Ambrus/Tibor
Bozi), 107 (Colton Harris-Moore, the Barefoot Bandit/
Marcus Donner/Reuters), 107 (police mugshot of Ned Kelly/
Ho New/Reuters), 110 (woman carrying laptop/Image
Werks), 121 (cabbage kimchi, Korean food/Topic Photo
Agency); Everpurse/www.everpurse.com p.131; Getty
Images pp.6 (Edinburgh at sunset/Sara Winter), 6 (Warsaw's
Old Town/Jorg Greuel), 12 (Tesla Motors Model S/Justin
Sullivan), 12 (Fairphone smartphone/Justin Tallis),
13 (clothes rail in shop/Mischa Photo Ltd), 14 (Times Square/
Siegfried Layda), 17 (rope way on Mount Kongo/ebiq),
18 (Richard and Mayumi Heene/RJ Sangosti), 20 (woman
playing violin in orchestra/Hill Street Studios),
20 (woodwind section/Erich Auerbach), 26 (pink
marshmallows/Floortje), 30 (professor and students in
lecture hall/Clerkenwell), 32 (bottle light, South Africa/
Gallo Images), 32 (Litre of Light project/Gallo Images),
34 (English suffragettes/Universal History Archive),
42 (lobster pots, Isle of Mull/VWB photos), 42 (Morocco/
Henglein and Steets), 44 (Incheon park/Sungjin Kim),
44 (Songdo/Ann Hermes/The Christian Science Monitor);
49 (businessman sitting at desk smiling/Thomas Barwick),
56 (traffic lights/Nick Dolding), 58 (Yangtze river drought/
ChinaFotoPress), 66 (The Galleria Vittorio Emanuele 11,
shopping centre, Milan/Tony C French), 67 (business
towers, Buenos Aires/Nikada), 73 (people waiting for an
interview/Diane Diederich), 78 (fire fighter holding baby/
Chris Briscoe), 83 (college student giving presentation/Hero
Images), 86 (close-up portrait of man/Paul Burns),
86 (portrait of a mature woman/Johnnie Davis), 91 (house
with face/Christian Beirle González), 91 (cheese grater
smiling/Paul David Galvin), 92 (Sardinian woman/RENAULT
Philippe/hemis.fr), 99 (sepak takraw ball game/Andrew
Watson), 102 (mosque at dusk/Allan Baxter), 104 (FC
Augsburg v Borussia Dortmund/Alexander Hassenstein/
Bongarts), 104 (Dortmund fans/John MacDougall/AFP),
108 (send it icon/Bryan Mullennix), 116 (Hong Kong tram/
Philippe Lopez), 116 (moths around light bulb/Jeffrey
Coolidge), 116 (Homeless man in the snow/Karen Bleier/
AFP), 120 (Psy performs on NBC's 'Today Show'/Gilbert
Carrasquillo), 121 (Samsung logo/Jung Yeon-Je),
122 (London Fashion Week/John Phillips), 123 (woman exits
Renner clothing store/Bloomberg), 123 (GAP shop/Justin
Sullivan), 123 (Zara shop/Bloomberg), 123 (Muji store/View
Pictures), 124 (Starbucks World Headquarters building,
Seattle/Kevin Schafer), 128 (woman in rice patties, Vietnam/
Kathy Dorsey), 128 (Fleet Street newsroom, 1970/
Popperfoto), 132 (lorry driving on icy road/James Balog),
133 (woman tending crops, Myanmar/Katie Garrod), cover
(light trails/teekid); Good & Proper Tea p.134 (Tea Van);
Hanwha Eagles Baseball Club/Eagles Fanbot Campaign
p.100 (robofans); Philip Hesketh p.118 (photo of author);
iStockphoto pp.36 (water wave/vovan13), 77 (rush hour in
Copenhagen/Hans Laubel); Kobal Collection pp.24 (Jaws
1975/Universal), 24 (Macbeth 1971/Columbia); 46 (Rio 2096:
A Story of Love and Fury/Buriti Filmes/Gullane Filmes/
Lightstar Studios), 46 (The Secret Life of Walter Mitty/Red
House Entertainment), 47 (Stepping on the Flying Grass/
Bumble Bee Studio/Humanplus Production/Kreasi Cinema/
Mediatama/Render Post), 55 (Spirited Away/Studio Ghibli/
NTV/Dentsu/Tohokushinsha Film); Oxford University Press
pp.34 (woman on computer/video still), 44 (city developers/
video still), 54 (film studies/video stills), p.63 (Woman using
mobile phone/Digital Vision), 64 (filing bottle/video still),
74 (Dean Ryan of Zsuzsanna Felvegi), 84 (Happiness in
Mexico/video stills), 94 (Debbie's selfie/video still); Rex
Features pp.8 (sales shopping/London News Pictures),
40 (chronic hoarder Richard Wallace/Jenny Goodall/Daily
Mail), 45 (island built out of water bottles/Sam Barcroft),
45 (Richie Sowas/Sam Barcroft), 57 (Amazon drone testing/
ZUMA), 58 (typhoon destruction, Japan/KeystoneUSA-
ZUMA), 97 (Ostrich pillow/REX); Rinspeed Inc
p.65 (Driverless car); Science and Society Picture Library
p.126 ('Alice and the Fairies', July 1917/National Museum of
Photography, Film & Television); Shutterstock
pp.6 (Monument Valley, Utah/tobkatrina), 8 (man shopping
online on tablet/LDprod), 12 (diamond engagement ring/
Torla), 16 (hippo with mouth open/Timothy Craig Lubcke),
18 (slices of watermelon/Alex Staroseltsev), 22 (carrot
illustration/Valentina Razumova), 22 (gold ring/Skylines),
24 (pumpkin carriage/Elena Schweitzer), 25 (locking door/

windu), 28 (restaurant kitchen/wavebreakmedia),
28 (restaurant meal/2nix Studio), 29 (burger and chips/
ilolab), 36 (floating market, Thailand/Anton Gvozdikov),
36 (Boat in San Francisco/Leonard Zhukovsky), 36 (water
splash/Fisher Photostudio), 39 (rice fields, Bali/Dudarev
Mikhail), 39 (bamboo forest/Ru Bai Le), 43 (hotel
receptionist/Gabriel Georgescu), 62 (young man looking at
tablet/Alexander Image), 63 (Businessman making call/
Dragon Images), 66 (Belem tower on Tagus river, Lisbon/
Mario Savoia), 66 (Grattan Bridge, Dublin/littleny), 66 (Big
Ben and red buses/PHOTOCREO Michal Bednarek),
66 (Manila, Philippines/joyfull), 66 (Melbourne skyline/
Gordon Bell), 66 (Parthenon in Acropolis, Athens/S.Borisov),
69 (dragonfly/paulrommer), 74 (Szeged, Hungary/joyfull),
75 (man working at home/gpointstudio), 76 (trolley bus,
Copenhagen/Evikka), 78 (ski rescue patrol/CandyBox
Images), 86 (portrait young man/Minerva Studio), 86 (young
woman portrait/pkchai), 86 (young Turkish man/Axel
Bueckert), 86 (senior woman portrait/Diego Cervo),
92 (woman on phone in office/Monkey Business Images),
92 (businessman portrait/EDHAR), 92 (portrait of young
man/eurobanks), 95 (portrait woman smiling/bbevren),
95 (portrait serious man/the808), 96 (tree growing from pile
of coins/wk1003mike), 98 (children in swimming pool/
dotshock), 99 (rugby match/Maxisport), 99 (mountain
biking/Warren Goldswain), 102 (Riga, Latvia/Christian
Mueller), 110 (student working in library/Ermolaev
Alexander), 110 (bicycle helmet/Andrey_Popov),
118 (employees in meeting/Pressmaster), 126 (great white
shark/Elsa Hoffmann), 126 (planets in space/Melkor3D),
127 (young man portrait outdoors/Adam Radosavljevic),
133 (young businesswoman/michaeljung); Sophos
p.114 (website); The Advertising Archives p.116 (Dettol
advertisement); TBWA Switzerland AG/McDonald's
Switzerland p.116 (McDonalds advert on road); Wiley
Publishing p.118 (Book cover, How to Persuade and
Influence People by Philip Hesketh).

Illustrations: Tatiana Arocha/Bernstein & Andriulli pp.8–9,
82–83; Mikel Casal/Eye Candy pp.70–71, 85; Clear as mud/
Folio Art p.60; Gill Button p.10; Paul Daviz p.48, Vicki
Gausden p.22, Simon Gurr p.130; Joanna Kerr pp.32, 35,
Ryo Takemasa/Dutch Uncle p.112, Fred van Deelen/The
Organisation pp.36, 66, 80.

Commissioned Photography: Mark Bassett p.26

*The authors and publisher are grateful to those who have given
permission to reproduce the following extracts and adaptations of
copyright material:* p.6 Adapted extract from "Manchester
man's charity quest to meet all of his 700 Facebook
friends" by Charlotte Cox, www.manchestereveningnews.
co.uk, 18 April 2013. Reproduced by permission of
Manchester Evening News. p.10 Adapted extracts from
"The Conversation: Is the Web Rotting Your Brain?" by
John Berman and Nicholas Carr, http://abcnews.go.com/
WN/Media/conversation-nicholas-carr-internet-brain/
story?id=10805528, 2 June 2010. Reproduced by permission
of ABC News. p.16 Adapted extract from "Experience: I was
swallowed by a hippo" by Paul Templer, www.theguardian.
com, 4 May 2013. Copyright Guardian News & Media Ltd
2013. Reproduced by permission. p.20 Adapted extract
from "Blink and The Wisdom of Crowds" by Malcolm
Gladwell, Slate, 12 January 2005 © 2005 The Slate Group.
All rights reserved. Used by permission and protected by
the Copyright Laws of the United States. The printing,
copying, redistribution, or retransmission of this Content
without express written permission is prohibited. p.48
Adapted extracts from "African videogames level up" by
Monica Mark, www.theguardian.com, 26 September 2013.
Copyright Guardian News & Media Ltd 2013. Reproduced
by permission. pp.50, 51 Adapted excerpts from "The
Rise of the Second Screen: Zeebox, GetGlue, Viggle, and
More" by Jose Castillo, first published by Information
Today, Inc., April/May 2013. www.infotoday.com. Used
with permission. All rights reserved. p.66 Adapted
extract from "Young Europeans flock to Argentina for job
opportunities" by Uki Goni, www.theguardian.com, 22
December 2011. Copyright Guardian News & Media Ltd
2011. pp.86, 87 Adapted extract from "Dove's new beauty
campaign confirms that we are more beautiful than we
think" by Katy Young, http://fashion.telegraph.co.uk,
22 April 2013. © Telegraph Media Group Limited 2013.
Reproduced by permission. p.208 Adapted extracts from
"One in four regrets rash messages on social network sites"
by Stephen McGinty, www.scotsman.com, 27 January 2012.
Reproduced by permission of The Scotsman Publications
Limited. pp.118, 119 Extracts from How to Persuade and
Influence People by Philip Hesketh, Capstone Publishing,
2010. Reproduced by permission of John Wiley and Sons
Inc.; permission conveyed through Copyright Clearance
Centre, Inc. p.96 Adapted extracts from "Kickstarter
entrepreneurs doing big business in the UK" by Jessica
Salter, www.telegraph.co.uk, 4 February 2013. © Telegraph
Media Group Limited 2013. Reproduced by permission.

Sources: www.oxfam.org.au, World Happiness Report 2013
edited by John Helliwell, Richard Layard and Jeffrey Sachs,
http://unsdsn.org., http://myhero.com, http://icelandreview.
com, www.kickstarter.com

With thanks to Katherine Griggs for the video pages.

With thanks to Jon Hird for the Grammar Reference pages.

Oxford University Press would like to thank: Alamy images,
Getty images, NASA, National Portrait Gallery, Museum of
London, Borussia Dortmund